Contents

1. The Environment: AS/400 and System/38. 1
1.1 Origins of AS/400. 1
1.2 Features of the AS/400. 2
    1.2.1 Libraries. 3
    1.2.2 External files: DDS and database files 4
    1.2.3 HELP ([CF4]) prompts. 7
    1.2.4 Subfiles 8
    1.2.5 Standard objects – e.g. QSYSPRT. 8
    1.2.6 CL commands. 9
    1.2.7 Journalling and commitment control 10
    1.2.8 The OVR (Over-Ride) family of commands 10
    1.2.9 Authorisation system 11
    1.2.10 Data Areas and Data Queues. 12
    1.2.11 Odds and ends. 12

2. Relational Databases 13
2.1 Problems with flat-files 13
2.2 Normalisation. 14
2.3 DB Types. 15
2.4 Rows and Tuples, Entities and Attributes. 16
2.5 Relational databases. 16
2.6 Userviews, dense keys 17
2.7 Data dictionary 18
2.8 Intersection data 18
2.9 Deadly embraces. 19

3. AS/400 and Relational DB: How they fit together 21
3.1 All data in DB 21

3.2 Logical files 22
3.3 Single level storage 24
3.4 Terminology 25
3.5 Intersection files 28

4. Database Design on the AS/400 29
4.1 Prior design or ...? 29
4.2 Data atoms 29
4.3 Attaching an Office/400 member. 30
4.4 Naming conventions 30
4.5 Reduce to 3NF 31
4.6 Recording the data atoms 31
4.7 Compile and use with SDA 32
4.8 *PRTF DDS 32
4.9 Documentation using SDA 32
    4.9.1 Value of documentation on disk 33
4.10 Formal specification shortcut 33
4.12 Feasibility studies 33

5. History of RPG 34
5.1 Introduction 34
5.2 Evolving dialects of RPG 35
5.3 Development 36
5.4 Today's situation 37
5.5 The Generator 37

6. RPG Names and Naming Conventions 38
6.1 Similarity to COBOL 38
6.2 Meaningfulness 39
6.3 Prefixing field names by file 39
6.4 Field definition 40
6.5 File names 42
6.6 Format names 42

7. The Coding Forms 44
7.1 The Building Blocks 44
    7.1.1 Fields 44
    7.1.2 Indicators 45
7.2 Arrays and Tables 47
7.3 Figurative Constants and Reserved Words 54
7.4 File pointers 56
7.5 Statements 56
7.6 H Header 59
7.7 F File 60
    7.7.1 The basic F-spec 60

7.7.2 F-spec continuations. 64
7.8 F* Indicator summary 65
7.9 L Line-counter 67
7.10 E Extension 67
7.11 I Input 68
   7.11.1 "Header" I-specs 68
   7.11.2 "Body" I-specs. 73
7.12 C Calculations. 75
   7.12.1 ACQ Acquire Program Device 78
   7.12.2 ADD Add. 78
   7.12.3 ANDxx And 79
   7.12.4 BEGSR Begin Subroutine. 80
   7.12.5 BITOF Set Bits to Off 80
   7.12.6 BITON Set Bits to On 81
   7.12.7 CABxx Compare and Branch 82
   7.12.8 CALL Call 82
   7.12.9 CASxx Case [conditional EXSR]. 83
   7.12.10 CHAIN Random Read 84
   7.12.11 CLOSE Close File 85
   7.12.12 COMIT Commit. 86
   7.12.13 COMP Compare. 86
   7.12.14 DEBUG Debug Function. 86
   7.12.15 DEFN Define Field 87
   7.12.16 DELET Delete Record 88
   7.12.17 DIV Divide. 88
   7.12.18 DO Do 89
   7.12.19 DOUxx Do Until 90
   7.12.20 DOWxx Do While 91
   7.12.21 DSPLY Display 91
   7.12.22 DUMP Dump Program 92
   7.12.23 ELSE Else. 92
   7.12.24 END End (of IF or DO group). 93
   7.12.25 ENDSR End Subroutine 93
   7.12.26 EXCPT Exception Output 94
   7.12.27 EXFMT Execute Format. 95
   7.12.28 EXSR Execute Subroutine. 95
   7.12.29 FEOD Force End of Data 96
   7.12.30 FORCE Force file for next cycle 96
   7.12.31 FREE Free program static storage 97
   7.12.32 GOTO Go To 97
   7.12.33 IFxx If 98
   7.12.34 IN Read Data Area. 98
   7.12.35 KFLD Key Field 99

- 7.12.36 KLIST Key List. 99
- 7.12.37 LOKUP Look Up. 100
- 7.12.38 MHHZO Move High to High Zone 103
- 7.12.39 MHLZO Move High to Low Zone. 103
- 7.12.40 MLHZO Move Low to High Zone. 103
- 7.12.41 MLLZO Move Low to Low Zone 104
- 7.12.42 MOVE Move. 104
- 7.12.43 MOVEA Move Array. 105
- 7.12.44 MOVEL Move Left 106
- 7.12.45 MULT Multiply. 107
- 7.12.46 MVR Move Remainder. 107
- 7.12.47 NEXT Next input for multiple-device file. 108
- 7.12.48 OCUR Get or Set Data-Structure Occurrence. 108
- 7.12.49 OPEN Open file. 109
- 7.12.50 ORxx Or 109
- 7.12.51 OUT Update Data Area. 110
- 7.12.52 PARM Parameter. 111
- 7.12.53 PLIST Parameter List 111
- 7.12.54 POST Post to INFDS [Information Data Structure]. 112
- 7.12.55 READ Read File 113
- 7.12.56 READC Read Changed record [from subfile] 113
- 7.12.57 READE Read Equal 114
- 7.12.58 READP Read Previous 115
- 7.12.59 REDPE Read Previous Equal. 115
- 7.12.60 REL Release Program Device 116
- 7.12.61 RETRN Return 116
- 7.12.62 ROLBK Roll Back. 116
- 7.12.63 SETGT Set Greater Than 117
- 7.12.64 SETLL Set Lower Limit 117
- 7.12.65 SETOF Set Indicator Off. 118
- 7.12.66 SETON Set Indicator On. 119
- 7.12.67 SHTDN Shut Down 119
- 7.12.68 SORTA Sort Array. 120
- 7.12.69 SQRT Square Root. 120
- 7.12.70 SUB Subtract. 120
- 7.12.71 TAG Tag [for GO TO] 121
- 7.12.72 TESTB Test Bit. 121
- 7.12.73 TESTN Test Numeric. 122
- 7.12.74 TESTZ Test Zone. 123
- 7.12.75 TIME Time and Date 124
- 7.12.76 UNLCK Unlock Data Area 125
- 7.12.77 UPDAT Update Record 125
- 7.12 78 WRITE Write Record. 126

	7.12.79 XFOOT Crossfoot (sum elements of array)	126
	7.12.80 Z-ADD Zero and Add	127
	7.12.81 Z-SUB Zero and Subtract	128
7.13	O Output	128
	7.13.1 "Header" O-specs	128
	7.13.2 "Body" O-specs	132
7.14	** Array content	135

8. The RPG Cycle ... 137
8.1 RPG II and RPG III ... 137
8.2 Primary and Secondary files ... 138
8.3 All programs read, process, output ... 138
8.4 Reading and "making available" ... 139
8.5 Use of Detail-time Ln indicators ... 141
8.6 The Cycle in detail ... 142
8.7 Structuring of programs ... 143
8.8 Level breaks on C-specs – detail time and total time ... 144
8.9 Matching ... 145
8.10 Implications with commitment control ... 146

9. Fully Procedural Programming ... 147
9.1 What it is ... 147
9.2 Programming without files ... 147
9.3 Structuring a Fully Procedural program ... 148
9.4 Uses of Fully Procedural programs ... 148
9.5 Output from Fully Procedural programs ... 148
9.6 Terminating a Fully Procedural program ... 149

10. Modular Programming ... 150
10.1 Principles and reasons ... 150
10.2 Coding the links – passing parameters ... 152
10.3 Multi-language programming ... 154
10.4 Effects of single-level storage ... 155
10.5 Multi-threading ... 157
10.6 Reclaiming resources ... 157

11. Workstation Programming ... 159
11.1 The screen ... 159
11.2 Screen files ... 159
11.3 DDS and SDA ... 160
11.4 EXFMT, WRITE and READ ... 162
11.5 Response times ... 163
11.6 PUTOVR (Put Over-ride) ... 164
11.7 Error Messages ... 165

12. Subfile Programming..166
12.1 What is a subfile?...166
12.2 Format names..167
12.3 Keywords..167
12.4 Identifying subfiles to RPG...170
12.5 The RPG READC (Read Changed) command.......................................171
12.6 Basics of hardware cost vs programmers' time...............................173
12.7 Indefinite length subfiles...173
12.8 Handling of ROLLUP/ROLLDOWN – auto vs manual...............................173
12.9 Search keys...174
12.10 Variable record lengths...175
12.11 Multiple active subfiles..175
12.12 Importance of field naming..176
12.13 Message subfiles..176

13. Journalling and Commitment Control 177
13.1 Problems with a corrupted database...177
13.2 Journalling the changes..177
13.3 Applying journal changes...178
13.4 Reason for commitment control..178
13.5 Commitment control...178
13.6 Rollback...178
13.7 Creating your own journal entries..179
13.8 BGN/ENDCMTCTL..179
13.9 Journals and receivers...179
13.10 Flip-flop logging...180
13.11 Sizing of logical transactions..181
13.12 Recording successful completions..181
13.13 Record locking..181
13.14 RPG cycle and commitment control..182
13.15 Locking levels: *CHG and *ALL...182
13.16 Locked records..182
13.17 The WAITRCD parameter...183
13.18 "Think time" and locking records..183
13.19 Impact on CPU load..183
13.20 Journals versus back-ups..183
13.21 Running batch without commitment control..................................183
13.22 Whip-round programs...184
13.23 Synchronised checkpoints..184
13.24 Recovery from hardware failure and database corruption....................185
13.25 Audit trails..185
13.26 Mirror databases..185

14. Debugging 187
14.1 Older systems – with the DEBUG verb 187
14.2 AS/400 debug system – STRDBG 188
14.3 Breakpoints 189
14.4 The Trace 192
14.5 AS/400 Dump 196
14.6 Messages 197
14.7 System-supplied data structures 202
14.8 Use of journals for debugging 202

15. Conversion from older, RPG II, machines 204
15.1 S/36 Environment on the AS/400 204
15.2 The existing system 205
15.3 A compromise approach 205
15.4 The transition – use of joined logical files 206

16. Conversion from Mainframe: CICS Implications 207
16.1 Why go from mainframe to AS/400? 207
16.2 Teleprocessing considerations 208
16.3 Pseudo-conversational CICS and its implications 209
16.4 CICS on the AS/400? 209

17. Standards and Conventions 210
17.1 Introduction – reasons for standards 210
17.2 PFs equivalent to entities 211
17.3 Intersection files 211
17.4 UNIQUE keyword and Physical Files 212
17.5 Naming and number of Logical Files 212
17.6 Work files 212
17.7 Program names 213
17.8 Library conventions 213
17.9 Library names 214
17.10 Program amendment notes 214
17.11 Format naming conventions 215
17.12 Data areas 215
17.13 The FRF (Field Reference File) 216
17.14 Use of PUTOVR in DSPFs 216
17.15 Indicator conventions 216
17.16 The GOTO command 217
17.17 Indicators 217
17.18 Logic cycle and commitment control 217
17.19 Use of OPNQRYF 217
17.20 Multiple definition of a file in a single program 217
17.21 Comments and paragraphing 217

17.22 Use of CASEQ rather than multiple IF/ELSE 218
17.23 Using *LIKE DEFN. 218
17.24 Costs/benefits of monitoring 219

APPENDIX A: The Versatile AS/400 copy command 220

APPENDIX B: Useful addresses 226

APPENDIX C: Bibliography 228

APPENDIX D: Examples 229
Example 1 229
Example 2 234
Example 3 235
Example 4 238
Example 5 243
Example 6 247
Example 7 249
Example 8 251

APPENDIX E: Version 2 – Upgrade to RPG 256
   E.1 SELEC Start a Select group 258
   E.2 WHxx When True, Select 258
   E.3 OTHER Other (catch-all) Selection 259
   E.4 CAT Concatenate. 260
   E.5 CHECK Check for existence of characters 261
   E.6 CLEAR Clear a Field or Data Structure 261
   E.7 ITER Iterate 262
   E.8 LEAVE Leave [a DOxx group]. 262
   E.9 RESET Reset a Field or Data Structure [to its initial value] 263
   E.10 SCAN Scan [for a character string] 263
   E.11 SUBST Substring. 264

APPENDIX F: The Coding Forms. 265

Index 271

1

The Environment: AS/400 and System/38

1.1 Origins of AS/400

F/S killed off, revived due anti-trust suit, became S/38, which became AS/400.

IBM's top-of-the-line mini is little understood by the DP community at large, but much admired by those who know it well. Compared to the competition, the AS/400 is like an atomic clock in a sundial factory.

It gives the impression that IBM looked at the best of everything they had done, and the best of everything all their competitors had done, and distilled it all into one machine, the System/38, which became the AS/400.

At the hardware level there is a substantial difference between a System/38 and an AS/400, but at the software level they are virtually the same.

The principal differences are in the use of command keys (the AS/400 has been brought into line with SAA standards) and in the command syntax: System/38 uses *filename.library* whereas the AS/400 uses *library/filename*.

In order to avoid clumsy and tedious repetition of the phrase "System/38 and AS/400", the name "AS/400" has been used in this book to mean either of these machines, unless explicitly stated otherwise.

Shortly after the introduction of the 360 mainframe, in 1964, the boffins at IBM's laboratories began work on their next generation operating system, which was intended to address all the shortcomings of the 360/370 family's operating systems.

It was called FS (for Future System), but by that time customers had millions of dollars invested in 360 and 370 programs, JCL, and expertise. They would not have been happy to have their collective boat rocked by a major conversion. Somebody high up in IBM got cold feet and FS was killed off.

Another undercurrent became interwoven, because it was just at this time that the US Justice Department made its attempt to use the anti-trust laws to split IBM in two. For some years customers found themselves called upon by two competing IBM salesmen – a farcical situation which was unfairly blamed on IBM.

The top brass at Big Blue decided to hedge their bets, and FS was revived and dusted off to give GSD the flagship it would need if forced to go it alone. This was the System/38 and, despite a weak start, it was by far the most advanced machine ever offered by IBM. It is the ghost of FS which has arisen to do what it was originally intended to do.

The System/38 was always something of a cult machine, and it was not until the change of name to AS/400 that the architecture was really given the full benefit of IBM's marketing power.

It is interesting to speculate where we would be now if FS had been unleashed in 1978 rather than 1988. . . . .

1.2 Features of the AS/400

❑ Integrated DBMS and TP monitor –
   the operating system, called CPF (Control Program Facility) on System/38 and OS/400 on AS/400 , has an integrated teleprocessing monitor, database manager and text editor, in marked contrast to tacked on products such as CICS, DL/I and ICCF, familiar to 370 users.

❑ Single-level storage –
   OS/400 uses what is called "single-level storage": and it is worth spending a few moments on this, because frequently even experienced OS/400 programmers seem not to understand it. (Readers who know Software AG's Adabas will recognise the "buffering algorithm" concept.) Essentially it amounts to an extension of the idea of fixed length paging used by 370 and later mainframes, though the pages are surprisingly small at 512 bytes each.
   When a block is read from disk it is held in a corresponding page in core until a page fault occurs and it is next in line for deletion. If a subsequent read calls for the same block of disk, OS/400 is smart enough to know that it is already in core, and that therefore there is no need for disk access.

Apart from the obvious benefits of this arrangement, it means that there is no need for a link editor to support the CALL mechanism. This is also true, for the same reason, of Natural programs whose compiled objects are stored within Adabas. Once a subprogram has been CALLed subsequent calls will almost certainly find it still in core. All programs on the AS/400, irrespective of language, are re-entrant (sometimes called multi-threadable).

One implication of all this is that there is absolutely no need to write huge monolithic programs, such as a 20,000-line RPG monster I once saw.

❑ Time-slicing (rather than interrupt-driven) –
  anyone who has worked on a mainframe running VM and CICS will know that machine load affects CMS response much less than CICS response. OS/400 allocates resources to interactive users in a VM-like way so, while slow response is certainly not unknown, it is much less of a problem than with CICS.

Most operating systems process a task until it becomes "ineligible" – usually because it is waiting for I/O. OS/400 (and VM) work by "time-slicing": each job is processed only for a predefined time, and then is suspended while use of the CPU passes to the next in line. This makes it much more difficult for a greedy job to monopolise the CPU.

❑ Everything on AS/400 is an object, and stored in a library –
  OS/400 views everything on the system – programs, queues, files, libraries, commands etc. – as "objects". All objects are stored in libraries.

Objects may have attributes. For example, programs may have the attributes RPG or CBL (COBOL), and files may be PF (Physical File), LF (Logical File), PRTF (Printer File), SPLF (Spooled File) etc. A Printer File may be thought of as a funnel through which data is passed to a Spooled File.

1.2.1 Libraries

IBM-objects prefixed with Q

Readers who have worked on IBM's mainframes or System/36s will be familiar with using libraries to contain programs. AS/400 takes the concept a stage further by storing all objects in libraries.

A library must be stored in a library which, in turn, must be stored in a library. We have a snake trying to eat its own tail. This problem is resolved by making the system library, QSYS, automatically known to OS/400. All other libraries must reside in QSYS.

Library QTEMP differs from all others in two significant respects:

1) There is a separate QTEMP for each active job in the system (OS/400 distinguishes between them transparently to the programmer)

2) Each QTEMP and everything in it is deleted as soon as its job terminates

It is intended as a catchall for all those little files etc. which soon clutter the disks of most computers, and which programmers "forget" to delete. It may help to think of it as an MS-DOS Ramdrive – lost when you switch off.

All IBM-supplied objects, such as QSYS and QTEMP, have names which begin with Q. There is nothing to prevent anyone else from creating an object whose name begins with Q, but the dangers are obvious. (DP managers should note a further danger: giving an object a name beginning with Q, and storing it in QSYS, is an obvious way for a hacker to hide his dirty tricks.)

Library lists

The fact that files are stored in libraries implies that we may have two versions of a file called DOG – one in MYLIB and one in YOURLIB. We distinguish between them by describing them as MYLIB/DOG or YOURLIB/DOG (on System/38 DOG.MYLIB or DOG.YOURLIB). This is tedious. OS/400 gets around the problem by attaching a library list to each job. This is exactly what it says: a list of library names, but the order in which they appear is important.

When an object is requested by means of an unqualified name, OS/400 searches the library list in sequence, beginning with the library at the top of the list, until it finds an object of the name and type requested.

If MYLIB appears in the library list ahead of YOURLIB, then a request for DOG will obtain MYLIB/DOG, but if YOURLIB is higher up in the list it will obtain YOURLIB/DOG.

More practically, suppose an insurance company has two versions of a file called CLAIMS, one in LIVELIB and one in TESTLIB. A programmer can switch backwards and forwards between the two versions, simply by changing his library list.

This is all very convenient; however, it contains the risk that he will accidentally update LIVELIB/CLAIMS, thinking he is working in TESTLIB. One way around this problem is to use the authorisation system, described in section 1.2.9 below. It is much easier to switch between using live and test versions of programs, files etc. if hard-coding of library names is avoided.

The figurative constant *LIBL enables you to make it explicitly clear in a CL program that the library list is to be searched. For example, code *LIBL/CLAIMS (or CLAIMS.*LIBL on System/38).

Sometimes you really do wish to use a version of a file which is not the highest version on your library list. The best way is to use an over-ride command – see section 1.2.8.

1.2.2 External files: DDS and database files

One of the AS/400s more attractive features is a powerful relational database. Without wishing to get into one of those boring arguments about exactly what makes a database relational, I would venture that the AS/400's satisfies Ted Codd's Twelve Principles, although sometimes in ways which might not be obvious to a newcomer to the machine. This is not the same as saying that it is wise to use all of those facilities, and an attempt to do so may cause performance problems. See the discussions of access paths below.

The OS/400 database stores data in "physical files", which may be accessed directly, or through "logical files". The mainframe database manager, Adabas, works in much the same way but calls its logical files "userviews" – arguably the Adabas term is more descriptive.

Physical files may be declared with an explicit record length, which is mostly to provide upward compatibility with earlier GSD offerings, alternatively the file is defined by describing its constituent fields.

Once the fields have been described within the definition of a physical file, any program using that file may declare it as "external", and the definition is then pulled in by the RPG compiler, rather as a file layout is pulled in by COBOL using a COPY statement. (The AS/400 COBOL compiler uses an option to the ASSIGN clause of the SELECT statement so that it too may pull in external definitions.)

A logical file may be declared over one single, or combinations of several, physical files, using any field or combination of fields as key(s). It may contain all, or any subset, of the fields in the underlying physical file(s), either exactly as they appear in the physical file, or in a concatenated form.

For example, the day, month and year might be declared separately in a physical file, but concatenated into a single date field in some or all of the logical files.

It is possible to give fields different names in the logicals to those used in the underlying physicals, though this facility should be used with circumspection, if at all.

Logical files may have different access authorisations from their underlying physical(s). It is possible severely to restrict access to the underlying physical, but to declare a logical containing only non- sensitive fields, and to which access is unrestricted.

For example, the payroll physical file may well contain non-sensitive information, such as home telephone numbers, as well as sensitive salary-related data. An unrestricted logical file might be generated for the purpose of creating a list of the telephone numbers. An omit/include facility is provided for logicals – in the telephone list example it might be desirable to omit the chief executive.

Logical files may share "access paths" – tree-structured indexes. This improves efficiency if one wishes to have two logicals with identical keys but (for example) different fields and/or authorisations.

In theory, an unlimited number of logical files may be declared over any given physical file, though in practice performance problems would result. IBM suggests not more than ten logicals per physical, but this is very much a rule of thumb, and all depends on the volatility of the file in question. In any case, what really matters is the number of access paths.

Think about it; the problem arises because OS/400 has to update all those indexes every time an entry for one of the key fields changes, or a record is added or deleted.

However, if the underlying physical file is used entirely, or almost entirely, in read-only mode – e.g. the client name and address file – then there is little or no updating to do, and so it doesn't matter how many logicals there are.

The fields within a file definition may have their attributes described directly, or by reference to a field in another file, or a combination of the two. The intention behind this is for every field in the database to be defined within a single physical file which forms, in effect, a data dictionary (and hopefully no one would be mad enough to try to put data in it!). All other physicals then refer to this field reference file so that any change may painlessly be rippled through the installation.

A "deadly embrace" situation can occur, in which Program A is waiting for a record held by Program B, which in turn is waiting for a record held by Program A. Unless something is done, both will wait for ever. OS/400's solution is to raise an error condition if a program has to wait longer than the stipulated period for a record. This period is one of the parameters of the CRTPF (Create Physical File) command, and the default value is 60 seconds.

Physical files usually contain only one member, but may be specified as multi-member files. (A multi-member file is analogous to a Partitioned Data Set in MVS.) Each member will contain a discrete set of data, but will have the same layout as all the other members clustered under that file name. A data capture file might contain a separate member for each data capture clerk. See section 1.2.8 for a description of how to use file over-rides to access a required file member.

Members should not be confused with formats, which are simply record layouts. Physical files may contain only one format, but logical files may draw formats from each of their underlying physical files.

Unlike OS/400, RPG objects if the format name is the same as the file name, and it is much easier to give files format names which differ from the file name than it is to rename formats in every RPG program. Chapter 17 suggests a scheme for naming files and formats.

Source code is always contained in source physical files, which differ only slightly from database physical files. They are always multi-member – each source program constitutes a member. Each has a standard three-field layout. The first two are six-digit fields containing header information: these contain the line sequence number and the date when the line was last updated. The third field contains the source, and is by default an 80-byte card image, though other lengths may be specified, up to a maximum of 256 bytes. Source physical files members may be accessed by a program for I/O in exactly the same way as database physical files members.

Like database files, screen and print files may pick up their field definitions directly from the field reference file. Alternatively – the preferred method – the definitions may be obtained from the database files from which their input is derived.

Properly used, this gives RPG a large measure of 4GL capability because, once the files have been declared as external, all fields are defined automatically, and moving of data between files is carried out without the need to code MOVE instructions.

All files are described by means of DDS (Data Description Specifications), which will appear very familiar indeed to anybody who has ever used any dialect of RPG. Screen file DDS may be created by means of SDA (Screen Design Aid). This is a two-way process, existing DDS may be displayed on the screen and modified, or brand new DDS may be created. SDA permits the programmer to retrieve field definitions from the field reference file, or from any other physical or logical file and, having done so, to paint them onto the screen, and to move them around, to suit users' whims.

Print files may be internal, where they are just like print files on any other machine; or external, in which case DDS handles all the tedious chores of field spacing, etc. It is strange that COBOL is largely shunned on a machine that offers – for the first time to my knowledge – a quick and easy way round COBOL's worst failing.

1.2.3 HELP ([CF4]) prompts

[CF4] is the best friend of anyone trying to learn OS/400. (And the same key is used on System/38. Hallelujah!)

If you know which command you want to use, but have forgotten the parameters, simply type the command name on the command line and press [CF4]. OS/400 will provide you with a series of prompt screens which lead you step by step through all that is needed.

Also, if you are not sure of the possible values for a given parameter, position the cursor on it and press [CF4], or alternatively type into the field a question mark ('?') followed by a blank, and press [Enter].

If you don't know which command to use, you can blank out the command line and press [CF4]. OS/400 will provide a menu of subjects. Select one of these, and more detailed sub-menus will be provided, until a point is reached at which you are invited to choose from a list of commands. When you have chosen one, OS/400 will take you straight into the prompt screens described above.

Newcomers to the AS/400 are sometimes discouraged by the prospect of having to learn a vast number of commands, but in fact it is very, very easy. Just use [CF4].

1.2.4 Subfiles

Interactive programming is an area where OS/400 really shines, because of a concept called the subfile (covered in detail in Chapter 12).

Suppose there is a need to display an invoice on a screen. There is a certain amount of header information followed by line items. The header information is handled as with any other system, but the line items are declared as a subfile. The input database file containing the line items is read in until there is a change of invoice number, writing a record to the subfile for each record read in. The page-size, or number of subfile lines which may be displayed at once, forms part of the subfile definition.

The subfile is then displayed, and the user may roll up and down. OS/400 intercepts the roll requests and handles them without the application program having to be involved at all. A message is issued if the user attempts to roll past the end of the subfile.

It is also possible to handle an end of subfile condition within the program. The appropriate roll key is enabled, and is then treated as a command key. Typically this would be done when it is desired to extend an input subfile.

A special type of subfile is provided for messages, so that many errors may be flagged to a single screen without having to worry about how they are going to fit onto the display. Such messages may contain "substitution variables", which facilitate sending meaningful messages such as "Acme Furnishers not on Customer file", rather than "Requested object not found".

1.2.5 Standard objects – e.g. QSYSPRT

IBM has provided a number of standard objects, which save the effort needed to create our own. These include standard diskette and tape files, QDKT and QTAPE, and standard output files for those commands which produce database output – see section 1.2.6.

By far the most frequently used object is QSYSPRT, the standard printer file. When an internal print file is to be used, it is still necessary to create a file (although without DDS) before running the program. If QSYSPRT is used the file already exists, courtesy of IBM. The only problem with this approach is that the resulting spooled file will be called QSYSPRT, and may be difficult to distinguish from hundreds of others also called QSYSPRT.

Suppose a print file's name with in a program is BIRD. You could use the CRTDUPOBJ (Create Duplicate Object) command to replicate QSYSPRT into QTEMP under the name BIRD, so that the spooled file would now be called BIRD.

An advantage of this method is that if the length of its standard stationery (for example), is changed for the installation, then all that needs to be done is to change QSYSPRT, and the change will "ripple" through automatically.

1.2.6 CL commands

Programs to implement, DB output, specimen files in QSYS. QCMDEXC. QCLSCAN.

IBM mainframe users grumble about the complexity of MVS and VSE JCL. Strange, then, that the AS/400's CL (Control Language) has 500+ verbs. (And you can create more of your own if you wish!)

The command names are formed of groups of letters, mainly three digits and mainly consonants, which are very easy to get used to. For example, think of:

```
STRSEU      str-seu     (Start Source Edit Utility)
DSPFFD      dsp-ffd     (Display File Field Description)
CHKOBJ      chk-obj     (Check Object [existence])
WRKSPLF     wrk-splf    (Work with Spooled Files)
```

Remembering the parameters of large numbers of commands is less of a problem than one might think. A powerful prompt facility, backed up by help screens, means that even newcomers to the machine seldom need to refer to the manuals.

Prompts are made available by means of a subject menu, and commands can be requested simply by supplying a character string representing the beginning of the command name; in addition, all the possible values for every parameter within a command can also be prompted.

CL may be run as an interpreted stream like 370 JCL and System/36 OCL, but usually it is compiled into programs of its own, rather like the work flow control statements on Burroughs Large Systems. It is certainly true that mastery of CL is the hallmark of the accomplished AS/400 programmer. The language is extremely powerful, and offers facilities undreamt of by the average mainframe programmer.

It would not be at all complicated to perform the following assignment:

❑ Find all programs using the Customer Master and compiled between 5th April 1991 and 14th May 1991

❑ Locate their source and recompile them

❑ Ensure that this is done between 9pm and 8am.

Decompiling is normally thought of as a highly complex task, yet CL programs may be decompiled by means of single CL verb, and the decompiling of files is no great problem. (A file decompiler is available – see Appendix B.)

All commands require programs to implement them, and these may be written in any language supported by OS/400, and may be multi-lingual modular programs as described in Chapter 10.

Some commands offer the option to produce output in the form of database files. Among the more commonly used of these are DSPOBJD (Display Object Description), DSPFD (Display File Description) and DSPJRN (Display Journal). In each case a specimen output file is to be found in QSYS.

IBM provides some useful service programs, including QCMDEXC and QCLSCAN: QCLSCAN provides a fast scanning facility, while QCMDEXC allows the programmer to execute CL commands from within a program written in any language. QCMDEXC is called QCAEXEC on System/38, and this name works on AS/400 too.

QCMDEXC is by far the most commonly used of these service programs, and an example of its use may be found at the end of Chapter 10. The only point to watch is that the command length parameter must be 15 digits long with 5 decimal places.

1.2.7 Journalling and commitment control

Journalling is optional, and may be of after-images only or both before- and after-images. If commitment control is used, before and after journalling is mandatory. Commitment control is used to prevent partially completed transactions from corrupting the database. The uses of journalling and commitment control include security, debugging, and the provision of audit trails. They are discussed in detail in Chapter 13.

1.2.8 The OVR (Over-Ride) family of commands

Suppose a program requests a database file called ABC. OS/400 simply searches the job's library list until it finds a library containing a file called ABC. If it does not find it an error condition is raised. But what if the file does exist in the database, but under the name XYZ? Arguably the programmer should change the program to read XYZ, but this is not always desirable.

The connection can be made by one of the over-ride family of CL commands, in this case OVRDBF (Over-ride Database File). The over-ride would be coded:

```
        OVRDBF     FILE(ABC)    TOFILE(XYZ)
```

and would be equivalent to DOS/VSE's

```
        //DLBL    ABC,'XYZ'
```

and to MVS's

```
        //ABC    DD    'XYZ'
```

and to System/36 OCL's

```
        //FILE  NAME-ABC,LABEL-XYZ
```

The OVRDBF command is also useful for connecting a program to a specific member in a multi-member file. Since multi-member files are not very often used in application programming this need usually arises when one wishes to process a member within a source file.

If we wish to read a source program called PQR in QRPGSRC in MYLIB, and have called the file QRPGSRC in our program, the following will do the trick:

    OVRDBF   FILE(QRPGSRC)   TOFILE(MYLIB/QRPGSRC)   MBR(PQR)

Assuming that MYLIB was at the top of the library list, this would have sufficed:

    OVRDBF   FILE(QRPGSRC)   TOFILE(*FILE)   MBR(PQR)

Note the use of the figurative constant *FILE where the file name is the same on the database and in the program. *FILE is the default. i.e. it was not necessary to code the TOFILE parameter at all.

The other widely used over-ride command is OVRPRTF (Over-ride Print File). When creating a print file it is possible to specify all sorts of characteristics: the type of stationery to be used, the length and width of the forms etc.

It is better not to specify these when the file is created, and instead to supply the parameters by means of an OVRPRTF. The advantage is that a program which requires special stationery may easily be tested using standard stationery simply by omitting the over-ride.

1.2.9 Authorisation system

Most authorisation systems are a pain in the neck. They obstruct upright citizens going about their lawful business far more than they discourage the ungodly. The authorisation system on the AS/400 is no exception. It extends to all object types — queues, programs etc. as well as files. There are a number of different types of authority: management and existence, as well as the usual data rights: read, add, update and delete.

Management authority means the right to view/copy the attributes of the object. Authorisation may be to individual users, or users may be collected into groups, and authority granted to the group. It is much easier to add a new member to a group than to go through each object to which the group is authorised adding the name of the new user. Authority may be granted by specifying each user and type of authority, or may be granted by means of a reference object. All authorities to the reference object are granted to the object being worked on.

The working guide-line for authorisation should be "need to restrict" rather than "need to know". Unless one is in a really sensitive environment — a bank, for example — there is a much greater need to prevent accidental updating than wilful interference.

A good example is the situation — discussed above, in section 1.2.1 — where a programmer is switching between live and test library lists, implying a risk of updating a live file by mistake. If he has read-only authority to the files, then there is no possibility of this happening.

1.2.10 Data Areas and Data Queues

Data areas will be familiar to any reader who has worked on a System/36, and are supported on the AS/400 mainly to ensure upward compatibility for any System/36 installations wishing to upgrade. A data area is simply a block of storage which may be accessed by programs and users. Unlike a file, it has only one "record". Its layout must be defined internally within a program.

In the past, data areas were sometimes used for passing parameters but, in RPG III, it is better to use the PARM pseudo command.

One use for data areas is best illustrated by means of an example. Suppose we work for the General Mining Corporation, and our trendy leaders decide to shorten the organisation's name to GenMinCo. Leaving aside the question of taste, we have a potential problem of going through hundreds of report programs changing the literals which provide the page headings. If the heading line is stored as a data area then a change to that data area will automatically change all page headings.

Data Queues are mentioned here only because they are sometimes confused with data areas. They provide very quick access to small amounts of data, but in practice are seldom encountered. Like data areas, their layouts must be defined internally, but unlike data areas, they may have more than one "record". There are a number of restrictions and caveats about the use of data queues, and anyone wishing to use them should study the manual first.

1.2.11 Odds and ends
Performance, cycling languages

The AS/400 is unquestionably a high-level machine. As such, most of the arguments hold good that were used twenty years ago to justify the swing from assembler languages to COBOL.

Now, no-one in his right mind would expect to get the same sort of performance out of a COBOL program as from the same application written in Assembler, and for that reason Assembler is still used for performance-critical jobs.

Yet one still finds installations which do things like prohibiting the RPG cycle, on the grounds that it is less efficient than procedural RPG III. If performance is that critical, the organisation should have bought a 43xx in the first place.

This brings to mind a rather curious situation. Most mainframe installations are swinging away from COBOL, which is a procedural language, to auto-cycling languages such as Natural.

GSD installations, having long used RPG II, with its built in cycle, are turning to full-procedural RPG III programs. Another case where the right hand doesn't know what the left is up to?

In Chapter 4 we shall discuss the methodology of database design on AS/400,and why it stands many established ideas on their heads.

2

Relational Databases

2.1 Problems with flat-files

Before databases came into widespread use, most organisations stored their data in flat-file systems. Many still do.

Each file is "owned" by a particular department – and frequently these departments are as protective of "their" files as a lioness is of her cubs. The data is not perceived as a resource to be used for the general good of the organisation.

A number of problems spring from this approach, one of the biggest being redundancy. In a large manufacturing company several departments will need to know the customers' names and addresses: e.g. marketing, sales, accounts, credit control and despatch.

If each one stores its own copy of the names and addresses there will clearly be a waste of disk space. But that is the least of our worries.

Suppose a customer moves, and gives his new address to a truck driver who happens to be making a delivery that day. The truck driver dutifully passes on the new address to his superiors in despatch – but they omit to notify the other departments, and the invoice goes to the customer's old address. Net result: delay in payment, possibly unnecessary work for credit control as a result and, worst of all, the customer decides that the company is run by a bunch of incompetent idiots with whom he will not again do business. Admittedly this is an extreme example.

There are other problems. One of the objectives in writing a payroll system is to be able to tell the manager of each department how much his staff are costing him. So we build an accumulator field into each employee's record on the salaries master file. At the end of each month we total these accumulator fields by department. Now suppose a clerk is moved to another department. His accumulated costs will be taken with him to his new department. His new manager will not be pleased.

One to many relationships have a nasty habit of turning into questions of "one to *how* many?". If we design a claims system for a medical malpractice insurer we shall probably ask ourselves what is likely to be the maximum number of doctors involved in a given incident.

We can think immediately of two – anaesthetist and surgeon – so we allow for four. And as sure as God made little green apples, next week we shall have a case with five.

The foregoing is by no means an exhaustive list of the difficulties caused by flat-file systems, and much effort has gone into developing the theory of databases which avoid them.

2.2 Normalisation

There are three main types of database, of which more anon. But whichever type is used, the importance of rendering the data into Third Normal Form (3NF) cannot be overstated.

It is appalling how many people working in database installations respond "What's that?" when 3NF is mentioned. Before we define 3NF it is necessary to understand the meaning of the term "data atom".

Our word "atom" comes from the Greek *atomos*, meaning indivisible. A date, for example, is not an atom: it can be divided into day month, and year.

This may sound like mere pedantry, but the purpose will become clear. (Don't forget that atoms can be concatenated into a single field.)

The formal definition of 3NF, (given by Chris Date of IBM) is:

> "A relation is in 3NF if it is in 2NF and every non-key attribute is fully dependent on the primary key."

2NF is defined as:

> "A relation is in 2NF if it is in 1NF and every non-key attribute is fully dependent on he primary key."

1NF is defined as:

> "A relation is in 1NF if all underlying domains contain atomic values only."

No, I don't carry that lot around in my head. Try this one:

"A file is in 3NF if its constituent fields are described by

```
the key                  (1NF)
the whole key            (2NF)
and nothing but the key  (3NF)
```

Less precise, but a good deal easier to remember.

Now we can see the point of that pedantic discussion of dates, above. Does 050427 mean 4th May 1927? Or 27th April 1905? Or 5th April 1927?

The only way we can know is by knowing the format of the date; in other words the data is described by something more than the key. 3NF will not be achieved if the file contains a non-atomic element.

Having emphasised the importance of normalising the data, it is necessary to add a caveat: do not over-normalise. Extreme fragmentation of the database can cause problems.

In the medical claims example in section 2.1 we should want to hold the telephone number of each surgeon. Now, it is conceivable that some surgeons would have more than one set of consulting rooms, and in theory we should hold the telephone number for each.

However, to go to the lengths of removing phone numbers to a separate entity would almost certainly be over-kill. Let common sense be your guide.

2.3 DB Types

Hierarchical, network, relational

There are three main types of database: hierarchical, network, and relational. The three types are represented on IBM mainframes by, respectively, DL/I, IDMS and Total, and Adabas.

In each case the DBMS (Database Management System) is grafted on to what was basically designed to be a flat file machine. The AS/400 database is of the relational type, and is an integral part of the machine.

Hierarchies are common in everyday life. Each city has many hospitals, each hospital has many wards, each ward has many beds.

It is also true that each surgeon has many wards, but these are usually distributed across several hospitals, so a ward will belong to a hospital in one hierarchy, but to a surgeon in another hierarchy.

There are a number of objections to hierarchical databases and when CODASYL, the governing body for COBOL, tried to establish a standard for databases it opted for the networked approach.

In a networked database each data item may be thought of as a node, which contains pointers to other nodes, and which in turn is pointed at by pointers in other nodes.

Each hospital node contains pointers to ward nodes. So does each surgeon node. Each ward node contains a pointer to a surgeon node and a pointer to a hospital node.

2.4 Rows and Tuples, Entities and Attributes

Many people are overawed by textbooks on relational database theory because they drone on learnedly about rows and tuples, and entities and attributes. Never fear!

Rows and tuples are, respectively, simply files and fields. And, for all practical purposes, so are entities and attributes. But it is important that we get the normalisation right.

2.5 Relational databases

Easier to understand: alternate indexes, keys not embedded

It may appear that there is no very great difference between a relational database and a flat-file system with alternate indexing.

In principle we could set up a relational database using System/36 or VSAM alternate indexes, but it would lack facilities such as journalling, "deadly embrace" resolution, data dictionary etc.

Because relational databases are more like flat-file systems than their competitors they are usually easier to understand for programmers who have been used to traditional methods.

One important difference between relational databases and their hierarchical and networked competitors, is that their indexes are stored separately from the data: they are not "embedded".

This is both good news and bad news. One of the worst things that can go wrong with a database is that the indexes get scrambled. On a relational database the solution is simple: delete the userviews and re-create them.

The bad news is that every database access requires two disk reads rather than one – one to pull in the index, and one to read the data. This has an obvious effect on performance, and is the main reason why in the early days of databases the relational model was regarded as very nice in theory but not really practical.

One of the major benefits of single-level storage is that it goes a long way to address this problem. On a tree-structured index there is a good chance that at least the upper levels of the tree will be on pages already in core.

2.6 Userviews, dense keys

One of the fundamental principles of databases is that each user may view the data as he wishes it to be, without concerning himself about the underlying structure.

The term "userview" comes from Adabas. CODASYL calls them "sub-schemas", and on the AS/400 they are Logical Files. Arguably the Adabas term is the most descriptive.

Suppose the SURGEON entity looks like this, its root key (printed in bold) being the Surgeon Number:

Number	Surname	Forename	Practice Address	Practice Phone	Medical School	Qualification	Home Address	Home Phone
S12345	SMITH	Lesley	123 Main St.	767314	Redbrick	MD	13 Easy St.	504042

(This is not properly normalised – what if the surgeon has more than one qualification?)

The Emergencies Department need to know how to get hold of a given surgeon quickly. They do not want to waste time looking up the surgeon number, and have no interest in qualifications, medical school etc. So they will probably want a userview that looks like this (again the keys are in bold):

Surname	Forename	Practice Phone	Home Phone
SMITH	**Lesley**	767314	504042

Most pre-database machines used ISAM (Indexed Sequential Access Method), albeit by some other trade name. The essence of this is that the data is physically arranged in key sequence, and that makes possible what is called a "sparse key".

Key entries are made one per disk track, recording the highest key on that track, rather than one per record, which is called a "dense key". Once data is keyed in some sequence other than that in which it is stored, dense keys are unavoidable.

Dense keys can cause severe performance problems unless avoiding action is taken. As we saw in previous sections, networked databases store their pointers with their data.

Relational databases did not become really practical until single-level storage (and large amounts of cheap core to support it) became available.

2.7 Data dictionary

The Data Dictionary has been described as a database in its own right; it contains details of the data items in the database.

In principle it should contain all the documentation on the database, including authorisation, mapping definitions, dependencies, cross referencing and so on.

Ideally all this information should be updated automatically rather than by depending on fallible and forgetful humans to make the necessary entries. In practice some capabilities may be implemented by discrete functions rather than contained within a formal data dictionary.

The acid test of a data dictionary is whether it is capable of supplying the DBA (Data Base Administrator) with the information he needs to determine the impact of any proposed change to the database.

2.8 Intersection data

Intersection Data is data that describes a particular instance of a combination of two entities.

If an operation goes wrong and there were three doctors involved, the patient's lawyers will probably sue all of them. They in turn will claim on their insurers. The insurer will want his database to hold each one's highest qualification on the date of the incident.

These cannot be stored in the DOCTOR entity because they may subsequently gain higher qualifications, and they cannot be stored in the CLAIM entity, because the number of doctors involved in a claim is unpredictable.

The answer is to store them as an intersection file, which would be given some more or less meaningful name, such as CLMDOC.

The relation would look like this:

CLAIM Entity

Claim Number	Claim Description	Other Details
C1	Amputated Wrong Leg	Date etc.
C2	Bungled delivery: Baby BrainDamaged	Date etc.
C3	Cancer not Diagnosed: Patient Died	Date etc.

DOCTOR Entity

Doctor Number	Highest Qual.	Other Details
D1	Ph D	name, etc.
D2	M.D.	name, etc.
D3	FRCS	name, etc.

CLMDOC Intersection.

Claim Number	Doctor Number	Hiighest Qual	Other Details
C1	D1	Ph D	salary grade, etc.
C1	D2	M.D.	salary grade, etc.
C1	D3	FRCS	salary grade, etc

When the intersection record is created the Highest Qualification field is copied from the Doctor entity. Once this has been done further updates of Highest Qualification in the Doctor entity will have no effect.

Note that the intersection file's root key is a combination of the root keys of the two entities which it links.

It is nearly always advisable to define the root key as unique (i.e. duplicates not allowed); if (say) C1D2 appeared twice it would mean that doctor D2 had been attached to the claim twice. Most DBMS's, including OS/400's, offer a facility to check that keys are unique.

Entity root keys should always be unique. If they are not the normalising is probably incorrect. Userviews – i.e. alternate indexes – will very seldom be unique. If they are the normalising is probably incorrect.

In the example in section 2.6 above we certainly could not allow two surgeons with the key S12345, but it is quite conceivable that there could be two called Lesley Smith.

2.9 Deadly embraces

We touched briefly on "deadly embraces" in section 1.2.2. Program A waits for a record held by Program B, which in turn waits for a record held by Program A. Unless something is done, both will wait for ever.

The easiest solution is a time-out, i.e. to raise an error condition if a program has to wait longer than the stipulated period for a record.

Suppose the read by Program B times out first. An error condition will be raised; if Program B has not monitored for this it will fall over, if it has then it can take appropriate action – probably to release all held records, wait a few seconds and then try again.

Meanwhile, because Program B has released the resource Program A was waiting for, Program A can go ahead normally.

In practice deadly embraces are very rare, and it is seldom worth the effort and expense of monitoring for time-outs.

3

AS/400 and Relational DB:

How they fit together

3.1 All data in DB

On an IBM mainframe, and on any other machine to which the DBMS was added as an afterthought, it is possible to have conventional flat-files outside the database. This is not so on an AS/400. Data on an AS/400 cannot be stored anywhere but the database.

That does not mean that it is impossible to store flat files on an AS/400, but simply that they will be regarded as database files. Of course, all the limitations of non-normalised data will still apply.

The most likely occasion when this might happen is when a file is part of a system which has been converted from an older, non-database machine.

If no DDS (Data Description Specifications) are available the file may simply be created with an explicit record length. If an attempt is then made to declare the file as external, it will be treated as having a single alphameric field of length equal to the record length, and having the same name as the file.

When a key is desired it is necessary to create DDS in order to describe the key to OS/400, but this may be quite simple. Suppose the record length is 120 characters and the key is required on the part number, which is on positions 4 to 9. The following will be adequate:

```
1.00 A          DATA1           3
2.00 A          PARTNO          6
3.00 A          DATA2         111
4.00 A*
5.00 A        K PARTNO                    UNIQUE
```

DATA1 and DATA2 are simply alphameric fields, each byte validly containing anything from X'00' to X'FF'. If, for example, positions 21 to 23 contain the hex pattern X'01234F', which happens to be a packed number, that is immaterial to OS/400. The programs that use DATA1 and DATA2 may, and almost certainly will, define them internally as many small fields.

PARTNO is defined on line 2 because OS/400 needs to know its attributes if it is to use it as a key, as requested in line 5. The character K to the left of PARTNO on line 5 tells OS/400 that PARTNO is to be used as a key. The keyword UNIQUE on the rightmost part of line 5 is advisable if the old ISAM file is to be emulated accurately.

3.2 Logical files

To implement userviews, field selection, joins (no update), number of logical files affect performance

Logical Files are used to implement userviews. Records may be selected by omit and/or include criteria, but you need to be careful with complex omit/include statements. The syntax is tricky.

Fields may be renamed, but this should be necessary only in exceptional circumstances. Generally it is better to change the programs to use the standard names, unless that is a really huge task.

Not everything that is possible is wise, and if renaming is really essential it is usually better to do it within RPG – see subsection 7.11.2. Try to get the opinion of an experienced AS/400 programmer before deciding which way to go.

Logical files (LFs) may be created over more than one Physical File (PF). If this is done without specifying a "join", the effect is to merge the two physical files. Joined logical files link two or more PFs by means of a common field – the names do not have to be same on all files, merely the attributes.

Take the example in section 2.8, and suppose we have been asked to list the names of all doctors involved in claims. One way to do it would be to read the intersection file CLMDOC, using the Doctor Number field on each record to read the appropriate record from the Doctor entity.

Alternatively we could use a joined LF to link CLMDOC to DOCTOR (which in practice would be a physical file – see section 3.4) and would need to define only one file – the joined LF – in our program.

The program would "see" a userview which looked like this:

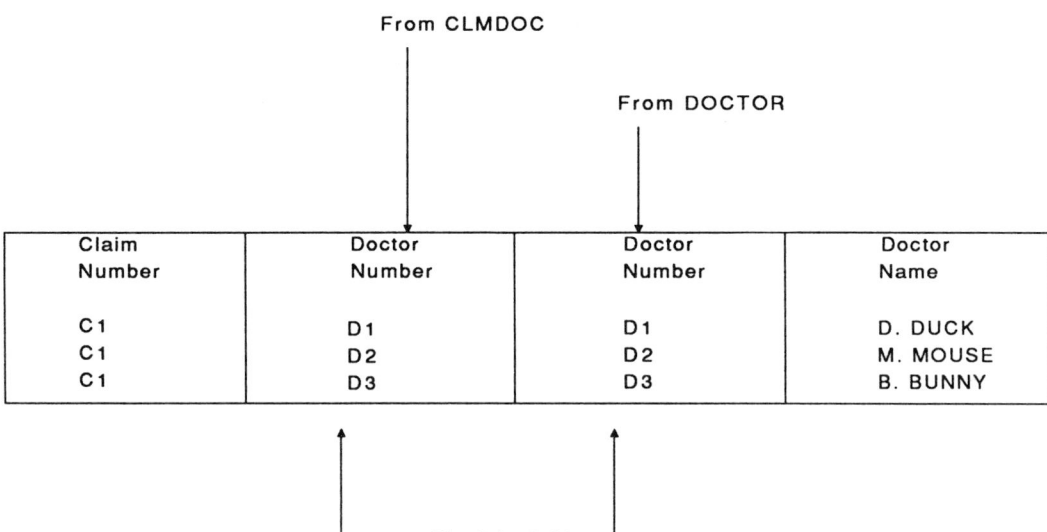

This facility is less useful than might at first appear. The time we save, by writing a simpler program, is lost in coding the DDS for the LF. As far as machine efficiency is concerned, it will be necessary to read the same number of physical records whichever option we choose.

There is some merit in creating a joined LF, if by doing so we can avoid writing a program altogether, and instead use a utility such as VIEW (see Appendix B). VIEW cannot handle more than one file, but that file can be a joined LF.

If we forget to delete the joined LF when we have finished with it, OS/400 will have the continuing overhead of maintaining it. (Don't forget that if it is in QTEMP it will be deleted automatically when the job finishes.)

The other factor which detracts from the usefulness of joined LFs is that they are read only: it is not possible to add or update records by means of a joined LF.

The CL command OPNQRYF (Open Query File) offers much the same facilities as LFs, in effect it creates temporary LFs. It does so without DDS, by means of complex command parameters. OPNQRYF was added to the operating system late in the life of System/38, i.e. shortly before the great cosmetic name-change to AS/400. On the other hand, LFs were there, right from the beginning.

As hinted at the beginning of this section, it is possible to create joined LFs over more than two physical files. Unfortunately joined LFs become exponentially more complicated as the number of physical files increases, and joining more than two PFs is seldom worth the bother.

Early versions of CPF required explicit specification if two LFs were to share an access path, but it is now done automatically wherever feasible, with obvious benefits for efficiency.

In theory, an unlimited number of LFs may be declared over a given PF, though in practice performance problems would result. IBM suggests not more than ten LFs per PF, but this is only a rule of thumb, and it all depends on the volatility of the file and the number of access paths.

OS/400 has to update all the indexes every time an entry for a key fields changes, or a record is added or deleted. If the underlying PF is used mainly in read-only mode then there is little or no updating to do, and so it doesn't matter how many LFs there are.

3.3 Single level storage

Performance implications

A Californian hot-rodding magazine once described an engine expert as being able to think like a hot petrol molecule flying through an intake valve.

By the same token a good AS/400 programmer should be able to think like a page in storage switching between disk and core. The effects of single-level storage may not be immediately obvious, but they permeate every aspect of the AS/400.

Files within the database consist of two elements: the records and the keys, and the keys may be further broken down into the different levels of the index, which is conceptually an inverted tree.

When a read is requested to a given record, the operating system has to start with the top level index for that file, follow down the appropriate branches of the tree, and finally retrieve the record itself. The chances are that each level of the index, and the record itself, will be on different pages. If every one of these pages had to be physically fetched from disk for every read we should have an impossible situation. As it is, at least the top level of the index is likely to be in core (depending on how often the file in question is used), and if we are lucky we may find all levels of the index and even the record itself already loaded. All this goes on completely transparently to the programmer.

A simple experiment will bring the point dramatically home. Choose a source file with a fairly large number of members and call it up using the STRSEU (Start Source Edit Utility) command – on the System/38 this is EDTSRC (Edit Source). Do not specify a member name.

You will be presented with a list of members in the file, and invited to select one. There will be more members than can fit onto the screen at once, so use the roll key to scroll through the entire list.

Now quit, by pressing [CF3] ([CF1] on System/38), and immediately do the same thing again. Note how the scrolling is much faster the second time around. This is because the pages containing the file header information, which STRSEU needs to create the list, are still in core from the first time.

Many older systems, and particularly older DBMSs, use DAM (Direct Access Method) in an attempt to improve performance. The basic idea is to use an algorithm to calculate the disk address of a record, and so avoid having to read an index.

It is possible to do this on an AS/400, but there is much less point in it because the index pages will usually be found to be already loaded.

3.4 Terminology

Rows are PFs, Tuples are Fields, the Data Dictionary is the FRF

This is a good moment to dispense with a small terminological difficulty. While "entity" and "attribute" have an impeccable pedigree in relational algebra, "attribute" already has a meaning in DDS, and assigning any other meaning to it can only lead to confusion. So don't do it.

One of the great truths of working with AS/400 is that PFs should correspond with the 3NF (Third Normal Form) groupings of the data; i.e. with the entities.

Two of Ted Codd's Twelve Rules are:

1)   All data should be represented as values within two-dimensional tables.

2)   Every value should be accessible via a combination of table name, primary key and column name

On an AS/400 these tables are, or at least should be, synonymous with PFs.

Physical files (and for that matter LFs) may be defined without keys, and it is sometimes suggested that the entity PFs should be so defined. Presumably this notion comes from the basic concept that a database is simply a pool of data, not arranged in any particular order.

The notion is sound enough in theory, but in practical day-to-day working it is often very useful to have the physical files keyed by their root keys, and to add the self-explanatory keyword UNIQUE.

If any attempt is then made to add rogue data to the PF, a duplicate key error will be raised. The program can contain a routine to handle it, or it can simply be allowed to crash. Certainly program crashes are undesirable but, compared to corrupting the database, they are much the lesser of two evils.

Tuples are simply fields, but the AS/400 field definition contains entries over and above what one would normally expect to find in a tuple. These include descriptive text, default column headings and, for numeric fields, whether they are to be stored as binary, packed or zoned.

Packed fields on the AS/400 are described in COBOL as COMPUTATIONAL-3, i.e. they take the form X'123F'. Note that unlike IBM mainframes, which use hex 'C' as the positive sign, AS/400 uses hex 'F', however the negative sign is the same as that on mainframes, hex 'D'.

Programmers converting to AS/400 from machines which use the COMPUTATIONAL-2 packed format should note that there is no language in RPG to handle COMP-2. There is in AS/400 COBOL but it is inefficient, and it is better to convert.

Better still, stay with zoned numerics. The disk and CPU overheads are quite small, and zoned is much easier to read on dumps etc.

The function of a **Data Dictionary** is largely performed on the AS/400 by the Field Reference File (FRF). This is implemented simply as a PF; the difference between it and any other PF is purely conceptual. That implies that it is possible to write data to it, and one might think that nobody would be mad enough to do so. Cater for the possibility anyway by restricting the number of records it may hold to one (OS/400's CRTPF (Create Physical File) CL command will not allow you to restrict it to zero).

All fields in the database should be declared in the first instance within a Field Reference File, and in practice it works well to give each major system its own FRF. For example, an insurance company might have separate FRFs for the Claims and Policy Holders databases.

DDS syntax permits referral within a file, a feature which may be used to set up root definitions.

Suppose we decide that all names in the database are to be 30 bytes long, and that we wish to store each policy holder's surname in a field called PHSNM. The FRF DDS would look like this:

```
1.00 A          NAME            30A
2.00 A                                  TEXT('Standard Name Field')
3.00 A                                  COLHDG('NAME')
4.00 A          PHSNM           R
5.00 A                                  REFFLD(NAME    *SRC)
6.00 A                                  TEXT('Policy Holders +
7.00 A                                        Surname')
8.00 A                                  COLHDG('POLICY'  'HOLDER'
9.00 A                                         'SURNAME')
```

Line 1 defines the root field NAME as 30 bytes alphameric. Line 2 associates with it the text 'Standard Name Field' and line 3 associates with it the column heading 'NAME'. If the TEXT and COLHDG keywords are omitted, the name of the field will be assumed for each: in other words, line 3 is redundant.

Line 4 defines field PHSNM and the letter R tells us that it is referenced. Line 5 gives the REFFLD keyword, which tells us to what it is referenced, and has the general form REFFLD (fieldname filename).

In this case the field is NAME and, because we wish to tell OS/400 that NAME is to be found within this file's own source, we use the figurative constant *SRC.

Lines 6 and 7, and 8 and 9 respectively supply field text and column headings for PHSNM. If they had been omitted the text and column headings for the reference field NAME would have been used, and if that too had been omitted the name of the field itself, PHSNM, would have been used.

Note that each of the words in the entry for lines 8 and 9 is enclosed in quotes. Various utilities – for whose use COLHDG is mainly intended – will stack these words one above the other, as in (a) below if coded as shown. If coded all within one set of quotes they would be shown as in (b).

```
     (a)                                         (b)


  POLICY                              POLICY HOLDER SURNAME
  HOLDER
  SURNAME
```

Over and above the considerations mentioned above, the very existence of a reference field often assists with documentation.

It may be thought excessive to go to the trouble of defining a one-byte root field FLAG, and then referencing all the one-byte flags to it, but doing so means a maintenance programmer can tell at a glance whether or not a given field is a flag.

As we saw in section 2.7, the data dictionary has tasks beyond merely defining fields. It is expected to provide information on cross referencing, dependencies etc. for the DBA.

These functions are supplied by a variety of CL commands, notably:

❑ DSPFD (Display File Description)

❑ DSPOBJD (Display Object Description)

❑ DSPPGMREF (Display Program References), and

❑ DSPDBR (Display Database Relations).

IBM supplies a DBA user profile called QSECOFR (Security Officer), and consequently the DBA on an AS/400 site is invariably referred to as SECOFR (pronounced SEC OFFER). Many experienced AS/400 programmers are not even familiar with the term DBA.

3.5 Intersection files

The purpose of intersection files was explained in section 2.8. The difference between an intersection file and any other PF is purely conceptual – OS/400 can see no difference at all.

Like any other PF, an intersection file may be declared without keys, though there would seem very little point in doing so; it may also have LFs based upon it. Most intersection files will require at least one such LF, to provide an inverted linkage.

Look at the example in section 2.8. The CLMDOC intersection file can tell us all the doctors involved in a given claim, but what if we want a list of all the claims in which a given doctor was involved?

The answer is an LF over CLMDOC, which would look like this:

Doctor Number	Claim Number	Intersection Details
D1	C1	intersection details
D1	C1	intersection details
D2	C78	intersection details
D3	C33	intersection details

There is no advantage to having multiple intersection files for the same intersection – a single PF, with as many LFs as are needed, is cleaner and more efficient.

4

Database Design on the AS/400

4.1   Prior design or .....?

Intuitive logic and the received wisdom at most database sites suggest that a proposed database and its associated applications should be defined in great detail before any attempt is made to "cut metal".

When one has at one's disposal the powerful tools of OS/400, such an approach is rather like using a mule team to drag a Ferrari around: you'll get from A to B all right – but what a waste!

4.2   Data atoms
Identifying and recording them

There are certain things which have to be done, regardless of the final design, so there is nothing to be lost by going ahead and doing them.

A vital task is to make a list of all data atoms required by the new application. (See section 2.2 for a discussion of data atoms.) Our list is likely to consist of a mixture of existing database items, plus new ones. There is not much we can do about existing ones, but we should record all new ones, reducing them to atoms as we go along.

We could do so on a grubby sheet of paper but, as it is no extra effort to type it straight into the computer, why not do so? One way would be to type it into a document in a word processor but, since IBM has thoughtfully provided a proper receptacle, let us make use of it.

Type each data atom straight into the Field Reference File DDS, where OS/400 requires you to give it a name and attributes (alpha or numeric, length, decimal positions etc.) and provides a slot 50 bytes long for descriptive text, which ultimately will appear in RPG III listings.

4.3 Attaching an Office/400 member
to expand each field definition

More than likely, 50 bytes is not sufficient to hold everything you wish to record about a data atom. To cater for this, create a source file with a member for each data atom, the member having the same name as the data atom.

An obvious extension to this idea is a single data entry program to link the source member with the Field Reference File and its DDS.

4.4 Naming conventions
for field names within files

Unless rigorous naming conventions are imposed, and the whole business properly co-ordinated, chaos will rapidly ensue.

Naming conventions always constitute a knotty and controversial problem and the RPG constraint of six digits for field names makes the problem worse.

Most sites use the first two digits as a file prefix then, as far as possible, use the next four digits as the field name proper. Clearly there are other possibilities, but this works as well as any. Whatever you do, avoid the temptation to use a prefix and a number. You should also avoid those prefixes already used by IBM in their command output files, such as JO for the output file from the DSPJRN (Display Journal) database file. (A set of model command output files is to be found in library QSYS.)

For example, the Sales file might be given a prefix of SL, and the Returned Goods file a prefix of RG. Customer would be CUST, so the customer field within the sales file would be SLCUST, and within the Returned Goods file it would be RGCUST.

A potential problem is: what if we change the attributes of CUST? A good designer will plan for this by having a "root" definition of CUST at the beginning of the Field Reference File definition, with SLCUST and RGCUST referred to it. This approach is discussed in section 3.4.

Another difficulty arises if the installation buys a package which uses some other convention, and all our carefully laid plans are likely to be ruined.

Note that DDS permits 10-character field names, with slightly more liberal name-forming rules than RPG. In other words, the RPG rules are a subset of the DDS rules.

Common sense suggests that an RPG installation should adhere to the RPG rules (otherwise the programmers will have to rename fields in the I-specs – see section 7.11 – each time a file is used).

You may notice the DDS keyword ALIAS, which allows a field to be given a 30-character name in addition to the normal DDS name. The 30- character limit should betray the purpose: it is for COBOL and PL/I programs, which permit 30-character names. When used in COBOL programs, any underscores are automatically converted to hyphens.

4.5 Reduce to 3NF
Key in physical file should correspond to 3NF key

Having prepared a list of data atoms, whether on the machine or elsewhere, the next thing to do is to reduce it to 3NF (third normal form). This applies to all databases on all machines.

Remember the informal definition of 3NF from section 2.2:

A file is in 3NF if its constituent fields are described by
- the key   (1NF)
- the whole key   (2NF)
- and nothing but the key   (3NF)

Now we can see why we had to reduce our initial list to data atoms. We should be unable to achieve 3NF if the FRF contained any non-atomic entries, such as dates. (Don't forget that atoms can be concatenated into a single field when creating a logical file.)

One of the great truths of working with AS/400 is that physical files should correspond with the 3NF groupings of the data.

As long as we get this right, the foundations of our database will be sound – though of course this is not to say that jerrybuilders cannot erect a ramshackle edifice upon them.

This is so important that it is worth repeating the advice in section 3.3: two of Ted Codd's Twelve Rules state:

1) All data should be represented as values within two- dimensional tables.

2) Every value should be accessible via a combination of table name, primary key and column name

On an AS/400 these tables should be represented by physical files.

4.6 Recording the data atoms
as physical file DDS

Once more, having arranged our data atoms into groups which are in 3NF, we need to record this somewhere. Again, we could use a grubby sheet of paper, but it is better to type it straight into the computer and, since these groups are exactly what our physical files ought to be, where better than as physical file DDS?

Note again that each step we have taken is a step which would have to be taken anyway, irrespective of the final design, so it is a complete waste of effort to prepare elaborate business and technical specifications before doing so.

4.7 Compile and use with SDA
involve users

Sooner or later all this DDS will have to be compiled, so do it now. The result is a collection of physical files whose constituent fields are ripe for painting onto screens using SDA (Screen Design Aid) and then saved as screen (i.e. *DSPF) DDS.

This gives us the opportunity to involve our user in the screen design process: we can sit him next to us and let him call the shots while we paint on fields, move them around, highlight them, add and change literals, what you will.

Nothing is more conducive to a smooth signoff than a user who feels he is signing off his own creation!

4.8 *PRTF DDS
*using SDA and converting from *DSPF DDS*

And what of the Cinderella of the development process, the printed reports? The tedious days of filling in a printer spacing chart are history. So is moving entries around by erasing them and pencilling them in again.

Simply develop the layout on SDA, then convert the resulting *DSPF DDS to (external) *PRTF DDS. Note that the *DSPF DDS should declare the screen type as *DS4 to get 132-character capability – the screen hardware must be able to support *DS4.

A conversion program is needed, also a utility to exercise the new DDS. These are quite simple to write, alternatively they may be purchased – see Appendix B.

Before proceeding with design of logical files and specification of programs, it remains to document what we have already achieved. Fortunately, there is little to be done.

4.9 Documentation using SDA

SDA will print the screens we have designed at the touch of a single command key; this is usually necessary for signoff purposes, and eventually to give the programmer a picture of what he is to do.

Everything else will already be residing in source members, and so may easily be printed – but why bother?

4.9.1 Value of documentation on disk

if world-wide distribution needed

On the contrary, the approach of keeping all documentation on the AS/400's disks offers some advantage if the new system is to be distributed to sites around the world.

Simply include the relevant source files on the installation tape and avoid the usual cumbersome business of reproducing and distributing manuals.

4.10 Formal specification shortcut

If management insists on a traditional formal specification (using forms developed by the DPM for the IBM 1401 – being the last machine he actually understood), then there is a short cut as follows.

Using SDA as outlined above, create an external print file to mirror the required form. Use the DSPFFD (Display File Field Descriptions) command to create database files containing the details of each of the physical files you have created.

Write a simple RPG program to read the DSPFFD output and the source file containing the amplified field descriptions, and write to your print file.

4.12 Feasibility studies

But what if all we were asked to do was a feasibility study, rather than a "do it"? The procedure outlined in this chapter would be at least as quick as any other, with the advantage that if the go-ahead is given the work is already done.

5

History of RPG

5.1 Introduction

George Santayana remarked that he who ignores history is doomed to repeat it. Henry Ford more famously stated that history is bunk.

Whatever the merits of that debate, anyone aspiring to be a good programmer should try to understand the underlying purposes of his tools, and how and why they evolved.

Knowledge engineers distinguish between deep and shallow knowledge. Shallow knowledge is "cookbook" knowledge: you do what the recipe says without understanding why. Deep knowledge implies an intimate understanding of the whys and wherefores of the subject.

In the case of RPG, this means having at least a nodding acquaintance with its past.

I find the history of RPG fascinating, and I enjoyed writing this chapter. Even if you do not enjoy reading it, I firmly believe you will be a better RPG programmer for having done so.

RPG is an old language – nearly as old as COBOL. For years its market penetration was only about 9% – much smaller than COBOL's – though with the tremendous success of the AS/400 this is increasing.

Although RPG is no more difficult than COBOL, RPG programmers have for many years enjoyed a salary premium over their COBOL counterparts. (In fact, in the mid-seventies, they actually earned more than mainframe assembler programmers, which was truly ridiculous, but only King Canute would argue with supply and demand.)

Unlike COBOL, it has never been protected by a standardisation body, though IBM's preponderance has exerted much the same influence. Even so, there are substantial variations between dialects of RPG, just as there are between dialects of COBOL.

Usually associated with IBM's GSD division, RPG is also implemented on their mainframes, and has been adopted by many other manufacturers, including ICL, Wang, Honeywell, and both the Burroughs and Univac components of Unisys.

It is available on IBM-compatible PCs, and there is at least one implementation under UNIX. PC-based emulators of both AS/400 and RPG III are marketed by California Software and Native Software, of Virginia.

5.2 Evolving dialects of RPG

Originally the language was simply called RPG. The first major improvement was RPG II, introduced around 1975, which introduced significant improvements such as array processing and data structures.

An even bigger enhancement came with RPG III, available only on System/38 and AS/400, and exploiting the advanced architecture of these most sophisticated of all IBM computers.

One of the most important improvements in RPG III over RPG II was the support for external files (see Chapter 1). Standardised field names go hand in hand with external files.

In RPG II field names were generally left to the individual programmer, and there was little or no reason to observe naming conventions, such as those outlined in Chapters 6 and 17. This can cause major headaches when converting an RPG II system onto an AS/400 – the problems are discussed in detail in Chapter 15.

When RPG first appeared it was claimed to be so simple that end-users would write their own programs, making programmers redundant. (The same rubbish is talked about 4GLs and CASE tools today.)

It was indeed (nearly) as simple as claimed, but simplicity was achieved only by limiting function. For example, there was no capability for array processing, so when this was required, it was necessary to use an Assembler sub-program – certainly a job requiring a trained programmer.

The years passed, the demand rose for the missing functions; and as they were added so the simplicity was lost. I freely predict that languages such as Synon/2 and its competitors will undergo the same life-cycle.

The observation underlying the original RPG was that virtually all programs operate in a *cycle* (Chapter 8 is devoted to the cycle). They read a record, do calculations based on the data just read, optionally produce output, then go back to read the next record. It should therefore be possible to produce a standard program, tailored by means of parameters, to suit individual requirements.

IBM was certainly not the first to try this approach; early Burroughs machines had a simple generator, called RG1, whose parameters were contained on just eight cards.

This proved too inflexible, and a variant called RG1A was introduced which generated an intermediate Assembler source deck, which the programmer then modified to incorporate the missing function.

Here one experiences a sense of *deja vu*: Synon/2 generates an intermediate RPG source deck....

The dividing line between RPG II and RPG III is difficult to draw precisely, because RPG II is a subset of RPG III, and a working RPG II program will compile and run quite happily using the RPG III compiler.

The waters are muddied still further because some RPG III features have been retro-fitted to some implementations of RPG II, giving rise to a sort of RPG $2^1/_2$. ($III^I/_{II}$?).

RPG III programmers who are fully conversant with RPG II tend to draw from each as appropriate to the task at hand, increasing the confusion.

The latest addition to the family is RPG 400. This is a classic case of "badge-engineering", and it will need a magnifying glass more powerful than mine to discover the differences. (See Appendix E).

About the most significant is that numeric fields may now be 30 digits long, rather than the 15 digits allowed in all previous versions. I can only comment that in 20 years of using the language I have never needed even 15.

Because they are so similar, most people in the industry use the term "RPG III" to cover both RPG III and RPG 400, and in this book we shall stick to that convention.

5.3 Development

from unit record machines...

Before computers as such came into widespread use, data processing was achieved by means of unit record machines, sometimes called Hollerith machines after their inventor, Herman Hollerith. These comprised (card) sorters, collators, and tabulators.

RPG was designed with an eye to selling computers by providing an easy upgrade path from unit record machines. It did so by emulating their way of working. Some of its features reflect this, notably the built-in level-breaking facility, and the rather odd way matching works (see Chapter 8).

Systems for unit record machines frequently utilised a number of different card types, identified by appropriate characters punched on the appointed columns.

RPG I-specs (for details of the various spec types see Chapter 7) mimic this selection ability, and it was so useful that files incorporating numerous different record types were much more common than in COBOL flat-file systems.

Each type is associated with one of the RPG "indicators", which is turned on automatically when it is read. Indicators are a major reason why many programmers dislike RPG. They are simply one-byte flags which contain X'F0' if off and X'F1' if on. Because it is so easy to set an indicator on when you mean to set it off, or test for on when you mean to test for off, indicators are a major source of bugs – almost as bad as GOTOs.

Relatively recent enhancements to the language provide IF and DO constructs, which greatly reduce the need to use indicators at all.

Various other factors – notably subfiles (see Chapter 12) – reduce the need still further. Fewer indicators means reduced debugging time and therefore higher productivity.

5.4 Today's situation
..... to modern "fully procedural" RPG

One of the most significant recent changes to the language is the introduction of fully procedural programs (see Chapter 9), meaning ones in which the cycle is shut off. Most RPG III programs are written this way.

Full procedural programming is much simpler for the neophyte, but in abandoning the cycle he forfeits both the matching facility and the automatic level breaking facility.

Given historical background we can understand some of the strange little quirks in today's RPG. For example, why the difference between table and array handling? Simply because tables were in the original RPG, and were not removed when RPG II came along for fear of causing upward compatibility problems with existing programs.

5.5 The Generator

Strictly speaking, there is no such thing as an RPG compiler. RPG stands for Report Program *Generator*, and the software in question is therefore just that: a program generator.

Just how far RPG has travelled from the original generator concept may be gauged by the fact that software is available – Synon/2 for example – to generate RPG programs. So the generator is now generated.

6

RPG Names and Naming Conventions

6.1 Similarity to COBOL

except 6-character, # and @ allowed, but no hyphen

The rules for forming RPG field names are broadly similar to those for COBOL. By far the most important difference is that they may not be longer than six characters – against 30 for COBOL. Worse still, subscripted names must be entirely contained within the six characters.

The character set for RPG field names comprises:

❑ the letters A through Z

❑ the numerals 0 through 9

❑ the special characters # and @

The first character of a field name must be A through Z or # or @. Embedded blanks are not allowed.

RPG has a number of reserved words and figurative constants, but nearly all of these begin with an asterisk – see section 7.3. The exceptions are PAGE, PAGE1 through PAGE7, and UDATE, UDAY, UMONTH and UYEAR.

The PAGE reserved words provide automatic page numbering with internally defined output files, while UDATE, UDAY, UMONTH and UYEAR contain the system date.

Only if a field is also a table, may its name begin with the letters TAB. Array elements are described using a comma between the array name and the subscript name.

If array ABC is to be subscripted by a field named X, the entry would be ABC,X. Note that array name, subscript name and comma together may not total more than six characters. For a detailed discussion see section 7.2.

6.2 Meaningfulness
Descriptive text in RPG III

RPG's worst failing is that field names have a maximum length of six characters, and are therefore necessarily cryptic, sometimes to the point of being meaningless or, worse, misleading.

Clearly, it is very difficult to come up with meaningful names under length restrictions as tight as these. Many hours can be saved later in the development cycle if a few minutes are devoted during the design stage to come up with understandable abbreviations.

I sometimes wonder why IBM did not take the opportunity of the huge leap from RPG II to RPG III to increase the permitted length of field names, however they chose instead to print alongside each database field 50 bytes of descriptive information drawn from the data dictionary.

Arrays and tables are defined on "E-specs" – see Chapter 7 – which provide a 17-character comment field. This should be used to give some clue as to what the array or table is.

About the worst response to the field naming problem is to throw in the towel and simply number them, using a letter in the first position to make the names legal.

6.3 Prefixing field names by file

As we saw in section 4.4, it is a good idea to make the first two characters of each database field name a prefix which tells us which file the field came from.

Of course, this reduces the number of characters available for the name proper to only four, which is really becoming tight, but it is still worth doing.

We used a prefix of SL for the Sales file, and RG for Returned Goods, which left us looking for a four digit abbreviation for "Customer Number". We came up with CUST, which may not constitute great literature, but is reasonably understandable.

It is possible to be imaginative, even within these tight constraints. One insurance company uses RIP, with permitted values of Y and N, to indicate whether a claimant is dead or not.

Prefixes containing # and @, and perhaps also Q and Z, should be reserved for workfields modelled on database fields. Always declare these using the DEFN verb – as described in Chapter 7.

6.4 Field definition

Move to rather than mapping as COBOL – Useful to avoid moves – exception is DS

There is a fundamental difference between COBOL and RPG in the way that fields are drawn from a record. Where COBOL simply maps over the record input area, RPG generates a move into a work area.

This means that if a field is defined twice, (say) as FLDA and FLDB, then changes to FLDB will not affect FLDA and vice versa, whereas in COBOL if FLDB REDEFINES FLDA, then any change made to either will affect both.

We can illustrate this as follows:

COBOL

```
            DATA DIVISION.
            .
            .
            01 RECXX.
               03 FLDA                          PIC X(3).
               03 FLDB     REDEFINES FLDA       PIC X(3).
            .
            PROCEDURE DIVISION.
               MOVE 'ABC'   TO FLDA.
               MOVE 'XYZ'   TO FLDB.
```

RPG

```
      IRECXX
      I                             1   3 FLDA
      I                             1   3 FLDB
      .
      .
      C                    MOVE 'ABC'     FLDA
      C                    MOVE 'XYZ'     FLDB
```

There is a subtle, but important, difference in the end result of these two apparently similar pieces of code. In the COBOL example, both fields will end up containing XYZ. In the RPG example, FLDA will contain ABC and FLDB will contain XYZ.

It follows that if the same field name is used in two files, then reading the second file will overwrite the contents of that field placed there by a read to the first file. In COBOL, a compiler error will result if the names are not qualified, and the qualification is used to ensure that overwriting does not occur.

When it comes to moving data from an input file to an output file, no MOVE commands are needed provided the same field names are used in both. In COBOL we might code:

```
            DATA DIVISION.
              .
              .
              .
            01 FILE-I.
               03 FLDPQR    PIC X(7).
              .
            01 FILE-O.
               03 FILLER    PIC X(10).
               03 FLDPQR    PIC X(7).
              .
            PROCEDURE DIVISION.
               MOVE FLDPQR IN FILE-I
                 TO FLDPQR IN FILE-O.
```

In RPG this is all that would be needed:

```
        IFILEI
        I                              1   7 FLDPQR
          .
          .
        OFILEO
        O                      FLDPQR    17
```

(In RPG, output positions are specified by end position, rather than by start position – this is discussed in more detail in Chapter 7.)

A further implication is that it is not necessary to map the entire record; it is possible to extract only those fields that concern us. Suppose we are interested only in positions 11 to 20, 31 to 40, and 51 to 60 of a 60-byte record. In COBOL we should have to code:

```
             01 INREC.
                03 FILLER    PIC X(10).
                03 FLDX      PIC X(10).
                03 FILLER    PIC X(10).
                03 FLDY      PIC X(10).
                03 FILLER    PIC X(10).
                03 FLDZ      PIC X(10).
```

The following RPG I-specs (Input Specifications) would suffice:
```
IINREC
I                               11  20 FLDX
I                               31  40 FLDY
I                               51  60 FLDZ
```

Another important difference is that RPG initialises fields, alphameric fields to blanks, and numeric fields to zeros. (Some COBOL compilers also do so, but in this they diverge from the ANSI definition.) Just to ensure total confusion, fields defined in *data structures* are not so initialised.

6.5 File names
8-character, operating system dependent, use of OVRDBF

RPG permits file names up to eight characters long, which must conform to RPG name forming rules. Obviously the rules for all operating systems will not necessarily be the same as RPG.

OS/400 permits names up to ten characters long, and the permitted characters are slightly different from RPG. Notably, underscores may be used as connectors. However, RPG naming rules are a subset of OS/400 naming rules. In other words, any valid RPG name will also be a valid OS/400 name, although not all valid OS/400 names are also valid RPG names. Common sense suggests that an AS/400 installation which uses RPG should stick to RPG rules for naming its files, and a naming scheme is suggested in Chapter 17.

If it is necessary to use a file in an RPG program which does not conform to RPG rules then the OVRDBF command provides a way out of the dilemma.

Suppose file CUST _ MAST is to be used in an RPG program. The underscore is illegal in RPG, and CUST _ MAST is nine characters long, which is one more than allowed, so we declare the file as CUSTMAST, for example. The connection is made by the CL command:

```
OVRDBF    FILE(CUSTMST)   TOFILE(CUST _ MAST)
```

See also section 1.2.8.

6.6 Format names
must not be the same as file names, so rename format if necessary

RPG does not allow record formats to have the same name as the file which contains them, although OS/400 does. It is much easier to give files format names which differ from the file name than it is to rename formats in every RPG program.

Sometimes a file is encountered which does have a format of the same name as itself – perhaps from a system which has been purchased from some other organisation – and it is then necessary to rename the format. See Chapter 7 for details.

Briefly, here is how to do it:
```
     FXYZ      IF  E              DISK
     F             XYZ            KRENAMEZYX
```

As always, if in doubt prompt with [CF4]. As long as you get the K (for Kontinuation) in position 53 the prompter will know what type of F-spec you want.

7

The Coding Forms

7.1 The Building Blocks

The main building blocks of RPG programs are fields and indicators, though indicators are much less important in RPG III than in previous versions of RPG.

7.1.1 Fields

Field naming rules and conventions were discussed in detail in Chapter 6, but may be summarised as follows. Field names may not be more than six characters long, and must consist of the letters of the alphabet, numerals, and the special characters #, @, and $. The first character must not be a numeral.

Fields may be alphameric or numeric. Alphameric fields may be up to 256 bytes long, and may contain any hex value. Numeric fields are limited to 30 digits (15 on System/38 and RPG II), of which up to nine may be decimal positions.

Numeric fields may be zoned, packed or binary. If packed they follow the convention that the half-byte containing the sign is at the end of the field. Packed fields with the sign at the beginning (COMPUTATIONAL-2 in COBOL terminology) are not supported by RPG. The AS/400 packed sign is always X'F' for positive and X'D' for negative.

Binary fields are supported, but are very rarely used in practice.

Alphameric fields are initialised to blanks and numeric fields to zeros, unless they form part of a data structure.

7.1.2 Indicators

An indicator is a special type of one-byte flag, which is always denoted by X'F1' when on and X'F0' when off. Indicator names are always two characters long, and the naming scheme is described below.

They are a fruitful source of program bugs – every bit as bad as GO TO instructions – mainly because it is so easy to set to ON or test for ON when you mean OFF.

Incidentally, the GSD dialects of COBOL contain language extensions to enable them to set and test indicators. This is necessary because System/36, System/38 and AS/400 all use indicators in their screen files for such purposes as conditioning display attributes.

RPG III programs tend to use many fewer indicators than equivalent RPG II programs. You may be sure that the subtle changes to the language that brought this about were not unintentional.

There are special indicators and general indicators. The general indicators are much more frequently used than the special indicators, particularly in RPG III. The distinction between indicators and fields is sharp in earlier versions of RPG, but somewhat blurred in RPG III. This is because in RPG III it is possible to refer to an indicator as if it were a field by prefixing it with *IN. Thus the match indicator may be used as a field simply by describing it as *INMR.

The general indicators may also be treated as an array of 99 elements, each one byte long: *IN,35 is exactly the same as *IN35. (See section 7.2 for a detailed discussion of arrays and subscripts.)

The principle advantage in referring to indicators as fields is that it is thereby possible to avoid the use of conditioning indicators (indicators in columns 9-17 of the C-spec, see section 7.12). The command:

```
C    35        ADD  1     COUNT
```

may be replaced by

```
C    *IN35     IFEQ '1'
C              ADD  1     COUNT
C              END
```

Of course, it is still possible to write IFEQ '1' when you intend IFEQ '0', or IFNE '1'.

In general, when a flag is needed a one byte field containing a naturally meaningful value is always better than an indicator. Suppose we need to remember whether a customer is married. In RPG II we might have used indicator 44 (the choice is arbitrary) with ON meaning married and OFF meaning not married. In RPG III we should prefer a field called MARIED – remember, six characters maximum – containing Y or N.

Judge for yourself which is less error prone, and which is easier for a maintenance programmer to follow:

```
C          44         ADD       1       COUNT
                or
C          MARIED     IFEQ      'Y'
C                     ADD       1       COUNT
C                     END
```

Special indicators include

level indicators	L0-L9 and LR
halt indicators	H1-H9
(page) overflow indicators	OA-OG and OV
command-key indicators	KA-KN and KP-KY
external indicators	U1-U8
match indicator	MR
first-page indicator	1P
return indicator	RT

The **level indicators** are discussed in detail in Chapter 8, *The RPG Cycle*, and they do not work in fully procedural programs – as discussed in Chapter 9; i.e. they do not work outside the cycle.

LR (Last Record) is important because it provides one way of telling the operating system to terminate the program, i.e. it is roughly equivalent to COBOL's STOP RUN. On earlier versions of RPG this was the only way to conclude a program. The relationship between the LR and RT indicators and the RETRN verb is discussed in Chapter 10, and the mechanism of terminating a program is discussed in Chapter 8.

If set, the **halt indicators**, H1-H9, will cause the program to crash and dump (though not immediately – this is discussed in more detail in Chapters 8 and 9) which is obviously not a very clean way of handling an error. However they are quick and easy to code, and are an acceptable way of handling a situation which simply should not occur at all – e.g. when we have a validated order record, but find that the customer number is not on the customer entity.

You should not use the same halt indicator for more than one error condition (unless you have to cater for more than nine error conditions).

Page overflow special indicators may be used only with internally defined print files. The most commonly used is OF, and the others are there only to cater for programs with multiple print files.

One particular overflow indicator may not be used for more than one file. External print files use one of the general indicators for overflow.

Page overflow indicators are set on when the last line to be printed (specified in the CRTPRTF (Create Print File) CL command) is passed. Note that special overflow indicators are set to off automatically when bottom of form is passed, whereas the programmer is responsible for setting the general indicators used with external print files to off. Ex RPG II programmers are particularly prone to forget to reset the overflow indicator when working with external print files.

The **command-key indicators** are set to on whenever the corresponding command key is pressed. [CF1] sets on KA, [CF2] sets on KB, etc. Most RPG III programmers prefer to use the DDS facility that associates a general indicator with a particular command key.

The **external indicators** U1-U8 exist purely to provide compatibility with much earlier machines. Some early computers had external switches which were set by the operator to provide crude run parameters. This facility was emulated by the U1-U8 special indicators. On an AS/400 there is no reason whatever to use them; all parameters should be passed by means of the PLIST/PARM operation codes (see sections 7.12.53 and 7.12.52). The only exception is where an RPG program written for an earlier machine is being run on the AS/400, in which case U1-U8 are initialised by one of the parameters on the SBMJOB (Submit Job) CL command.

On System/36 and on VSE mainframes U1-U8 are initialised by means of the UPSI byte (that is why there are only 8 of them: 8 bits to a byte). On System/36 the UPSI byte is set by the //SWITCH OCL statement, and in VSE by the //UPSI JCL statement.

The match indicator, MR, is set on when a record in the primary file matches a record in a secondary file – see Chapter 8 *The RPG Cycle*, and does not work in fully procedural programs (i.e. it does not work outside the cycle) – see Chapter 9.

The **first-page indicator**, 1P, is meaningful only with internally defined output files used within the cycle. It provides a way of ensuring that the first page's headings print before the first detail line.

Note that any value determined by a calculation entry – e.g. the time or date accessed by a TIME command – is not available at 1P time, unless the special subroutine *INZSR is used.

Use of RT, the **return indicator**, is discussed in detail in Chapter 10 *Modular Programming*. It provides a way of terminating a program without releasing its dynamically allocated storage. In many cases this will substantially improve performance.

With the exception of 1P, indicators are initialised to OFF.

7.2 Arrays and Tables

Probably the most puzzling thing about arrays and tables is the reason why RPG should have both. The answer is that the earliest versions had only tables, but when arrays were added it was necessary to retain tables for upward compatibility.

What are the differences? Like an array, a table is a list of values. Unlike an array, subscripting is not allowed. Individual entries cannot be addressed by the table name and a pointer to the position in the table.

Table names must always begin with TAB, whereas array names are not allowed to begin with TAB.

The delimiter between an array name and its subscript is a comma, (,) not brackets, as in most programming languages. The array name, comma and subscript must be written without any embedded blanks.

If we wish to refer to the N-th element in array ABC we write:

```
ABC,N
```

In COBOL this would be

```
ABC (N)
```

When an individual element of an array is referenced, the array name, delimiter and subscript must all fit within the six character limitation for RPG field names.

This means in practice that we have to be very careful how we name both arrays and subscripts. A system of three characters for the array name, and two characters for the subscript name (plus the comma, making six) works as well as any.

Sometimes – surprisingly, not very often – it is just not possible to get any sort of meaningful subscript name into only two characters. A useful technique in this situation is to use a normal six character name for manipulating the subscript, then move it to a two character name immediately before using it.

Suppose we have an array named TXT, but are having trouble remembering that BP means Beginning Pointer. Give it a more meaningful name, say BEGPTR. Then process like this:

```
          C         *LIKE     DEFN BEGPTR    BP
                             .
                             .
                    (manipulate BEGPTR)
                             .
                             .
          C                   MOVE BEGPTR    BP
          C                   MOVE TXT,BP    XYZ
```

Note that BP is defined by means of a DEFN pseudo command (see section 7.12.15). If a maintenance programmer coming after us decides to enlarge BEGPTR he might miss the need to enlarge BP.

If we had explicitly defined BP, the consequences would be potentially catastrophic – the high order digit might be lost. As it is the dimensions of BP will be adjusted automatically. In programming, prevention is always cheaper than cure.

Tables and arrays may both be in "alternating" form. The concept is best illustrated by means of an example. We might have two tables, Table A containing:

```
CAD
DEM
GBP
USD
```

and Table B containing:

```
Canadian Dollars
German Marks
British Pounds
U.S. Dollars
```

We might wish to combine these as the alternating table:

```
CAD Canadian Dollars
DEM German Marks
GBP British Pounds
USD U.S. Dollars
```

In the earliest forms of RPG the only way it was possible to convert from the currency code to the currency name was by means of a LOKUP command (subsection 7.12.37) issued against an alternating table:

```
C           MOVE  'DEM'   PQR
              .
              .
C     PQR   LOKUP TABA    TABB    44
C           MOVE  TABB    FLDXYZ
```

The lookup would get a hit on the second entry in the table (indicator 44 tells us whether or not there was a hit). The next statement, moving TABB to FLDXYZ, would get the second iteration of TABB, and so FLDXYZ would contain 'German Marks'.

Today we would of course use arrays. There is no longer any need to do this sort of thing, nor has there been for many years, but the old constructs are retained in the hallowed name of upward compatibility.

Nevertheless, we might wish to load the arrays by means of input in alternating format, in which case we would simply declare the arrays as alternating when coding the E-spec.

It is not often that there is any advantage in using tables rather than arrays.

RPG's array handling is in many ways much more powerful than most other languages. A very useful command, which is not used anything like as much as it should be, is XFOOT (section 7.12.79), which allows you to sum all the elements of an array with a single command.

When an array name is specified without a subscript, in arithmetic or move operations, it is interpreted as meaning that the operation should be performed on each element of the array.

This is particularly useful for adding groups of accumulators. If we have two arrays, A1 and A2, then the command:

```
     C               ADD    A1        A2
```

will add each element of A1 to the corresponding element of A2.

It is also possible to output entire arrays with a single statement, but again only with internally defined files.

Alphameric arrays are output without any spaces between the elements, but numeric arrays have two spaces placed between the elements after doing any editing requested.

If you wish to output an alphameric array with spaces between the elements it is quite easy to fool the compiler. All that is needed is to specify a second array, as much bigger than the first as is desired, and then move the contents of the first to it:

```
                           .
                           .
      3.00    E            TXT1     11  5
      4.00    E            TXT2     11  7
                           .
                           .
     33.00    C            MOVE     TXT1         TXT2
                           .
                           .
     85.00    O                 TXT2        77
```

Statement 3.00 defines array TXT1 with 11 elements each of 5 bytes; statement 4.00 defines array TXT2 with 11 elements each of 7 bytes. At statement 33.00 each element of TXT1 is moved to the corresponding element of TXT2. The rules for the MOVE command tell us that the move will be right justified, leaving the high order two bytes of each element of TXT2 still containing their initial blanks. (Contrast with:

```
C                MOVEA    TXT1      TXT2
```

which would over-write the first 55 bytes of TXT2 with the 55 bytes of TXT1.)

At statement 85.00 the entire array TXT2 is output on positions 1 to 77 of the output record, looking for all the world as though it was TXT1 that was output, with two blanks separating the elements.

Early forms of RPG did not allow arrays of structures – an array was simply a list of elements. An array of structures is a group of data items repeated as often as desired, for example, in COBOL:

```
01 ARRAY-XYZ.
   05 XYZ OCCURS 22 TIMES.
      10 SURNAME     PIC X(15).
      10 FORENAME    PIC X(15).
      10 ADDR-1      PIC X(20).
      10 ADDR-2      PIC X(20).
      10 ADDR-3      PIC X(20).
      10 ADDR-4      PIC X(20).
```

RPG III offers multiple occurrence data structures, which are defined, like all data structures, on I-specs, rather than on the E-specs used for arrays (see section 7.10).

One of the worst failings of RPG is that multidimensional arrays are not supported. (But can you imagine trying to get array name plus multiple subscripts and commas all into six characters?)

Over the years cunning programmers have devised a method of doing it anyway, but it is a real Heath Robinson lash-up. (For the benefit of American readers, Heath Robinson is Rube Goldberg's English cousin.) Here it is, for what it is worth.

Suppose we need to work with a 3x4 matrix, in other words with 12 elements. We declare a single dimension array , call it ABC, and then manipulate the subscript such that RPG will always fetch us the correct element.

To do this we declare a two digit subscript, XY, and treat the first digit as the X axis subscript and the second digit as the Y axis subscript. We also need two single digit fields, X and Y, which are combined to form XY.

If we need to refer to the element which is second on the X axis and third on the Y axis we code:

```
ABC,23
```

In COBOL this would be:

    ABC (2, 3)

Rather than a literal we wish to use the symbolic field XY and do so like this:

    C   MOVE   2   X
    C   MOVE   3   Y
    C   MOVEL   X   XY
    C   MOVE   Y   XY
    C   MOVE   ABC,XY   etc

Note how MOVEL is used to move the contents of X to the high-order position of XY, while MOVE is used to move the contents of Y to the low-order position of XY. Alignment rules for MOVE and MOVEL are described in sections 7.12.42 and 7.12.44 respectively.

In COBOL all that would be needed would be:

    ABC (X, Y)

Alert readers will have noticed that our matrix comprises only 12 elements, but we are referring to element 23.

We have to declare as many elements as will be generated by the maximum value of X in the high-order position, and the maximum value of Y in the low-order position. In other words, ABC must be declared with 34 elements.

That means considerable wastage: (34 − 12 =) 22 elements.

Note that if we had declared our matrix instead as 4x3 − also 12 elements − the wastage would be even greater: (43 − 12 =) 31 elements.

Well, I did warn you it was a Heath Robinson contraption.

Data may enter a table or array in one of four ways:

    1) As the result of a command in the C-specs

    2) Directly from an input file, via the I-specs.

    3) At run time, before processing begins, from a file designated as a table file by a T in column 16 of the F-spec.

    4) At compile time, by means of source statements following the program source, and preceded by a header statement containing '**' in Columns 1 and 2.

Option (1) is self explanatory. Option (2) is more interesting, though seldom used in RPG III, and is best illustrated by means of an example:

The Coding Forms

```
     1.00    FXYZFILE   IP       80              DISK
                                  .
     3.00    E                   TXT      22  5
                                  .
                                  .
     6.00    IXYZFILE   NS    01
     7.00    I                             1   5 TXT,1
     8.00    I                             6  10 TXT,1
     9.00    I                            40  45 TXT,5
    10.00    I                            17  21 TXT,7
```

Every time a record is read from XYZFILE elements 1,2,5 and 7 of array TXT will be loaded from the fields in the record stipulated by statements 7.00 through 10.00.

Note that the elements of the array can be specified in any order, and that their contents can be drawn from any part of the record.

It is even possible to specify the same element more than once. Each specification will over-ride the one that went before it.

It is still easier to load the entire array from contiguous fields on the input record:

```
    1.00  FXYZFILE   IP     80            DISK
                                .
    3.00  E                    TXT    12 5
                                .
                                .
    6.00  IXYZFILE   NS    01
    7.00  I                              1  60 TXT
```

The array is specified on line 3.00 as consisting of 12 elements of 5 bytes each, for a total of 60 bytes. When the array name is specified on without a subscript, (statement 7.00) the 60 bytes specified on statement 7.00 will over-write the entire array.

This can also be done with numeric arrays. If array text had been defined as 5 digits numeric, then statement 7.00 would have looked as though it was defining a numeric field 60 digits long, which of course violates RPG rules. The compiler is able to recognise that an array is involved, and that therefore there is no violation.

Probably the main reason that this technique is not often used in RPG III is that array elements are not allowed as fields on external files.

Option (3) is a hangover from the earliest days of RPG, before Option (4) became available. It is still occasionally useful for loading moderately volatile arrays.

Before any other processing takes place any files specified with a T in column 16 of the F-spec are read into the appropriate array or table.

Option (4) is today by far the most common way of loading arrays. It is explained in section 7.14.

7.3 Figurative Constants and Reserved Words

Figurative constants are names which stand for values. In RPG they stand out because they begin with an asterisk, and anyway they are easy to remember because there are only five of them. They are:

*BLANK   Plural *BLANKS.

              Valid only with alphameric fields.

              Equivalent to COBOL SPACE/SPACES.

*ZERO   Plural *ZEROS (NB: Not *ZEROES).

              Valid with both alphameric and numeric fields.

              Equivalent to COBOL ZERO/ZEROS/ZEROES.

*HIVAL   means X'FF....FF' with an alphameric field,

              99.......99 with a numeric field.

              Equivalent to COBOL HIGH-VALUES.

*LOVAL   means X'00....00' with an alphameric field,

              -99.......-99 with a numeric field.

              Equivalent to COBOL LOW-VALUES.

*ALL   e.g. MOVE *ALL'XYZ' will fill the receiving field with

              a repeating pattern of XYZXYZ....XYZ

              Equivalent to COBOL ALL (as in MOVE ALL)

RPG has fewer **reserved words** than COBOL, and it is less difficult to avoid using one by mistake. Many of them begin with an asterisk, and most of them are an alternative to explicit field names in the PSDS (Program Status Data Structure) – see section 7.11 and Chapter 14.

There are two groups of reserved words which do not begin with asterisks. They are the page numbering group and the date group.

The page numbering reserved words are PAGE, and PAGE1 through PAGE7. They are intended as a means of automatic page numbering for internally defined print files. Whenever they are encountered in an output specification they are automatically incremented before being output. They may be set or reset by MOVE etc. commands within the RPG program. Although intended for page numbering, they may be used anywhere where serial numbering is required.

Page numbering in an externally defined print file is handled by the DDS keyword PAGNBR.

The only point to watch when using the PAGE family is that a different one must be used for each print file. Remember that they are incremented each time they are output, so if a given PAGE variable is used for more than one file the next number will be given to the next file that requests a number, with the result that page numbering will go something like this:

File	Page Numbers
PRINTA	1, 3, 6, 9
PRINTB	2, 4, 5, 7, 8

The date group of reserved words comprises UDATE, UDAY, UMONTH and UYEAR, and is used to make the machine date available to RPG. UDATE is a six-digit numeric, and the others are each two-digit numeric fields.

The format of UDATE is determined by the system value which has been set at your installation, and may be mmddyy (American format), ddmmyy (British format), or yymmdd (sensible format). It may be over-ridden by an entry in Column 19 of the H-spec.

UDAY, UMONTH and UYEAR may not appear in a data structure, so if you need American or British format elsewhere in the program you will have to move them to work fields within a data structure:

```
I    DS
I                  1   6 TODAY
I*
I                  1   2 UY
I                  3   4 UM
I                  5   6 UD
                   .
                   .
                   .
C        MOVE UYEAR    UY
C        MOVE UMONTH   UM
C        MOVE UDAY     UD
```

Julian dates are directly supported by RPG only if the job attribute QDATFMT is set for a Julian date (see section 7.12.75), but are very easily obtained by means of the CVTDAT (Convert Date) CL command. See Example 2 in Appendix D.

7.4 File pointers

The machine "remembers" where it last accessed each file by using file pointers. For example, if the second record in a file has just been read the pointer will point to the border between the second and third records, as follows:

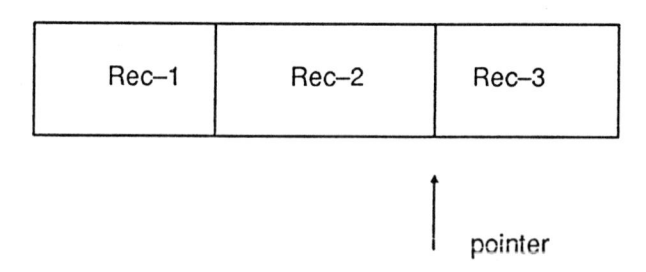

```
+-------+-------+-------+
| Rec-1 | Rec-2 | Rec-3 |
+-------+-------+-------+
                ↑
                pointer
```

If another READ is issued, then the third record will be retrieved; but if a READP (Read Previous) is issued the second record will be read again.

When a file is opened by RPG (either automatically or under user control) the pointer is set to the beginning of the file. It may subsequently be set by the following commands:

```
CHAIN     (see section 7.12.10)
READ      (see section 7.12.55)
READE     (see section 7.12.57)
READP     (see section 7.12.58)
REDPE     (see section 7.12.59)
SETGT     (see section 7.12.64)
SETLL     (see section 7.12.65)
```

If a CHAIN does not find its target, or if a read encounters end of file, etc., the relevant pointer's setting is destroyed, and it must be reset by a SETLL, SETGT or successful CHAIN before another read may be performed.

The pointer is destroyed when the file is closed, either by an explicit CLOSE command (see section 7.12.11) or when the program terminates.

7.5 Statements

Introduction

RPG source statements, like those of COBOL, consist of 80-character card images. In both cases this reflects the Hollerith cards which were widely used when the languages were conceived, and is perpetuated today when there is no longer any reason for an 80-character restriction.

Both also have line numbers in the first few columns of each source statement. These were to facilitate sorting if the card deck should become muddled, and similarly do not have much relevance today!

Like COBOL, any statement with an asterisk on column 7 is a comment.

Fixed format

Unlike COBOL, RPG is a fixed format language, into which entries are made on rigidly defined columns. A number of different form types exist, each of which is identified by the appropriate character on column 6.

Each form type is discussed in detail in the sections which follow.

One disadvantage of the fixed format system is that adjacent fields often appear without any intervening blanks, which can be very confusing to read. Look at the following statements:

```
F                          RRN11 KSFILE DSPR1S1
         and
I                      1   2 X1
I                      1   20X2
         and
C        MOVE XXX          YYY
C        MOVELXXX           YYY
```

The F-spec looks as though KSFILE is all one entry – in fact it is two entries, K and SFILE.

The first I-spec is clear enough – field X1 is an alphameric field on positions 1 and 2 of the record – but what about X2? Or is it 20X2? Is it on positions 1 to 20 of the record? Or what? In fact field X2 is being defined as a numeric field with zero decimal positions, on positions 1 and 2 of the record.

The move from XXX to YYY is clear enough – but what about the next line? Is field LXXX being moved? In fact it is a MOVEL (Move Left) command, and if only we could code it like this it would be much clearer:

```
C        MOVEL XXX         YYY
```

A useful tip

Here is a tip. When this sort of thing happens, pencil a line between the two fields.

This is particularly useful while you are still unfamiliar with RPG, and also when you are involved in complicated debugging, and do not want to be distracted by having to separate fields mentally. The reduction in eye strain has to be experienced to be believed.

Coding forms

Early computers lacked both the processing power and the special low level scanning instructions found today, so RPG's rigid format gave it a significant advantage in compile times, though this has now almost disappeared.

Some say that this fixed format makes RPG difficult to use, but I have never found it so, particularly with the special formatting text editors now available.

It is strange that IBM did not take the opportunity of the huge leap from RPG II to RPG III to increase the permitted length of field names. They chose instead to print alongside each database field 50 bytes of descriptive information drawn from the data dictionary.

The major RPG statement types are:

```
H - Header Specs
F - File Specs
E - Extensions to File Specs
I - Input Specs
C - Calculations
O - Output Specs
```

Examples of the coding forms appear in Appendix F.

The observation underlying the original RPG was that virtually all programs operate in a *cycle*. They read a record, do calculations based on the data just read, optionally produce output, then go back to read the next record. It should therefore be possible to produce a standard program, tailored by means of parameters, to suit individual requirements.

The I, C and O specs – input, calculations and output, correspond to the three stages of this process, The H, F and E specs stand aside from the actual processing, but provide definitions necessary for the others to proceed.

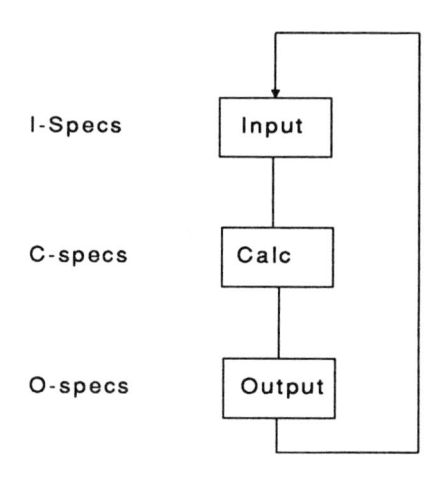

```
I-Specs    ┌───────┐
           │ Input │◄──┐
           └───┬───┘   │
               │       │
C-specs    ┌───┴───┐   │
           │ Calc  │   │
           └───┬───┘   │
               │       │
O-specs    ┌───┴───┐   │
           │Output │───┘
           └───────┘
```

In COBOL terms, the H, F and E specs correspond roughly to the IDENTIFICATION and ENVIRONMENT DIVISIONS.

The cycle has since been partially abandoned, but the pattern of coding forms remains the same.

SEU (Source Edit Utility)

Because RPG is a fixed format language the various coding forms are annotated with numerous columns and fields. They look intimidating – but really they are quite simple.

They are made even simpler by the prompting facilities offered by SEU (the Source Edit Utility).

Either type a P into the first character of the line, or hit [CF4] with the cursor anywhere on the line, and SEU will copy the statement to a prompt area at the bottom of the screen, where it is neatly broken up into its component parts, depending on statement type.

SEU is one of the best text editors around, and clearly owes much to the CMS text editor found on the VM hypervisor on mainframes. However, programmers used to VSE's ICCF will miss the "stacking" copy.

Sad to relate, although the AS/400 text editor is streets ahead of the competition, SEU is one area where IBM took a giant leap backwards when System/38 became AS/400. In a bid to make it idiot proof, IBM merely made it infuriating for experienced users – meaning anyone with more than two days on the machine. For example, on System/38 switching between upper and lower case involves but a single keystroke; on AS/400 it is a morning's work wandering around the various service screens.

7.6   H Header

The Header statement is identified by an H on column 6. One only is permitted in each program, and it is implementation dependent – in other words, the format differs between RPG III and RPG II, and between different dialects of RPG II.

It is used to provide various parameters needed to generate and run the program. Examples are the date format (DMY, MDY or YMD), and whether to use decimal commas rather than decimal points.

In some earlier versions of RPG, a missing H-spec would cause a terminal compilation error. RPG III has default values for all H-spec entries, and very few RPG III programmers bother with H-specs at all.

Every now and again one comes across a DP manager who is particularly concerned about some some or other parameter. If you encounter one of these, you will almost certainly be given a model H-spec which is to be copied into all programs, or the default values will have been changed.

Either way, all you have to do is follow orders. It is not necessary to know the meaning of all the entries.

7.7 F File

The F-spec corresponds almost exactly with the SELECT verb in COBOL. It is used to describe to the compiler which files are to be used; one F-spec is required per file, just as one SELECT per file is required by COBOL.

The F-spec is identified by an F on column 6, and RPG III F-specs are unique among RPG statements in that continuation lines are allowed. These are specified by a K – presumably standing for Kontinuation – in column 53.

7.7.1 The basic F-spec

Columns 7 to 14 contain the file name and, if possible, this should be the same as the name by which the file is identified to OS/400. If it is imperative to use a different name, then the connection is made by means of a CL OVRDBF (Over-ride Database File) command – see section 1.2.8.

For internally described files, OS/400 needs to make the connection only at run time. However, for externally described files, OS/400 needs to make the connection both at run time and at compile time. This is because the information needed to generate I-specs and O-specs comes from the file header.

When compiling with externally described files which need over-rides, use SEU (Source Edit Utility) to create a source member which contains a // JOB statement, all the OVRDBF statements required, and a CRTRPGPGM (Create RPG Program) CL command. Then submit this using a SBMDBJOB (Submit Database Job) command, rather than a SBMJOB (Submit Job) command. SBMDBJOB will run the CL stream you have created in interpretive mode, like OCL on a System/36, or JCL on a mainframe.

Column 15 specifies whether the file is to be input, output, update, or combined (input and output), the entries being I,O,U,C respectively.

Column 16 is left blank for output files, and may otherwise contain:

```
P for Primary
S for Secondary
R for Record address
T for Table
F for Full function
```

Record address files were used to implement tag sorting, a technique which has no relevance on an AS/400 (the tree structured index of a Logical File is itself a set of tags). The facility is included only to provide upward compatibility.

Table files are used to load tables or arrays at run-time, but before the main processing begins, and are described in section 7.2. They are left over from the past, and are rarely used today.

Primary and secondary files are permitted only with the cycle, and are described in detail in Chapter 8. In earlier forms of RPG, omission of the primary file would cause a terminal compile error, but in RPG III all that happens is that the cycle is switched off.

That leaves us with **Full function**. On earlier versions of RPG there was a further entry: C for Chain, which is not supported by RPG III. Some dialects of RPG II support both C and F; C permits reading only by the CHAIN command, while F also permits the use of commands such as SETLL. C is equivalent to ACCESS IS RANDOM in COBOL, while F is equivalent to ACCESS IS DYNAMIC. When converting an RPG II program to run on an AS/400 any C entries must be changed to F.

Column 17 is normally left blank, but may contain an E, provided the file being described is primary or secondary, i.e. provided the program is using the cycle. The E means that when end of file is encountered on that particular file, the program is to terminate immediately rather than follow the usual rules for a cycling program.

Column 18 is also usually left blank. It may contain A for Ascending sequence, or D for Descending which, again, is applicable only to primary or secondary files. In practice there is very seldom any point in using this entry on an AS/400. It was quite useful back in the days when decks of punched cards were being matched and might have been incorrectly sorted.

Column 19 contains an E if the file is externally described, and an F if internally described.

Why F for internal? Some machines support variable length records (the AS/400 does not), and in the dialects of RPG II used by those machines programmers are required to enter F for Fixed length or V for Variable length.

The E entry is good news for lazy programmers. It means that there is no need to worry about specifying record and block lengths, key positions and lengths, etc. The compiler will do all that. Better still, it will also generate I-specs and/or O-specs for all fields within the file.

The only remaining entries for external files are:

```
Column    Entry and Purpose
31        K or blank. Specifies whether file keyed
33-34     Overflow indicator (print files only)
40-46     Device type
```

The only point to watch is that if the K on column 31 is not specified even a keyed database file will be retrieved in RRN (relative record number) sequence.

Unlike earlier versions of RPG, CHAIN commands to a file not specified as keyed will not cause a terminal compilation error, but will be presumed to refer to RRN.

The remainder of this subsection refers to Internal files only

Columns 20 to 27 OS/400 looks after block length, so columns 20 to 23 are left blank. The record length is required in columns 24 to 27.

Column 28 contains an L if to be processed between limits in conjunction with record addresses, also known as tags (see column 16). The facility is included only to provide upward compatibility. Otherwise it is left blank.

Columns 29 and 30 contain the length of the key field or record address field (if any).

Column 31 contains the record address type (if the file is keyed), otherwise it is left blank. In practice the entry is invariably A, for alphameric, but it is possible to have packed keys, in which case the entry is P.

Column 32 contains the File Organisation. This is blank for an unkeyed file or I if Indexed (i.e. keyed). If the file is a record address tag file enter a T (see also columns 16 and 28).

Columns 33 and 34 contain the overflow indicator if the file is a print file, otherwise it is blank. Overflow indicators are discussed in detail in section 7.1.

Columns 35 to 38 contain the key field starting position (if a keyed file), otherwise it is left blank.

Column 39 contains an E or an L to indicate whether further information about the file is provided in either an E-spec or an L if an L-spec; otherwise it is left blank.

An E is required only if the file is a table file (T on column 16) or a record address file (see also columns 16, 28 and 32); whereas an L is needed only if the file is a line counter print file (see section 7.9).

Columns 40 to 46 give the device type, which may be one of the following:

```
PRINTER
DISK
WORKSTN
SPECIAL
SEQ
```

A DISK file is any file on the database, including flat files (see section 3.1).

WORKSTN is an abbreviation for Work Station, which is GSD-speak for a screen.

SPECIAL is very rarely encountered, and means that the device is to be accessed via non-IBM software. See also column 54.

SEQ is an abbreviation for Sequential. At run-time OS/400 will look at the file header to discover what type of device the file resides upon.

Earlier version of RPG included the option of TAPE. In years gone by, when disks were small and expensive, it was not uncommon to see an RPG program writing to a tape. Today, any file which is destined for tape (or diskette) should be created as a database file, and then copied to the appropriate device by CPYTOTAP or CPYTODKT CL commands respectively.

In a small installation, where programmers do their own tape mounting, it probably doesn't matter very much if tape output is created directly by RPG.

But in a large installation you will probably incur the wrath of the operators if you ask them to drop everything to mount a tape for your program. They much prefer to be given the name and library of a disk file to be copied to tape or diskette at their convenience.

Columns 47 to 52 should be left blank. In some dialects of RPG II a symbolic device entry is required.

Column 53 should also be left blank. (A K entry is valid only for external files.)

Columns 54 to 59 are blank unless the device type on columns 40 to 46 is SPECIAL, in which case this field is used to name the software which will interface with the special device.

Columns 60 to 65 must be blank.

Column 66 is blank unless the file is to be extended, in which case it takes an A. When an A is coded in this column it is permissible to issue a write to a file which has been declared as input by means of an I in column 15.

Note that AS/400 disk files, unlike disk files on many other machines, are not automatically cleared when they are opened for output. If it is desired that the file be cleared then this must be done by means of a CLRPFM (Clear Physical File Member) CL command, before invoking the RPG program.

Columns 67 to 70 must be blank.

Columns 71 and 72 contain the file conditioning entry, if required, otherwise it is left blank. This field may contain any of the special indicators U1 through U8 (see section 7.1). If the indicator is ON the file will be treated like any other; if OFF the file will be ignored. This is true of both RPG II and RPG III. RPG III permits a further entry, UC, which looks like another special indicator, but is not. It stands for "User Control", and means that the file will not be opened automatically when the program is initiated, like other RPG files. Instead, it must be opened by an OPEN command (see section 7.12.49)

This feature is often used in RPG III.

7.7.2 F-spec continuations

F-spec continuations should be blank except for

Columns 19 to 28 contains an external record format name if the continuation operator (in columns 54 to 59) is RENAME or IGNORE, otherwise left blank.

Columns 47 to 52 contains the name of a numeric field which is to hold the relative record number of a subfile – see Chapter 12 – if the continuation operator (in columns 54 to 59 is SFILE. For all other continuation operators it should be blank. Although not required by OS/400, it is strongly recommended that this field bc 4 digits long.

Column 53 contains K, for Kontinuation.

Columns 54 to 59 contains the continuation operator. Permitted values are:

```
          COMIT
          ID
          IGNORE
          IND
          INFDS
          INFSR
          NUM
          PASS
          PLIST
          PRTCTL
          RECNO
          RENAME
          SAVDS
          SFILE
          SLN
```

Most of these are very seldom used in practice, and we shall not discuss them further here. The exceptions are:

```
          COMIT
          IGNORE
          INFDS
          INFSR
          RENAME
          SFILE
```

COMIT (note the spelling) is used with commitment control, described in Chapter 13. It must be specified for any file for which the COMIT and ROLBK verbs are to be used.

IGNORE is used to ignore formats which exist in a file, but which are not wanted in this program. No I-specs or O-specs are generated for the format specified in columns 19 to 28, resulting in a smaller and more efficient program.

INFDS names in columns 60 to 65 a file information data structure for the file.

INFSR names in columns 60 to 65 a subroutine which is to be executed if an error occurs in an I/O operation to the file. This mode of operation is similar to an ON CONDITION in PL/I, or a MONMSG ahead of all other executable statements in a CL program.

RENAME renames the format named in columns 19 to 28 to the name specified in columns 60 to 65.

A **SFILE** line is required for each subfile – see Chapter 12 – in a display file.

Each one names in columns 47 to 52 the field which is to hold the relative record number of the subfile whose subfile format is named in columns 60 to 65. For example:

```
FXYZFILE    CF       E                WORKSTN
F                                     RRN11 KSFILE DSPR1S1
F                                     RRN21 KSFILE DSPR2S1
```

7.8 F* Indicator summary

A special hot corner in Hell is reserved for programmers who don't document indicators properly. There are few prospects more daunting than to be asked to maintain a program which uses every indicator in sight without offering the slightest clue as to what any of them might mean.

IBM offers an indicator summary form, but this is no more than a stylised comment – it has an asterisk on column 7. If I had my way, I should make that indicator comment form into a spec type in its own right, and the use of any indicator not thus defined would result in a terminal compile error. Are you listening, Rochester?

There are even some people around who seem to think their employers have to pay for every indicator used, and so attempt to re-use them. Very occasionally re-use of indicators cannot be avoided, though when this situation arises it is almost always a sign that the program is too big, and should be split – see Chapter 10.

As mentioned above, the IBM indicator summary form is no more than a stylised comment, specifically a stylised F-spec comment. It seeks to separate the indicators into various categories – ID, calculations etc. – which is more useful in RPG II than in RPG III. In doing so it reduces the amount of space available for the description – and that, after all, is the whole point of the exercise. For RPG III, it is probably better to devise your own layout. IBM's use of an F-spec comment is a broad hint that the indicator documentation should appear somewhere near the file specs, at the beginning of the program. Most installations place them immediately following the file specs.

There is very little prospect of using indicators in a way such that the number is directly meaningful, but you should at least try to group them in meaningful ways.

For example, suppose we have a group of fields, FLDA through FLDD, and each of them requires a CHANGE indicator, and also indicators so that they may be displayed in reverse image or highlighted on the screen.

We might adopt an indicator scheme something like this:

```
31   CHANGE for FLDA
32   RI for FLDA
33   HI for FLDA

41   CHANGE for FLDB
42   RI for FLDB
43   HI for FLDB
 .
 .
71   CHANGE for FLDE
72   RI for FLDE
73   HI for FLDE
```

We can tell at a glance that any indicator beginning with a 3 refers to FLDA, with a 4 to FLDB etc., and that any indicator ending with a 1 is a CHANGE, any indicator ending with a 2 is for Reverse Image, any indicator ending with a 3 is for Highlighting.

The IBM summary form lists all the possible indicators, the intention being that they should be crossed off as they are used, to avoid inadvertently using a given indicator twice. This is a good idea in theory, but in practice, as long as we are careful to list the indicators in a sensible sequence – usually in numerical sequence, with all special indicators either at the beginning or the end – it all usually sorts itself out.

Most RPG III programmers use the DDS facility to associate a general indicator with a command key, in preference to the command key special indicators. The main reason is that this allows 50 bytes of comment (in the DDS) which is pulled into the generated I-spec when the program is compiled.

It doesn't really matter how you document indicators. Just make very sure you do it.

7.9 L Line-counter

The Line-counter specification form (L-spec) exists in RPG III only for compatibility with earlier versions of the language. It is used to associate specified line numbers on the printed form with channels on a carriage tape (or its electronic equivalent).

When an L-spec is used, the corresponding F-spec must have an L on column 39.

On AS/400, form size is described by means of the appropriate parameter on the CRTPRTF (Create Print File) CL command. For non-standard forms it is better to use the OVRPRTF (Over-ride Print File) CL command – see also Chapter 17.

To skip to a certain line before printing, use the appropriate DDS for an external print file, and an entry in columns 19-22 of the O-spec for an internal print file.

7.10 E Extension

The E-spec, or File Extension form is something of a misnomer, because today it is seldom used for file extensions. These are specified by means of an F-spec with a K on column 53 – the Kontinuation form (see section 7.7).

In the early days of RPG, the standard way of loading a table was through a table file with an extension specification, as described in section 7.2. Note that when this technique is used, the file's F-spec must have a T on column 16 and an E on column 39, and the file name must be repeated on columns 11-18. Columns 19-26 are very rarely used today, and even in the past were used mainly for processing tag files (see section 7.7.1).

Arrays, as opposed to tables, came late to the RPG language, and it was natural for the language designers to require them to be specified on the same form as tables. As explained in section 7.2, the old way of loading tables and arrays, via Table Files, was replaced by new and better techniques. That is why E-specs are now used almost entirely for defining arrays.

Defining an array on an E-spec is quite straightforward. The name is entered on columns 27-32, the number of elements in the array on columns 36-39, and the entry length on columns 40-42. Optional entries include the number of entries per record, on columns 33-35, which refers to arrays loaded at compile time (see sections 7.2 and 7.14), and is also needed for arrays loaded by Table Files. Leave these columns blank for all other arrays. The number of decimal positions should be entered on column 44. A blank on column 44 means that the array is not numeric. Column 43 should also be left blank unless you know exactlywhat you are doing: entries other than blank are very rarely required.

An A or D – for Ascending or Descending – is required on column 45 if the high/low facility of the LOKUP verb (see section 7.12.37) is to be used. In early versions of RPG, an entry in this column would generate a binary search (equivalent to a SEARCH ALL in COBOL) when a LOKUP was executed, but for some strange reason this useful facility was dropped.

Comments should be made on columns 58-74 to amplify the necessarily cryptic names of arrays. Alternating arrays and tables (described in section 7.2) are described in columns 46-57, using fields which mirror those of the main array description. The RPG compiler will quite happily handle arrays coded as alternating which have no relevance to one another but, unless you really want the alternating facility, it is better to give each array an E-spec of its own.

There are not many pitfalls on the E-spec. Probably the most common error is to confuse the number of elements (columns 36-39) and the length of an element (columns 40-42). Make sure that your description on the E-spec agrees with the data following the ** statement (section 7.14).

7.11 I Input

In RPG III, Input Specifications (I-specs) are used almost exclusively for defining working storage data structures. This is another apparent misnomer brought about by the gradual change in the language design over the years.

The original purpose of I-specs – to describe the layout of input records – has not been lost, but in today's RPG those I-specs are generated by the compiler from the definitions of external files.

Nevertheless, I-specs are occasionally wanted even with external files, to amend or amplify the external description. It is convenient to think of I-specs as comprising two basic types: header and body entries.

7.11.1 "Header" I-specs

Header I-specs vary according to their main purpose; the three main types are:

1) To indicate to the compiler that the following body entries refer to a working storage data structure rather than a file layout

2) To connect internal file descriptions to the appropriate file

3) Where an external file's format is to be amended and/or amplified, to connect the appropriate record format to the I-specs

Data structure headers always have the letters DS in columns 19 and 20. The data structure may optionally be named, in which case the name appears in columns 7-12.

The fields within a data structure may be internally or externally defined, and the body entries follow the rules for the appropriate type of file.

If the data structure is to be externally defined, then an E is required in column 17, and the name of the file from which the external definition is to be derived in columns 21-30. These columns are blank for internally defined data structures.

In RPG III, but not in RPG II, data structures may have multiple occurrences, in other words there may be an array of structures. The number of occurrences is entered in columns 44-47. If these columns are left blank the data structure is assumed to have only one occurrence.

The following shows a multiple occurrence data structure, first in COBOL, then in RPG:

COBOL

```
01 ARRAY-XYZ.
    05 XYZ OCCURS 22 TIMES.
        10 SURNAME      PIC X(15).
        10 FORENAME     PIC X(15).
        10 ADDR-1       PIC X(20).
        10 ADDR-2       PIC X(20).
        10 ADDR-3       PIC X(20).
```

RPG

```
IXYZ DS                 22
I                        1  15 SURNAM
I                       16  30 FORNAM
I                       31  50 ADDR1
I                       51  70 ADDR2
I                       71  90 ADDR3
```

A further entry, on columns 48-51, allows us to specify the length of the data structure. If left blank, the data structure length defaults to the highest To position specified on the body entries. In the example above, the data structure would be given a default length of 90 bytes.

There are two special types of data structure:

1) The Program Status Data Structure (PSDS)
2) The File Information Data Structure (INFDS)

The PSDS

There may be only one PSDS per program, and it is identified by an S in column 17 of the "header" I-spec. The PSDS contains information about the program, supplied by OS/400, which is mainly useful in debugging and/or error recovery. Those uses are detailed in Chapter 14.

There are also some uses for normal processing. For example, it is often desirable to display the user's user-id on the screen, (for one thing it helps supervisors spot clerks who are "borrowing" one another's passwords). The user-id may be accessed as follows:

```
I       SDS
I                      254 283 USERID
```

Tables of the start and end positions of all the fields in the PSDS, the meaning of the various status codes etc., occupy several pages of the manual, and it would be pointless to reproduce them here.

The "body" I-specs (see section 7.11.2) may be supplied as shown above, exactly as for any other body I-spec, but for some entries a figurative constant may be supplied in place of start and end positions. The following are both valid ways to access the program status code:

```
I          SDS
I                              11    150STATCD
I          SDS
I                              *STATUS     STATCD
```

The INFDS

Every file defined to the program may have an INFDS. It is defined by means of an F-spec kontinuation (see section 7.7.2), with a matching name in a data structure "header" I-spec:

```
FXYZFILE   IF     E              DISK
F                                             KINFDS INFXYZ
"
"
IINFXYZ    DS
I                              11    150STATCD
```

Each INFDS contains information about its file, supplied by OS/400, which is mainly useful in debugging and/or error recovery. Since the same information is equally available from a dump, the INFDS is of limited use for everyday programming.

Uses other than debugging include receiving feedback from devices of type SPECIAL (on columns 40-46 of the F-spec), and testing whether or not a file is open:

```
FXYZFILE   IF     E              DISK
F                                             KINFDS INFXYZ
"
"
IINFXYZ    DS
I                               9    9 XYZOPN
"
"
C          XYZOPN   IFNE  '1'
C          OPEN     XYZFILE
C          END
```

Tables of the start and end positions of all the fields in the INFDS, the meaning of the various status codes etc., are described in detail in the manual, so again, it is unnecessary to reproduce them here.

The "body" I-specs (see section 7.11.2) may be supplied as shown above, exactly as for any other body I-spec, but for some entries a figurative constant may be supplied in place of start and end positions. The following are both valid ways to access the file status code:

```
IINFXYZ    DS
I                              11 150XYZSTA

IINFXYZ    DS
I                              *STATUS XYZSTA
```

Where the purpose of the header is to connect internal file descriptions to the appropriate file, columns 7-14 must contain the name of a file specified in the F-specs. Note that internal files' I-specs require a file name, whereas external files' I-specs require a format name.

Before computers came into widespread use, data processing was achieved using unit record machines: card sorters, collators, and tabulators. RPG was designed with an eye to selling computers by providing an easy upgrade path from unit record machines. These frequently utilised a number of different card types, identified by appropriate characters punched on the appointed columns.

RPG I-specs mimic this selection ability by means of three record identification entries – columns 21-27, 28-34, and 35-41 – which allow you to select the required record type(s), and set on the requested indicator, called a "resulting indicator".

They are very seldom used on the AS/400, and as the coding is self-evident, we shall pass over them quickly.

The three entries have an AND relationship to one another, and continuation statements are possible, which may have either an AND or an OR relationship to the first statement.

That sounds a bit of a mouthful, so let's clarify it by an example. The COBOL statement:

```
IF (COL1 = 'A' AND COL2 = 'B' AND COL3 = 'C' AND COL4 = 'D') OR
   (COL1 = 'E' AND COL2 NOT = 'F') .....
```

would translate into RPG I-specs as:

```
      IFILEA     NS   01   1 CA  2 CB  3 CC
      I          AND       4 CD
      I          OR        1 CE  2NCF
```

We assume that the file is FILEA, and that Indicator 01 is to be used as the resulting indicator.

Each OR line may have its own resulting indicator, if desired.

The NS entry in columns 15 and 16 calls for a word of explanation. Unit record machines were programmed by means of plug boards, known as panels. The boards contained rows of holes rather like microphone jack points, which were connected as required by short lengths of wire with a plug at each end. The panel itself was then plugged into the machine. Programs that were too complex to "rewrite" were stored in the form of panels which were kept plugged for that particular purpose.

Consider a wages application. Punched cards containing employee information had to be merged with those containing information from the clock card. Employees without clock cards were permitted, but clock cards without employees were not, and so the cards had to be correctly paired off. The panels were plugged so that an error was raised if any of these conditions were not met.

The RPG I-spec contains a "sequence" field, into which generations of programmers have simply been told to type NS (for Non Sequenced) because it doesn't affect them.

The facility is there to mimic such checks from the plugged panels, and any alpha value – not only NS – will switch it off. Columns 17 and 18 are meaningful only if columns 15 and 16 have a numeric entry. Note how the final "Not F" is coded (NCF): the C stands for character; alternative entries are Z for zone and D for digit. If Z (or D) is specified then only the zone (or digit) part of the literal is compared against the input.

We may define as many record types as we wish, but we must remember that RPG tests each record against the literals in the order in which they are specified, and stops testing when it gets a "hit".

Suppose we have Name records identified by an N on column 1, and Address records identified by NA on columns 1 and 2. The following will not work, because NA records will satisfy the first test. Indicator 01 will be set on and the testing will terminate.

```
      IFILEA    NS    01    1 CN
                         .
                (body entries)
                         .
                         .
      I         NS    02    1 CN  2 CA
                         .
                (body entries)
                         .
```

We should do the test for NA first. Note that if columns 7-14 are left blank the compiler will assume that the file is the same as that in the previous header I-spec.

Where the purpose of the header is to connect amendments to an external file description with the appropriate file format, columns 7- 14 must contain the name of the format. Note that external files' I-specs require a format name, whereas internal files' I-specs require a file name.

About the only reason for supplying a header I-spec for an external file is to be able to have a resulting indicator, which is coded on columns 19 and 20, just as for internal files. For external files, no selection of record type is allowed.

7.11.2 "Body" I-specs

A "Body" I-spec looks very much like an entry in the file layout form found in the documentation of most installations. It contains start and end positions for the field, and its name.

Remember that there is a fundamental difference between COBOL and RPG in the way that fields are drawn from a record. Where COBOL simply maps over the record input area, RPG generates a move into a work area.

This means that if a field is defined twice, for example, as FLDA and FLDB, then changes to FLDB will not affect FLDA and vice versa, whereas in COBOL if FLDB REDEFINES FLDA, then any change made to either will affect both. See section 6.3.

Also, because start and end positions are explicitly specified, it is necessary to define only those fields which are actually required.

For internally defined files, columns 7-42 are left blank. Column 43 will contain a P if the field is packed, a B if it is binary. Otherwise it is left blank, except for those rare occasions when we require an L, for preceding (left) sign, or an R for trailing (right) sign.

Columns 44-47 and 48-51 contain respectively the From and To positions within the record. If the field is numeric, column 52 contains its number of decimal positions, if not, column 52 is left blank.

The field name appears in columns 53-58, and must of course adhere to RPG naming rules.

Columns 59-60 and 61-62 contain level and matching specifications, if required, and are only valid within the cycle. They are discussed in detail in Chapter 8.

Columns 65-66, 67-68 and 69-70 may contain indicators which are set to on if the field is, respectively, plus, minus or blank/zero.

The Field Record Relation entry is the only one that is the least bit tricky. It is used to instruct the compiler that the field in question is to be updated only when the specified resulting indicator is set to on.

The concept is best illustrated by an example.

```
IFILEA      NS      01      1 CA    2 CB    3 CC
I           AND             4 CD
I           OR      02      1 CE    2NCF
I                                           1       15      SURNAM  02
I                                           16      30      FORNAM  02
I                                           31      50      ADDR1
I                                           51      70      ADDR2
I                                           71      90      ADDR3
```

Only if position 1 contains an E and position 2 does *not* contain an F, will indicator 02 be set to on, and only if indicator 02 is set to on will fields SURNAM and FORNAM be updated.

In principle there is nothing wrong with Field Record Relation indicators, but in practice they are very easy to miss when maintaining a program, so are best avoided. Prevention is better than cure.

A much cleaner solution for the above is:

```
IFILEA      NS      01      1 CA    2 CB    3 CC
I           AND             4 CD
I                                           31      50      ADDR1
I                                           51      70      ADDR2
I                                           71      90      ADDR3
I           NS      02      1 CE    2NCF
I                                           1       15      SURNAM
I                                           16      30      FORNAM
I                                           31      50      ADDR1
I                                           51      70      ADDR2
I                                           71      90      ADDR3
```

"Body" I-specs for external files are used mainly to add level or matching indicators to the basic I-spec which the compiler generates from the file header. See statements A000000 to A000003 of Example 4 in Appendix D. All that is required is to code the required field name (without start and end positions) and the required indicators. The compiler does the rest.

The other important use is to rename fields. The two most common reasons why fields need to be renamed are:

    1) The DDS name does not conform to RPG rules (e.g. it is more than 6 characters long)

    2) The DDS name is duplicated in another file which is also being used by the program.

We can now see the importance of having a carefully thought out and installation wide naming plan. (See Chapters 6 and 17.) If we do not have such a plan we shall find ourselves having to write masses of renaming I-specs every time we define a file to a program, thus negating most of the value of having external files. Renaming a field is easy. Simply type the DDS name into columns 21-30, and the required RPG name in columns 53-58.

7.12 C Calculations

The C-spec corresponds closely to the PROCEDURE DIVISION in COBOL. It is identified by a C in column 6 and in RPG III is easily the most important spec type.

It consists essentially of a verb and three operands – known as Factor 1, Factor 2 and Result. At first, working with the verb in the middle of the operands seems a bit strange, but one soon gets used to it.

Attached to the Result field is a definition field in which the length and number of decimal positions may be specified.

The compiler does not mind how many times a particular field is defined, provided that the definitions do not clash with one another, but it is bad practice to define any field more than once. (What happens when you want to change the definition?)

In RPG III, fields are defined by means of the result definition less frequently than in RPG II, because of the existence of the DEFN (Define) pseudo-verb, which should be used wherever it is sensible to do so.

A field which appears in the I-specs is considered to be defined to RPG, and need not be defined again in C-specs.

Right next to the Result definition, in column 53, is the half adjust field, which is used for rounding results of arithmetic operations to the dimensions of the Result field. Enter an H if half adjustment is required, otherwise leave blank.

An H on column 53 corresponds to the COBOL ROUNDED option. The COBOL statement:

    MULTIPLY A BY B GIVING C

is equivalent to the RPG:

    C   A   MULT B   C

whereas:

    MULTIPLY A BY B GIVING C ROUNDED

is equivalent to the RPG:

    C   A   MULT B   C   H

Do *not* enter an H in column 53 of a DIV (Divide) statement if the next statement is an MVR (Move Remainder) – see section 7.12.46.

Indicators

In addition to the basic operator and operands, RPG C-specs have conditioning and resulting indicators.

Operations may be conditioned to the setting of an indicator or group of indicators, and may set indicators for use elsewhere in the program.

As discussed in section 7.1.2, indicators are a fruitful source of bugs. With the introduction of the IFxx and DOxx constructs, they are used very much less in RPG III than in RPG II.

The "xx" can take the following meanings:

```
        EQ      Equal
        GT      Greater than
        LT      Less than
        GE      Greater than or equal to
        LE      Less than or equal to
```

IF and DO have been retro-fitted to some dialects of RPG II, creating a sort of RPG $2^{1}/_{2}$.

The "pure" RPG II:

```
C               SALARY    COMP    40000         73
C       73                ADD     1     COUNT
```

may – and should – be replaced by:

```
C               SALARY    IFGT    40000
C                         ADD     1     COUNT
C                         END
```

Conditioning indicators in columns 9-17 should not be used at all in new programs, and indeed there should be an installation standard against doing so – see Chapter 17.

Columns 7 and 8 are used mainly for the Lx indicators in the cycle – see Chapter 8. In RPG II all statements that formed part of a subroutine were required to have SR in columns 7 and 8; to ensure upward compatibility this is still allowed in RPG III, but is no longer a requirement.

About the time when the original RPG became RPG II, the language was amended to allow and-ing and or-ing of conditioning indicators. This was achieved by coding AN (no D) or OR in columns 7 and 8:

```
C           71
CAN         72
COR         73              ADD    1      COUNT
```

It is an excruciatingly horrible construct, and there is certainly no reason whatever to use it in RPG III.

Standard practice in free format languages is to indent nested IFs and ELSEs. This is obviously impossible in a fixed format language like RPG, so the compiler provides an indication of nesting level on the right of the compilation listing:

```
C           SALARY          IFGT 40000            B001
C           SEX             IFEQ 'M'              B002
C                           ADD  1    MCOUNT      002
C                           ELSE                  X002
C                           ADD  1    FCOUNT      002
C                           END                   E002
C                           END                   E001
```

The COBOL equivalent is:

```
IF SALARY GREATER THAN 40000
    IF SEX EQUAL 'M'
        ADD 1 TO M-COUNT
    ELSE
        ADD 1 TO F-COUNT.
```

Like having the verb in the middle, the RPG way is a little odd until one gets used to it, but is very effective indeed. Level indication is provided explicitly by the compiler, rather than depending on the programmer's indentation, so mistakes are much easier to trap.

In RPG III resulting indicators in the C-specs are flagged by a '1', '2' or '3' to the right of the compilation listing, indicating respectively that indicators are coded in columns 54-55, 56-57 and 58-59. This is a great help when checking to see if an indicator has been coded in the wrong position.

Verbs

RPG has a dauntingly large number of verbs – considerably more than COBOL – but not all of them are in everyday use. Presumably people learning the language will wish to concentrate on the more commonly used verbs, so I have attempted to indicate (in bold) the frequency of use in each of the verb descriptions which follow. Naturally these gradings are somewhat subjective – e.g. some programmers might reverse my gradings of Do While and Do Until.

Some verbs are environment dependent: COMIT and ROLBK will be used quite frequently in installations which use commitment control, but not at all by those which don't.

The rest of this section describes the verbs and how they are used on the coding form (an example of which is given in Appendix E). They are listed in alphabetical order. A small table at the beginning of each description summarises the type of entry allowed for Indicators (with the relevant column numbers), the Factor 1, Factor 2 and Result fields; and indicates the purpose of the Resulting Indicators (again showing the column numbers). In the case of verbs where Resulting Indicators are not applicable, the entry is shown as blank.

The following abbreviations have been used for the different types of entry for Indicators, Factor 1, Factor 2 and Result fields:

Blk   leave blank

Opt   entry optional

Req   entry required (i.e. mandatory)

7.12.1 ACQ Acquire Program Device

Usage: Very frequent, Frequent, Occasional, Seldom, **Very seldom**

Indicators		Fact 1	Fact 2	Result	Resulting Indicators		
7 - 8	9 - 17				54 - 55	56 - 57	58 - 59
Opt	Opt	Req	Req	Blk	Blk	Err	Blk

Used for attaching the device named in Factor 1, to the WORKSTN file named in Factor 2.

If the device is not available, the indicator specified in columns 56- 57 will be set to on. If no indicator is specified then the INFSR (file error subroutine) – see section 7.7.2 – will be invoked. If neither indicator nor INFSR is specified then the program will crash.

7.12.2 ADD Add

Usage: **Very frequent**, Frequent, Occasional, Seldom, Very seldom

The Add verb has two formats:

Indicators		Fact 1	Fact 2	Result	Resulting Indicators		
7 - 8	9 - 17				54 - 55	56 - 57	58 - 59
Opt	Opt	Opt	Req	Req	Result +ve	Result -ve	Result zero

1) If Factor 1 is blank, Factor 2 is added to Result and the sum placed in Result

2) If Factor 1 is not blank, Factor 1 is added to Factor 2 and the sum placed in Result

In RPG III the first format is by far the more common, but in some dialects of RPG II only the second format is available.

If one or more indicators is specified in columns 54-59 they are set according to the algebraic value of Result.

7.12.3 ANDxx And

Usage: **Very frequent**, Frequent, Occasional, Seldom, Very seldom

Indicators		Fact 1	Fact 2	Result	Resulting Indicators		
7 - 8	9 - 17				54 - 55	56 - 57	58 - 59
Opt	Blk	Req	Req	Blk	Blk	Blk	Blk

The literal or variable specified in Factor 1 is compared to the literal or variable specified in Factor 2. The result of this comparison is logically and-ed to the results of the previous comparison(s).

It is better to use ANDxx where applicable, rather than multiple IFs. For example:

```
C           SALARY    IFGT 40000
C           SEX       ANDEQ 'M'
C           EYES      ANDEQ 'BLUE'
C                     ADD  1    COUNT
C                     END
```

is cleaner than:

```
C           SALARY    IFGT 40000
C           SEX       IFEQ 'M'
C           EYES      IFEQ 'BLUE'
C                     ADD  1    COUNT
C                     END
C                     END
C                     END
```

7.12.4 BEGSR Begin Subroutine

Usage: **Very frequent**, Frequent, Occasional, Seldom, Very seldom

Indicators		Fact 1	Fact 2	Result	Resulting Indicators		
7 - 8	9 - 17				54 - 55	56 - 57	58 - 59
Opt	Blk	Req	Blk	Blk	Blk	Blk	Blk

BEGSR is required at the beginning of every subroutine. The name specified in Factor 1 is used as a target by EXSR and CASxx commands, and is rather similar to a COBOL paragraph name.

Many programmers like to begin all subroutine names with SR so that they all appear together in the sorted cross reference listing produced by the RPG III compiler.

Factor 1 should contain the figurative constant *PSSR (Program Status Subroutine) if this is a program error handler. The *PSSR receives control whenever an error occurs and no error indicator has been specified.

In earlier versions of RPG, it was necessary to code SR in columns 7 and 8 of all subroutine statements. This requirement has been dropped, but programs written to the old standard will compile successfully.

7.12.5 BITOF Set Bits to Off

Usage: Very frequent, Frequent, Occasional, **Seldom**, Very seldom

Indicators		Fact 1	Fact 2	Result	Resulting Indicators		
7 - 8	9 - 17				54 - 55	56 - 57	58 - 59
Opt	Opt	Blk	Req	Req	Blk	Blk	Blk

The BITOF and BITON commands enable the RPG programmer to manipulate data at bit level – a luxury which is not afforded to his COBOL counterpart.

The Result field must specify the name of a one byte variable. The bits specified in Factor 2 are set to off.

Unfortunately the Factor 2 entry must number the bits from 0 to 7 rather than 1 to 8.

The following will load the value X'77' into the field HEX77:

```
C           MOVE    *HIVAL   HEX77 1
C           BITOF   '04'     HEX77
```

The first line defines HEX77, with a length of one character alphanumeric, and loads X'FF' (i.e. B'1111 1111') into it.

The second line sets off the first and fifth bits, thus leaving a value of X'77' (B'0111 0111').

7.12.6 BITON Set Bits to On

Usage: Very frequent, Frequent, Occasional, **Seldom**, Very seldom

Indicators		Fact 1	Fact 2	Result	Resulting Indicators		
7 - 8	9 - 17				54 - 55	56 - 57	58 - 59
Opt	Opt	Blk	Req	Req	Blk	Blk	Blk

As with the BITOF command, BITON enables the RPG programmer to manipulate data at bit level – a luxury which is not afforded to his COBOL counterpart.

The Result field must specify the name of a one byte variable. The bits specified in Factor 2 are set to on.

Again, the Factor 2 entry must number the bits from 0 to 7 rather than 1 to 8.

The following will load the value X'22' into the field HEX22:

```
C           MOVE    *LOVAL   HEX22 1
C           BITON   '26'     HEX22
```

The first line defines HEX22, with a length of one character alphanumeric, and loads X'00' (i.e. B'0000 0000') into it.

The second line sets on the second and sixth bits, thus leaving a value of X'22' (B'0010 0010').

7.12.7 CABxx Compare and Branch

Usage: Very frequent, Frequent, Occasional, Seldom, **Very seldom**

Indicators		Fact 1	Fact 2	Result	Resulting Indicators		
7 - 8	9 - 17				54 - 55	56 - 57	58 - 59
Opt	Opt	Req	Req	Opt	HI	LO	EQ

The CABxx commands are simply GOTO commands in sheep's clothing. Like GOTO itself, CABxx should be used with great caution – see Chapter 17.

The literals, variables or figurative constants in Factors 1 and 2 are compared, and if the compare is satisfied control is transferred to the TAG specified in Result.

If indicators are specified in columns 54-59 they are set depending on whether the Factor 1 is greater than, less than, or equal to Factor 2.

The CAB is thus effectively a combined COMP and GOTO. When Result is left blank it amounts to a COMP.

This treacherous command's potential to cause mayhem is quite extraordinary.

7.12.8 CALL Call

Usage: Very frequent, **Frequent**, Occasional, Seldom, Very seldom

Indicators		Fact 1	Fact 2	Result	Resulting Indicators		
7 - 8	9 - 17				54 - 55	56 - 57	58 - 59
Opt	Opt	Blk	Req	Opt	Blk	Err	LR

The use of the CALL command is covered in detail in Chapter 10.

Factor 2 contains the name of the program to be CALLed, which may be in the form of a literal, field or array element. The latter two options offer some tantalising possibilities.

Various third party utilities can read the source code to produce a system structure chart. However, if you use anything other than a literal, they will have nothing to work on.

Parameters to be passed to the CALLed program are specified by means of PARM statements, which may follow directly after the CALL, or may be specified elsewhere, headed by a PLIST.

When the PLIST option is chosen, the name of the PLIST must be entered in the Result. At first sight, the PLIST option seems a neat way of handling parameters, but most experienced RPG III programmers seem to revert to using PARM statements directly after the CALL.

Resulting indicators may be specified in columns 56 and 57, to test whether the CALLed program terminates in an error; and in columns 58 and 59, to test whether the CALLed program terminates with LR set. In practice these resulting indicators are not often used. It is better for each CALLed program to do its own error monitoring, and if the RCLRSC (Reclaim Resources) CL command is used, as outlined in Chapter 10, there is no need to know about the CALLed program's LR.

7.12.9 CASxx Case [conditional EXSR]

Usage: Very frequent, **Frequent**, Occasional, Seldom, Very seldom

Indicators		Fact 1	Fact 2	Result	Resulting Indicators		
7 - 8	9 - 17				54 - 55	56 - 57	58 - 59
Opt	Opt	Opt	Opt	Req	HI	LO	EQ

When used properly, the CASxx command permits testing a variety of conditions in a very concise and cleanly structured way. Essentially, Factor 1 and Factor 2 are compared, and if the comparison is satisfied, the subroutine named in Result is executed.

There are many options for using conditioning and resulting indicators, and for leaving Factors 1 and 2 blank, but these are best ignored, except for the use as an "error bucket" as described below.

CAS commands are considered to occur in groups, even though a group may comprise a single CAS command. Each group *must* be terminated with an END statement.

The CAS group:

```
     C           SALARY    CASGT40000         SRXYZ
     C                     END
```

is equivalent to:

```
     C           SALARY    IFGT  40000
     C                     EXSR  SRXYZ
     C                     END
```

When only a single test is involved there is little advantage of using a CAS statement. It comes into its own when we are asked to test a number of possibilities.

Suppose we are asked to test for the colour of peoples' eyes. The valid possibilities are blue, brown, green and grey. Anything else is an error.

This is an elegant way of doing it:

```
C           EYE         CASEQ'BLUE'         SRBLUE
C           EYE         CASEQ'BROWN'        SRBRWN
C           EYE         CASEQ'GREEN'        SRGREN
C           EYE         CASEQ'GREY'         SRGREY
C                       CAS                 SRERR
C                       END
```

When there is a successful comparison, the stipulated subroutine is executed, and processing then continues with the statement following the END statement. In the example, the second to last statement calls for unconditional execution of the subroutine SRERR, but this will only be carried out if all the other tests have failed.

7.12.10 CHAIN Random Read

Usage: Very frequent, **Frequent**, Occasional, Seldom, Very seldom

Indicators		Fact 1	Fact 2	Result	Resulting Indicators		
7 - 8	9 - 17				54 - 55	56 - 57	58 - 59
Opt	Opt	Req	Req	Opt	Miss	Err	Blk

A read is issued to the file (or format) in Factor 2 using the key value in Factor 1.

If the record is not found the indicator specified in columns 54 and 55 will be set to on. If there is an error, the indicator specified in columns 56 and 57 will be set to on. The Miss indicator is compulsory, but the Error indicator is optional.

If the file is not keyed, then Factor 1 must contain the required RRN (Relative Record Number). When a CHAIN is issued against a subfile format (see Chapter 12) the RRN is always used.

Result may contain the name of a data structure into which the record from an internally defined file is placed. There is seldom any point in using this option. Coding the data structure I-specs is no more and no less difficult than coding the record I-specs.

When a CHAIN is issued using a partial key, the first record to satisfy the search argument is retrieved. Note that when a compound key is specified for an externally defined file it must be a KLIST name.

An unsuccessful CHAIN will destroy the file's pointer (see section 7.4) while a successful CHAIN will set it so that a subsequent read will retrieve the next record.

Suppose file FILXYZ contains three records, AA, AB and AC. The CHAIN will retrieve the first record and the READ the second record.

```
C            'A'       CHAINFILXYZ              71
C                      READ FILXYZ                  72
```

If the data is not needed, and all that is required is an existence check, the SETLL command (section 7.12.64) should be used in preference to CHAIN. This is because CHAIN causes data to be passed from the disk to the program buffer, whereas SETLL merely interrogates the index to find out if the record exists.

If you discover a CHAIN being used in this way and decide to change it to a SETLL to improve performance, be careful. CHAIN sets on an indicator for a Miss, whereas SETLL sets on an indicator for a Hit. Any subsequent tests of that indicator will therefore need to be reversed.

7.12.11 CLOSE Close File

Usage: Very frequent, Frequent, **Occasional**, Seldom, Very seldom

Indicators		Fact 1	Fact 2	Result	Resulting Indicators		
7 - 8	9 - 17				54 - 55	56 - 57	58 - 59
Opt	Opt	Blk	Req	Blk	Blk	Err	Blk

When a program terminates with LR on, RPG automatically closes any files which are open, so this command is not very often required.

The name of the file to be closed is entered in Factor 2, and an error indicator may be specified in columns 56-57.

The CLOSE command destroys the file pointer.

Note that if it is required to reposition a file pointer at the beginning of the file, a SETLL command (see section 7.12.64) with a search argument of *LOVAL is much more efficient than a CLOSE followed by an OPEN.

7.12.12 COMIT Commit

Usage: Very frequent, Frequent, **Occasional**, Seldom, Very seldom

Indicators		Fact 1	Fact 2	Result	Resulting Indicators		
7 - 8	9 - 17				54 - 55	56 - 57	58 - 59
Opt	Opt	Opt	Blk	Blk	Blk	Err	Blk

The use of COMIT is covered in detail in Chapter 13. Factor 1 may contain an entry for a commitment boundary identifier. The file pointer(s) are not affected by COMIT.

7.12.13 COMP Compare

Usage: Very frequent, Frequent, Occasional, **Seldom**, Very seldom

Indicators		Fact 1	Fact 2	Result	Resulting Indicators		
7 - 8	9 - 17				54 - 55	56 - 57	58 - 59
Opt	Opt	Req	Req	Blk	HI	LO	EQ

The contents of Factor 1 are compared with the contents of Factor 2, and indicators set accordingly. At least one resulting indicator must be coded.

COMP was very frequently used in RPG II but has been largely superseded by IFxx in RPG III.

7.12.14 DEBUG Debug Function

Usage: Very frequent, Frequent, Occasional, Seldom, **Very seldom**

Indicators		Fact 1	Fact 2	Result	Resulting Indicators		
7 - 8	9 - 17				54 - 55	56 - 57	58 - 59
Opt	Opt	Opt	Opt	Opt	Blk	Blk	Blk

The use of DEBUG is covered in detail in Chapter 14.

DEBUG was a valuable tool in earlier versions of RPG, but has been largely superseded by the AS/400's advanced debugging environment.

Result may contain the name of a variable whose contents are to be output to the file specified in Factor 2. If Factor 2 is blank, the variable is output to the requesting terminal.

The contents of Factor 1 are used as an identifier for the field in Result. If Factor 1 is left blank, the statement sequence number is output in its place.

7.12.15 DEFN Define Field

Usage: Very frequent, **Frequent**, Occasional, Seldom, Very seldom

Indicators		Fact 1	Fact 2	Result	Resulting Indicators		
7 - 8	9 - 17				54 - 55	56 - 57	58 - 59
Opt	Blk	Req	Opt	Req	Blk	Blk	Blk

DEFN has two purposes:

1) To define a field using the attributes of another field

2) To associate a variable with a data area.

When used to define a field, Factor 1 should contain the figurative constant *LIKE, Factor 2 the name of the field being used as a model, and Result the name of the field being defined.

This technique should be used wherever a new field has some logical association with an existing field, particularly a database field.

If the attributes of the field named in Factor 2 are changed – perhaps because of a database change – the attributes of the field in Result will automatically change too.

The fact that a DEFN has been used, is a form of documentation in itself: it offers a maintenance programmer a clue that there is a link between the two fields.

The length may be over-ridden by an entry in columns 49-51, but this facility is not often used.

*LIKE DEFN statements may appear anywhere in the program, but it is good practice to group them together at the beginning of the C-specs.

When used to associate a variable with a data area, Factor 1 should contain the figurative constant *NAMVAR, Factor 2 the name of the data area, and Result the name of the variable being associated. If Factor 2 is left blank it will be assumed to be the same as Result.

7.12.16 DELET Delete Record

Usage: Very frequent, Frequent, **Occasional**, Seldom, Very seldom

Indicators		Fact 1	Fact 2	Result	Resulting Indicators		
7 - 8	9 - 17				54 - 55	56 - 57	58 - 59
Opt	Opt	Opt	Req	Blk	Miss	Err	Blk

This command is used to delete a record from an update file (U in column 15 of the F-spec).

Factor 2 must contain the name of the file or record format, and Factor 1 may contain a key. If Factor 1 is left blank the last record read will be deleted.

The file pointer is left pointing at the record following the deleted record.

If Factor 1 is provided, then an indicator must be entered in columns 54-55. An error indicator may optionally be entered in columns 56-57.

7.12.17 DIV Divide

Usage: Very frequent, Frequent, **Occasional**, Seldom, Very seldom

Indicators		Fact 1	Fact 2	Result	Resulting Indicators		
7 - 8	9 - 17				54 - 55	56 - 57	58 - 59
Opt	Opt	Blk	Blk	Req	Result +ve	Result -ve	Result zero

The DIV verb has two possible formats:

1) If Factor 1 is blank, Result is divided by Factor 2 and the answer placed in Result

2) If Factor 1 is not blank, Factor 1 is divided by Factor 2 and the answer placed in Result

In RPG III the first format is by far the more common, but in RPG II only the second format is available.

If one or more indicators is specified in columns 54-59 they are set according to the algebraic value of Result. A program exception will result if Factor 2 contains zero, so it is sound practice to test Factor 2 before each DIV command.

An H may be entered in column 53 to half-adjust the answer. If the next command is to be an MVR (Move Remainder) – see section 7.12.46 – then column 53 should be left blank.

7.12.18 DO Do

Usage: Very frequent, Frequent, Occasional, **Seldom**, Very seldom

Indicators		Fact 1	Fact 2	Result	Resulting Indicators		
7 - 8	9 - 17				54 - 55	56 - 57	58 - 59
Opt	Opt	Opt	Opt	Opt	Blk	Blk	Blk

Each DO statement must have an associated END statement. The statements between the DO and its END are called a 'do group'. Processing is best described by an example:

```
C            4          DO    24    XYZ    B001
C                        .                  001
C                   (processing)             001
C                        .                  001
C                       END    2            E001
```

The COBOL equivalent is:

```
PERFORM (paragraph name)
VARYING XYZ FROM 4 BY 2 UNTIL XYZ = 24.
```

The PL/I equivalent is:

```
DO XYZ = 4 TO 24 BY 2;
   .
   (processing)
   .
END;
```

The starting value specified in Factor 1 of the DO, is placed in the Result variable of the DO, and then incremented by the value specified in Factor 2 of the END, until it exceeds the value specified in Factor 2 of the DO. After each increment, the do group is executed.

If Factor 1 of the DO is blank the starting value is assumed to be 1.

If Factor 2 of the DO is blank the limit value is assumed to be 1.

If the Result of the DO is blank RPG will generate an internal control field.

If Factor 2 of the END is blank the increment is assumed to be 1.

Factors 1 and 2 of the DO, and Factor 2 of the END, may contain variables rather than the literals shown.

That all sounds terribly complicated but the example above is a "worst case". In practice DO loops tend to be a lot simpler, as follows:

```
C                             DO   20    X        B001
C           ABC,X             IFEQ 'P'             B002
C                             MOVE 'Q'  ABC,X     002
C                             END                 E002
C                             END                 E001
```

This will inspect the first 20 entries of array ABC, changing each to Q if it contains P. The Result field of DO statements is nearly always used to subscript an array (as shown).

7.12.19 DOUxx Do Until

Usage: Very frequent, Frequent, Occasional, **Seldom**, Very seldom

Indicators		Fact 1	Fact 2	Result	Resulting Indicators		
7 - 8	9 - 17				54 - 55	56 - 57	58 - 59
Opt	Opt	Req	Req	Blk	Blk	Blk	Blk

Each DOUxx statement must have an associated END statement. The statements between the DOUxx and its END are called a do group.

Factor 1 is compared with Factor 2 and the do group statements are processed until the Do Until condition is satisfied, however the first test is not performed before the do group has been executed once.

The test may be supplemented with ANDxx and ORxx statements:

```
        C     HAIR            DOUEQ'BLONDE'        B001
        C     EYES            ANDEQ'BLUE'          001
        C                     ADD  1    COUNT      001
        C                     END                  E001
```

The DOUxx command is very similar to the DOWxx command – see next section. The difference between them is that DOUxx always processes the do group once.

NOTE:

Programmers familiar with COBOL should not fall into the trap of assuming that DOUxx (Do Until) is similar to COBOL's PERFORM UNTIL; DOWxx (Do While) is the equivalent.

Any programmer who has used, or is ever likely to use, either COBOL or PL/I will avoid a lot of confusion by using DOWxx rather than DOUxx.

7.12.20 DOWxx Do While

Usage: Very frequent, **Frequent**, Occasional, Seldom, Very seldom

Indicators		Fact 1	Fact 2	Result	Resulting Indicators		
7 - 8	9 - 17				54 - 55	56 - 57	58 - 59
Opt	Opt	Req	Req	Blk	Blk	Blk	Blk

Each DOWxx statement must have an associated END statement. The statements between the DOWxx and its END are called a do group.

Factor 1 is compared with Factor 2 and the do group statements are executed for as long as the Do While condition is satisfied.

The test may be supplemented with ANDxx and ORxx statements:

```
C          HAIR      DOWEQ'BLONDE'         B001
C          EYES      ANDEQ'BLUE'            001
C                    ADD   1     COUNT      001
C                    END                   E001
```

The DOWxx command is very similar to the DOUxx command – see previous section. The difference between them is that DOUxx always processes the do group once.

See also Note at end of section 7.12.19.

7.12.21 DSPLY Display

Usage: Very frequent, Frequent, Occasional, Seldom, **Very seldom**

Indicators		Fact 1	Fact 2	Result	Resulting Indicators		
7 - 8	9 - 17				54 - 55	56 - 57	58 - 59
Opt	Opt	Opt	Opt	Opt	Blk	Err	Blk

This command allows the program to send a message and receive a reply. It was quite popular in some dialects of RPG II, but in RPG III there are better ways of sending messages, and it is seldom encountered.

The Factor 1 entry contains the message, and Factor 2 designates where the message is to go. Result provides a field to receive the reply.

Factor 2 is normally left blank. The default is the invoking workstation if the program is interactive, and QSYSOPR (the system operator) if it is a batch program.

7.12.22 DUMP Dump Program

Usage: Very frequent, Frequent, Occasional, Seldom, **Very seldom**

Indicators		Fact 1	Fact 2	Result	Resulting Indicators		
7 - 8	9 - 17				54 - 55	56 - 57	58 - 59
Opt	Opt	Opt	Blk	Blk	Blk	Blk	Blk

There is very little call for this command in an AS/400 environment. If a dump is required following a program crash, it is generally one of the options offered by the system error message.

For debugging purposes there are many powerful alternatives available, which are discussed in Chapter 14.

Factor 1 may be used to specify an identifier for the dump.

7.12.23 ELSE Else

Usage: **Very frequent**, Frequent, Occasional, Seldom, Very seldom

Indicators		Fact 1	Fact 2	Result	Resulting Indicators		
7 - 8	9 - 17				54 - 55	56 - 57	58 - 59
Opt	Blk	Blk	Blk	Blk	Blk	Blk	Blk

ELSE is a pseudo-verb – it generates a directive to the compiler rather than executable code.

The nesting level indication on the right of the compilation listing is prefixed by an X to indicate the position of an ELSE:

```
C         FLDXYZ        IFEQ  'RED'            B001
C                       ADD   1      RED       001
C                       ELSE                   X001
C                       ADD   1      NOTRED    001
C                       END                    E001
```

In a complex nested IF, this can be quite useful for checking that the ELSE references the correct IF.

7.12.24 END End (of IF or DO group)

Usage: **Very frequent**, Frequent, Occasional, Seldom, Very seldom

Indicators		Fact 1	Fact 2	Result	Resulting Indicators		
7 - 8	9 - 17				54 - 55	56 - 57	58 - 59
Opt	Opt	Blk	Opt	Blk	Blk	Blk	Blk

END is a pseudo-verb – it generates a directive to the compiler rather than executable code.

The END statement is used to terminate a DO or IF group. Note that Factor 2 is optional, but only for the DO command – see section 7.12.18.

Conditioning indicators are valid for END, but anyone who uses them should be hung, drawn and quartered – not necessarily in that sequence.

7.12.25 ENDSR End Subroutine

Usage: **Very frequent**, Frequent, Occasional, Seldom, Very seldom

Indicators		Fact 1	Fact 2	Result	Resulting Indicators		
7 - 8	9 - 17				54 - 55	56 - 57	58 - 59
Opt	Blk	Opt	Opt	Blk	Blk	Blk	Blk

The ENDSR command terminates a subroutine begun by a BEGSR command – see section 7.12.4.

Factor 1 may contain a name, which is in effect a TAG name – see section 7.12.71.

If the subroutine is a *PSSR (error subroutine), Factor 2 may contain the name of the point to which control is to be returned.

In earlier versions of RPG, it was required to code SR in columns 7 and 8 of all subroutine statements. This requirement has been dropped, but programs written to the old standard will still compile successfully.

7.12.26 EXCPT Exception Output

Usage: Very frequent, Frequent, **Occasional**, Seldom, Very seldom

Indicators		Fact 1	Fact 2	Result	Resulting Indicators		
7 - 8	9 - 17				54 - 55	56 - 57	58 - 59
Opt	Opt	Blk	Opt	Blk	Blk	Blk	Blk

EXCPT allows output to be performed from within the C-specs, rather than having to wait until the O-spec part of the cycle is reached.

It is sometimes confused with WRITE (see section 7.12.78) which has a similar purpose; EXCPT refers to internal files, whereas WRITE applies to external files.

In earlier versions of RPG, EXCPT had no operands. When an EXCPT was issued RPG would write every E-type output line (see section 7.13.1) whose conditioning indicators were set. It was necessary to be very careful that the correct indicators, and only those indicators, were set.

This problem has been greatly alleviated by providing the facility for "exception names", which are entered in columns 32-27 of the header O- spec (see section 7.13.1), and referenced by Factor 2 of EXCPT.

If several header O-specs have the same name, they will all be output when referenced by an EXCPT.

The old form of coding (choice of indicator is arbitrary):

```
        C                           SETON 51
        C                           EXCPT
        C                           SETOF 51
         .
         .
        O         E 2 1 51
                        (body entries)
         .
```

may be replaced by:

```
C                       EXCPT HDG1
 .
 .
O     E 2 1             HDG1
                        (body entries)
 .
```

7.12.27 EXFMT Execute Format

Usage: Very frequent, **Frequent**, Occasional, Seldom, Very seldom

Indicators		Fact 1	Fact 2	Result	Resulting Indicators		
7 - 8	9 - 17				54 - 55	56 - 57	58 - 59
Opt	Opt	Blk	Req	Blk	Blk	Err	Blk

The EXFMT command is equivalent to a WRITE command immediately followed by a READ command. It is valid only with Workstation files, i.e. for interactive programs, which are covered in Chapter 11.

Factor 2 specifies the name of the format which is to be written and then read. An error indicator may be specified, but this option is seldom used.

Note that a subfile format name may not be specified. You should use the subfile control format name – see Chapter 12.

7.12.28 EXSR Execute Subroutine

Usage: Very frequent, **Frequent**, Occasional, Seldom, Very seldom

Indicators		Fact 1	Fact 2	Result	Resulting Indicators		
7 - 8	9 - 17				54 - 55	56 - 57	58 - 59
Opt	Opt	Blk	Req	Blk	Blk	Blk	Blk

The subroutine whose name appears in Factor 2 is executed. Conditioning indicators are permitted, but it is bad practice to use them.

If conditioning is required use either IF or CASxx statements – see sections 7.12.33 and 7.12.9 respectively.

The RPG statement:

```
C                   EXSR      ABCRTN
```

is the same as the COBOL:

```
PERFORM ABCRTN.
```

7.12.29 FEOD Force End of Data

Usage: Very frequent, Frequent, Occasional, Seldom, **Very seldom**

Indicators		Fact 1	Fact 2	Result	Resulting Indicators		
7 - 8	9 - 17				54 - 55	56 - 57	58 - 59
Opt	Opt	Blk	Req	Blk	Blk	Err	Blk

The FEOD command forces an end of file, for the file named in Factor 2.

There may have been some point to this command in earlier versions of RPG, but it is difficult to see any use for it in RPG III.

7.12.30 FORCE Force file for next cycle

Usage: Very frequent, Frequent, Occasional, Seldom, **Very seldom**

Indicators		Fact 1	Fact 2	Result	Resulting Indicators		
7 - 8	9 - 17				54 - 55	56 - 57	58 - 59
Opt	Opt	Blk	Req	Blk	Blk	Blk	Blk

This command may be used only in the cycle – see Chapter 8. It interferes with the cycle's normal method of selecting the file from which the next record is to be read.

If you need to use it, you should seriously rethink your program design....

7.12.31 FREE Free program static storage

Usage: Very frequent, Frequent, Occasional, Seldom, **Very seldom**

Indicators		Fact 1	Fact 2	Result	Resulting Indicators		
7 - 8	9 - 17				54 - 55	56 - 57	58 - 59
Opt	Opt	Blk	Req	Blk	Blk	Err	Blk

This command de-allocates the storage allocated to the program named in Factor 2.

It is not often used because it is easier to use a CL RCLRSC (Reclaim Resources) command following each menu CALL. See section 10.6.

7.12.32 GOTO Go To

Usage: Very frequent, Frequent, Occasional, Seldom, **Very seldom**

Indicators		Fact 1	Fact 2	Result	Resulting Indicators		
7 - 8	9 - 17				54 - 55	56 - 57	58 - 59
Opt	Opt	Blk	Req	Blk	Blk	Blk	Blk

The GOTO command transfers control to the TAG statement named in Factor 2. Note that GOTO is all one word, apart from that the command is identical to COBOL's GO TO.

It was widely used in RPG II but, with the introduction of IF, DO and CASxx commands, is quite unnecessary in RPG III.

A few years ago a statistical survey of COBOL bugs revealed that about 75 per cent were caused by faulty GO TO commands, and there is no reason to think that RPG is much different. You have been warned!

See also Chapter 17.

7.12.33 IFxx If

Usage: **Very frequent**, Frequent, Occasional, Seldom, Very seldom

Indicators		Fact 1	Fact 2	Result	Resulting Indicators		
7 - 8	9 - 17				54 - 55	56 - 57	58 - 59
Opt	Opt	Req	Req	Blk	Blk	Blk	Blk

Each IFxx statement must have an associated END statement. The statements between the IFxx and its END are called an if group. Factor 1 and Factor 2 are compared, and if the comparison is satisfied the if group is executed. The test may be supplemented with ANDxx and ORxx statements.

Processing is best described by an example:

```
C          FLDABC    IFEQ FLDXYZ          B001
C          FLDPQR    ORNE FLDJKL          001
C                    .                    001
C                    (processing)         001
C                    .                    001
C                    END                  E001
```

The COBOL equivalent would be:

```
IF (FLDABC = FLDXYZ) OR (FLDPQR NOT = FLDJKL)
    PERFORM (paragraph name)
```

Note that in RPG the verb appears between the operands, which looks a little strange at first, but one soon gets used to it.

Conditioning indicators may be used on IFxx statements, but it is looking for trouble to do so.

7.12.34 IN Read Data Area

Usage: Very frequent, Frequent, Occasional, **Seldom**, Very seldom

Indicators		Fact 1	Fact 2	Result	Resulting Indicators		
7 - 8	9 - 17				54 - 55	56 - 57	58 - 59
Opt	Opt	Opt	Req	Blk	Blk	Err	Blk

Factor 2 must contain either a name specified in a *NAMVAR DEFN statement (see section 7.12.15), or the figurative constant *NAMVAR, in which case all data areas defined in the program are read.

Factor 1 may contain the figurative constant *LOCK, which locks the data area until an OUT command (see section 7.12.51) is issued for it.

Data areas are mainly a legacy from earlier GSD machines. There is little advantage in using them on an AS/400, and they can cause problems with commitment control – see Chapter 13.

7.12.35 KFLD Key Field

Usage: Very frequent, Frequent, **Occasional**, Seldom, Very seldom

Indicators		Fact 1	Fact 2	Result	Resulting Indicators		
7 - 8	9 - 17				54 - 55	56 - 57	58 - 59
Opt	Blk	Blk	Blk	Req	Blk	Blk	Blk

This is explained in section 7.12.36, which follows.

7.12.36 KLIST Key List

Usage: Very frequent, Frequent, **Occasional**, Seldom, Very seldom

Indicators		Fact 1	Fact 2	Result	Resulting Indicators		
7 - 8	9 - 17				54 - 55	56 - 57	58 - 59
Opt	Blk	Req	Blk	Req	Blk	Blk	Blk

KLIST and KFLD are pseudo-verbs – they generate directives to the compiler rather than executable code.

When a file has a composite key it is necessary to define a search argument in the form of a list of fields, each holding the corresponding part of the key of the required record.

The list is headed by a KLIST statement, which is followed by as many KFLD entries as necessary.

Suppose we wish to use the logical file ORDER1, built over the ORDER entity, and keyed by Part number and Date. The key would look like this:

```
C          KORD1     KLIST
C                    KFLD           PARTNO
C                    KFLD           ORDYY
C                    KFLD           ORDMM
C                    KFLD           ORDDD
```

KLISTs can be used with CHAIN, DELET, READE, REDPE, SETGT and SETLL commands.

KLISTs can appear anywhere in the C-specs, but in the interests of tidy programming, should be grouped together at the beginning of the C- specs – see Chapter 17.

7.12.37 LOKUP Look Up

Usage: Very frequent, Frequent, **Occasional**, Seldom, Very seldom

Indicators		Fact 1	Fact 2	Result	Resulting Indicators		
7 - 8	9 - 17				54 - 55	56 - 57	58 - 59
Opt	Opt	Req	Req	Opt/Blk	HI	LO	EQ

The LOKUP verb causes a search to be made of a table or array – see section 7.2. The search argument is entered in Factor 1 and may be a field (including an array element), a literal or a figurative constant.

If a Table is to be searched then Factor 2 contains the name of the Table, and Result may contain the name of an Alternating Table, if required.

If an Array is to be searched then Factor 2 contains the name of the element of the array with which the search is to begin.

Be sure that the subscript is set to the desired value before the LOKUP commences. (It is particularly easy to forget this, particularly if the LOKUP is to begin from the first element, as is usually the case.)

At least one resulting indicator must be specified to indicate the success or otherwise of the LOKUP. This is nearly always Equal (columns 58-59). The HIGH option (columns 54-55) causes the LOKUP to end when it finds the entry that is nearest to, but higher than, the search argument. The LOW option (columns 56-57) causes the LOKUP to end when it finds the entry that is nearest to, but lower than, the search argument.

The LOKUP verb equates to the COBOL SEARCH verb. For example, the RPG:

```
C                       MOVE   1              X
          .
          .
C            FLDA       LOKUP  ARR,X                   44
C                       MOVE   ARR,X          FLDXYZ
```

is equivalent to the COBOL:

```
SET X TO 1.
SEARCH ARR VARYING X
  WHEN FLDA = ARR (X)
    MOVE ARR (X) TO FLDXYZ.
```

There is no equivalent to COBOL's SEARCH ALL in RPG II or III, though there was in the earliest forms of RPG. (SEARCH ALL provides a binary search, rather than the linear search provided by LOKUP and SEARCH).

For small arrays it doesn't make much difference which form is used, but for really large arrays there is a vast improvement in performance when binary searches are used.

I vividly remember being called in to investigate a performance problem with an RPG II program running on an IBM 4331. Every record in an enormous file was being checked against several very large arrays, using LOKUP. The installation had a COBOL compiler, but none of the programmers knew COBOL. I replaced each LOKUP by a CALL to a COBOL program which did a binary search (i.e. a SEARCH ALL) on the array. Run time fell from 10 hours CPU bound to 3 hours with plenty of spare CPU capacity!

It is possible to use LOKUP to implement a form of decision table processing (sometimes called truth table processing).

Suppose we have a list of observations of creatures. Some are invalid, the rest are either bat, dog or man. We are asked to decide which is which, process accordingly, and reject the errors. Our basic decision table would look like this:

```
     Fur     | Y Y Y Y N N N N
     Tall    | Y Y N N Y Y N N
     Wings   | Y N Y N Y N Y N
     --------------------------
     Bat     | . . . . . . X .
     Dog     | . . . X . . . .
     Man     | . . . . . X . .
     Invalid| X X X . X . . X
```

We can refine this a little: anything that is not either bat, dog or man is invalid:

```
Fur    | Y N N
Tall   | N Y N
Wings  | N N Y
-------------
Bat    | . . X
Dog    | X . .
Man    | . X .
```

From this we generate an alternating table:

```
YNN Bat
NYN Dog
NNY Man
```

The RPG is now very simple:

```
C          INPUT     LOKUPTABYN     TABTYP         44
C*
C          *IN44     CASNE'1'       ERROR
C          TABTYP    CASEQ'Bat'     SRBAT
C          TABTYP    CASEQ'Dog'     SRDOG
C          TABTYP    CASEQ'Man'     SRMAN
C                    END
```

Obviously this example is trivial (we should hardly bother with a table for an "action stub" with only three entries) but the principle should be clear.

A minor variation would be to set up subprograms rather than subroutines. The alternating table might become:

```
YNN PROGBAT
NYN PROGDOG
NNY PROGMAN
```

and the RPG would become:

```
C          INPUT     LOKUPTABYN     TABTYP         44
C*
C          *IN44     IFNE'1'
C                    EXSR ERROR
C                    ELSE
C                    CALL TABTYP
C                    END
```

The comments in section 7.12.8 concerning the use of variable names in Factor 2 of CALL statements are also relevant.

7.12.38 MHHZO Move High to High Zone

Usage: Very frequent, Frequent, Occasional, Seldom, **Very seldom**

Indicators		Fact 1	Fact 2	Result	Resulting Indicators		
7 - 8	9 - 17				54 - 55	56 - 57	58 - 59
Opt	Opt	Blk	Req	Req	Blk	Blk	Blk

The zone portion of the high order byte of Factor 2 is moved to the zone portion of the high order byte of Result.

If you can think of a use for this command (or its cousins, MHLZO and MLHZO in the next two sections), 'pass Go and collect $200'.

7.12.39 MHLZO Move High to Low Zone

Usage: Very frequent, Frequent, Occasional, Seldom, **Very seldom**

Indicators		Fact 1	Fact 2	Result	Resulting Indicators		
7 - 8	9 - 17				54 - 55	56 - 57	58 - 59
Opt	Opt	Blk	Req	Req	Blk	Blk	Blk

The zone portion of the high order byte of Factor 2 is moved to the zone portion of the low order byte of Result.

7.12.40 MLHZO Move Low to High Zone

Usage: Very frequent, Frequent, Occasional, Seldom, **Very seldom**

Indicators		Fact 1	Fact 2	Result	Resulting Indicators		
7 - 8	9 - 17				54 - 55	56 - 57	58 - 59
Opt	Opt	Blk	Req	Req	Blk	Blk	Blk

The zone portion of the low order byte of Factor 2 is moved to the zone portion of the high order byte of Result.

7.12.41 MLLZO Move Low to Low Zone

Usage: Very frequent, Frequent, Occasional, Seldom, **Very seldom**

Indicators		Fact 1	Fact 2	Result	Resulting Indicators		
7 - 8	9 - 17				54 - 55	56 - 57	58 - 59
Opt	Opt	Blk	Req	Req	Blk	Blk	Blk

The zone portion of the low order byte of Factor 2 is moved to the zone portion of the low order byte of Result.

7.12.42 MOVE Move

Usage: **Very frequent**, Frequent, Occasional, Seldom, Very seldom

Indicators		Fact 1	Fact 2	Result	Resulting Indicators		
7 - 8	9 - 17				54 - 55	56 - 57	58 - 59
Opt	Opt	Opt	Req	Req	Result +ve	Result -ve	Result z/blk

The contents of Factor 2 are moved to the field in Result. Provided that Factor 2 and Result are the same length, there are no difficulties, and it proceeds in the same way as a COBOL MOVE.

If Result is *shorter* than Factor 2, then the rightmost (low order) digits of Factor 2 are moved to Result.

If Result is *longer* than Factor 2, then the contents of Factor 2 are moved to Result, right justified. The remaining leftmost (high order) digits of Result are not affected.

This MOVE marches to a different drummer than the MOVE in most other languages – so be careful.

Factor 2 may be numeric and Result alphameric, or vice versa, which means that the MOVE command may be used for converting data from one format to the other.

In particular, be careful of using the following to reset a counter:

    C   MOVE 0COUNT

If COUNT is only one digit long all will be well, but if it is longer, and contains, for example, 123 before the move, then it will contain 120 afterwards – not quite what would usually be intended.

In RPG II most programmers used the Z-ADD command (see section 7.12.80) to avoid the problem, but with the introduction of RPG III and figurative constants it is perhaps better to use:

    C   MOVE *ZERO COUNT

If Factor 2 and Result are both unsubscripted array names, then each element of the Factor 2 array will be moved to the corresponding element of the Result array.

7.12.43 MOVEA Move Array

Usage: Very frequent, Frequent, Occasional, **Seldom**, Very seldom

Indicators		Fact 1	Fact 2	Result	Resulting Indicators		
7 - 8	9 - 17				54 - 55	56 - 57	58 - 59
Opt	Opt	Blk	Blk	Req	Result +ve	Result -ve	Result zero

This command moves data from field to array, or from array to field, or from array to array. The move proceeds character by character, from left to right, ignoring array element boundaries.

If Result is *longer* than Factor 2, the move will terminate when the last byte of Factor 2 has been moved, leaving the rightmost (low order) bytes of Result unchanged.

If Result is *shorter* than Factor 2, the move will terminate when the last byte of Result has been filled.

If Factor 2 and Result are of different lengths the move will not necessarily terminate on an element boundary. Both Factor 2 and Result may contain subscripted array names. This implies that the sending and/or receiving operands may be in the middle of an array.

Numeric MOVEAs are allowed on the AS/400 only. In this case, the array elements and fields must have the same dimensions.

The most frequent use of the MOVEA is for text processing, when a field of 30 characters, for example, is redefined as an array of 30 elements of one byte each. Suppose we are given a 30-character field, called TEXT, and asked to set to blank any character which is not an upper-case letter.

The following code might be used:
```
E                        TABABC    26  26
E                        TXT       30   1
                          .
                          .
C                        MOVEA TEXT       TXT,1
C*
C                        DO    30         X
C          TXT,X         LOKUP TABABC               44
C          *IN44         IFNE  '1'
C                        MOVE  *BLANK     TXT,X
C                        END
C                        END
C*
C                        MOVEA TXT,1      TEXT
                          .
                          .

**
ABCDEFGHIJKLMNOPQRSTUVWXYZ
```

7.12.44 MOVEL Move Left

Usage: **Very frequent**, Frequent, Occasional, Seldom, Very seldom

Indicators		Fact 1	Fact 2	Result	Resulting Indicators		
7 - 8	9 - 17				54 - 55	56 - 57	58 - 59
Opt	Opt	Opt	Req	Req	Result +ve	Result -ve	Result z/blk

The contents of Factor 2 are moved to Result. Provided that Factor 2 and Result are the same length, there are no difficulties, and the move proceeds in the same way as a COBOL MOVE.

If Result is *longer* than Factor 2, then the leftmost (high order) digits of Factor 2 are moved to Result. The remaining rightmost (low order) digits of Result are not affected.

If Result is *shorter* than Factor 2, then the contents of Factor 2 are moved to Result, but truncated on the right-hand side.

The MOVEL behaves like a COBOL MOVE except that excess characters on the right of the receiving field remain unchanged, rather than being padded with blanks.

Factor 2 may be numeric and Result alphameric, or vice versa, which means that the MOVEL command may be used for converting data from one format to the other.

Contrast this command with MOVE (see section 7.12.42). One of the most common – and difficult to spot – errors in RPG is a MOVE, when a MOVEL is intended.

7.12.45 MULT Multiply

Usage: Very frequent, Frequent, **Occasional**, Seldom, Very seldom

Indicators		Fact 1	Fact 2	Result	Resulting Indicators		
7 - 8	9 - 17				54 - 55	56 - 57	58 - 59
Opt	Opt	Blk	Req	Req	Result +ve	Result -ve	Result zero

The MULT verb has two formats as follows:

1) If Factor 1 is blank, Result is multiplied by Factor 2 and the answer placed in Result

2) If Factor 1 is not blank, Factor 1 is multiplied by Factor 2 and the answer placed in Result

In RPG III, the first format is by far the more common, but in some dialects of RPG II only the second format is available.

If one or more indicators is specified in columns 54-59, they are set according to the algebraic value of Result.

An H may be entered in column 53 to half-adjust the answer.

7.12.46 MVR Move Remainder

Usage: Very frequent, Frequent, Occasional, **Seldom**, Very seldom

Indicators		Fact 1	Fact 2	Result	Resulting Indicators		
7 - 8	9 - 17				54 - 55	56 - 57	58 - 59
Opt	Opt	Blk	Blk	Req	Result +ve	Result -ve	Result zero

For obvious reasons, this verb must follow the DIV command (Divide – see section 7.12.17). Any remainder that is left after carrying out the division is placed in Result.

The DIV verb must not have half-adjust specified (H on column 53). If it does the compiler will not complain, but the result may be incorrect.

This is the only example in RPG where two commands work as a pair.

7.12.47 NEXT Next input for multiple-device file

Usage: Very frequent, Frequent, Occasional, Seldom, **Very seldom**

Indicators		Fact 1	Fact 2	Result	Resulting Indicators		
7 - 8	9 - 17				54 - 55	56 - 57	58 - 59
Opt	Opt	Req	Req	Blk	Blk	Err	Blk

The next input for the multiple-device file specified in Factor 2 is fetched from the device specified in Factor 1.

If an error occurs, the indicator specified in columns 56-57 will be set to on. If no indicator is specified, then the INFSR (file error subroutine) – see section 7.7.2 – will be invoked. If neither indicator nor INFSR is specified, the program will crash.

7.12.48 OCUR Get or Set Data-Structure Occurrence

Usage: Very frequent, Frequent, **Occasional**, Seldom, Very seldom

Indicators		Fact 1	Fact 2	Result	Resulting Indicators		
7 - 8	9 - 17				54 - 55	56 - 57	58 - 59
Opt	Opt	Opt	Req	Opt	Blk	Err	Blk

The OCUR command is used with multiple occurrence data structures (see section 7.2), and has two distinct formats:

1) When there is an entry in Factor 1, the current occurrence is **set** to the value specified in Factor 1. The indicator specified in columns 56-57 is set to on if an attempt is made to set the current occurrence out of range.

2) When there is an entry in Result, the current occurrence is **retrieved** and placed in Result.

In both cases Factor 2 gives the name of the multiple occurrence data structure being referred to.

See Example 4 in Appendix D.

7.12.49 OPEN Open file

Usage: Very frequent, Frequent, **Occasional**, Seldom, Very seldom

Indicators		Fact 1	Fact 2	Result	Resulting Indicators		
7 - 8	9 - 17				54 - 55	56 - 57	58 - 59
Opt	Opt	Blk	Req	Blk	Blk	Err	Blk

When a file is opened, a control block is built in which the operating system stores the information it needs (such as the file pointer). The operating system is unable to satisfy I/O requests if this block does not exist. In RPG II, and by default in RPG III, all files are opened automatically at program initialisation *unless* UC is coded in columns 71-72 of the F-spec, in which case the file is not opened.

An OPEN may be issued against any file which is not open. It may never have been opened, or it may have been opened (explicitly or by default) and then closed. OPEN positions the file pointer to the beginning of the file. If, later on, it is desired to re-position the pointer to the beginning of the file, do not CLOSE and re-OPEN the file – it is very inefficient. Instead use:

```
C           *LOVAL    SETLL filename
```

7.12.50 ORxx Or

Usage: **Very frequent**, Frequent, Occasional, Seldom, Very seldom

Indicators		Fact 1	Fact 2	Result	Resulting Indicators		
7 - 8	9 - 17				54 - 55	56 - 57	58 - 59
Opt	Blk	Req	Req	Blk	Blk	Blk	Blk

The literal or variable specified in Factor 1 is compared to the literal or variable specified in Factor 2. The result of this comparison is logically or-ed to the results of the previous comparison(s).

It is better to use ORxx where applicable, rather than multiple IFs. This for example:

```
C          SALARY    IFGT 40000
C          SEX       OREQ 'M'
C          EYES      OREQ 'BLUE'
C                    ADD  1       COUNT
C                    END
```

is cleaner than:

```
C          SALARY    IFGT 40000
C                    ADD  1       COUNT
C                    END
C*
C          SEX       IFEQ 'M'
C                    ADD  1       COUNT
C                    END
C*
C          EYES      IFEQ 'BLUE'
C                    ADD  1       COUNT
C                    END
```

7.12.51 OUT Update Data Area

Usage: Very frequent, Frequent, Occasional, **Seldom**, Very seldom

Indicators		Fact 1	Fact 2	Result	Resulting Indicators		
7 - 8	9 - 17				54 - 55	56 - 57	58 - 59
Opt	Opt	Opt	Req	Blk	Blk	Err	Blk

Factor 2 must contain either a name specified in a *NAMVAR DEFN statement (see section 7.12.15), or the figurative constant *NAMVAR, in which case all data areas defined in the program are updated.

Factor 1 may contain the figurative constant *LOCK, which maintains the lock after the data area has been updated.

Data areas are mainly a legacy from earlier GSD machines. There is little advantage in using them on an AS/400, and they can cause problems with commitment control – see Chapter 13.

7.12.52 PARM Parameter

Usage: Very frequent, **Frequent**, Occasional, Seldom, Very seldom

Indicators		Fact 1	Fact 2	Result	Resulting Indicators		
7 - 8	9 - 17				54 - 55	56 - 57	58 - 59
Opt	Blk	Opt	Opt	Req	Blk	Blk	Blk

See section 7.12.52 which follows.

7.12.53 PLIST Parameter List

Usage: Very frequent, **Frequent**, Occasional, Seldom, Very seldom

Indicators		Fact 1	Fact 2	Result	Resulting Indicators		
7 - 8	9 - 17				54 - 55	56 - 57	58 - 59
Opt	Blk	Req	Blk	Blk	Blk	Blk	Blk

PLIST and PARM are pseudo-verbs – they generate directives to the compiler rather than executable code.

When parameters are passed to a program (see section 10.2) it is necessary to define them in a list. Any parameters to be passed to the CALLed program are specified by means of PARM statements, which may follow directly after the CALL, or may be specified elsewhere, headed by a PLIST. If the PLIST option is chosen, the name (in Factor 1) of the PLIST must be entered in the Result of the CALL statement. The PLIST option seems a neat way of handling parameters, but most experienced RPG III programmers use PARM statements directly after the CALL.

The CALLed program also has to know about the parameters. A special form of the PLIST is used, which has the figurative constant *ENTRY in Factor 1.

Suppose three fields, X, Y, and Z are to be passed. In the calling program we would code:

```
CALL    'SRA1'
PARM    'JKL'      X
PARM               Y
PARM               Z
```

In the called program we would code:

```
*ENTRY    PLIST
          PARM      A
          PARM      B
          PARM      C
```

The value JKL is loaded into field X before it is passed.

Note that the fields are called A,B,C in the called program, but X,Y,Z in the calling program. There is no compulsion to use the same names (though it usually makes the programs easier to understand).

While the names do not matter, it is imperative that the fields are of the same length and type, and appear in the same sequence in both parameter lists.

If a numeric field is passed it must be packed in both lists or zoned in both lists. A practical tip is to avoid passing numeric fields at all: convert to alpha before passing, and convert back to numeric after receiving. The extra effort is trivial.

While the compiler will allow PLISTs to be coded anywhere in the C- specs, it is good practice to put them at the beginning, with the DEFNs and KLISTs.

7.12.54 POST Post to INFDS [Information Data Structure]

Usage: Very frequent, Frequent, Occasional, Seldom, **Very seldom**

Indicators		Fact 1	Fact 2	Result	Resulting Indicators		
7 - 8	9 - 17				54 - 55	56 - 57	58 - 59
Opt	Opt	Opt	Opt	Opt	Blk	Err	Blk

The POST command has two uses:

1) To force an immediate update the file information data structure (INFDS) – which is automatically updated after each I/O operation.

2) To update the INFDS for a program device.

Option (1) is obtained by specifying a file name in Factor 2. The information will be posted to the INFDS specified in Result or, if Result is blank, in the INFDS associated with the file.

Option (2) is obtained by specifying a device name in Factor 1, and the name of the INFDS in Result.

If an error occurs, and no error indicator has been specified, control will pass to the INFSR subroutine, failing which the program will crash.

7.12.55 READ Read File

Usage: **Very frequent**, Frequent, Occasional, Seldom, Very seldom

Indicators		Fact 1	Fact 2	Result	Resulting Indicators		
7 - 8	9 - 17				54 - 55	56 - 57	58 - 59
Opt	Opt	Blk	Req	Opt	Blk	Err	EOF

A record is read from the file specified in Factor 2. The file pointer is used to determine which record to read, and is positioned pointing at the next record following a successful READ.

If the pointer does not exist (the file has not been OPENed or the pointer has been destroyed) the error indicator will be set to on. If no error indicator is specified the program will crash unless a file error subroutine (INFSR) has been specified.

In practice, provided the program is intelligently structured, so that you do not make elementary blunders, like trying to do a READ against a file which is not open, the error condition virtually never arises.

If the READ encounters end-of-file the EOF indicator will be set to on. The EOF indicator is required, and the program will not compile if it is omitted.

If the file is externally described, Factor 2 may contain a format name rather than the file name.

7.12.56 READC Read Changed record [from subfile]

Usage: Very frequent, **Frequent**, Occasional, Seldom, Very seldom

Indicators		Fact 1	Fact 2	Result	Resulting Indicators		
7 - 8	9 - 17				54 - 55	56 - 57	58 - 59
Opt	Opt	Blk	Req	Blk	Blk	Err	EOF

The READC command is valid only with subfiles – see Chapter 12.

After a subfile control format has been written, and read back, by an EXFMT command (see section 7.12.27) the subfile may be read to analyse changed records.

The name of the subfile format – not the control format – must be specified in Factor 2.

The READC will access only those subfile records which have been changed; in other words if no subfile records have been changed the first READC will set on the end-of-file indicator. The EOF indicator is required, and the program will not compile if it is omitted.

If an error occurs, the error indicator will be set to on. If no error indicator is specified the program will crash.

7.12.57 READE Read Equal

Usage: Very frequent, Frequent, Occasional, **Seldom**, Very seldom

Indicators		Fact 1	Fact 2	Result	Resulting Indicators		
7 - 8	9 - 17				54 - 55	56 - 57	58 - 59
Opt	Opt	Req	Req	Opt	Blk	Err	EOF

The READE is somewhat like a READ combined with a compare. Records are read from the file specified in Factor 2 for as long as they match the key specified in Factor 1.

If the file is externally described, Factor 2 may contain a format name rather than a file name.

The EOF indicator is set on when the first unmatched record is encountered, and that record is not returned to the program. The EOF indicator is required, and the program will not compile if it is omitted.

The file pointer is positioned pointing at the next record following a successful READE group; however, if physical end-of-file is encountered, the EOF indicator will be set to on and the pointer destroyed.

When an error occurs the error indicator will be set to on. If no error indicator is specified the program will crash unless a file error subroutine (INFSR) has been specified.

Again, provided the program is intelligently structured, so that you do not make elementary blunders like trying to do a READE against a file which is not open, the error condition virtually never arises.

The purpose of the READE is to provide a way of creating a structured read loop. Suppose we are asked to process all records containing a requested part number; the following will do it:

```
     C          REQPNO         READE  FILXYZ    71
     C          *IN71          IFNE   '1'                 B001
     C                         (process)                  001
     C                         END                        E001
```

An alternative way is:

```
C         REQPNO        SETLL    FILXYZ
C                       READ     FILXYZ          71
C*
C         REQPNO        DOWEQ    FILPNO              B001
C         *IN71         ANDNE    '1'                 001
C                       (process)                    001
C                       READ     FILXYZ          71  001
C                       END                          E001
```

The second alternative more closely resembles COBOL, and is less likely to cause confusion for anyone who has been, or is likely to be, a COBOL programmer. That is why READE has been allocated a usage of "Seldom".

7.12.58 READP Read Previous

Usage: Very frequent, Frequent, Occasional, **Seldom**, Very seldom

Indicators		Fact 1	Fact 2	Result	Resulting Indicators		
7 - 8	9 - 17				54 - 55	56 - 57	58 - 59
Opt	Opt	Blk	Req	Opt	Blk	Err	EOF

The READP command is almost identical to the READ command (see section 7.12.55) except that it works in reverse, i.e. the file pointer moves towards the beginning of the file. It is not allowed for Workstation files.

7.12.59 REDPE Read Previous Equal

Usage: Very frequent, Frequent, Occasional, **Seldom**, Very seldom

Indicators		Fact 1	Fact 2	Result	Resulting Indicators		
7 - 8	9 - 17				54 - 55	56 - 57	58 - 59
Opt	Opt	Req	Req	Opt	Blk	Err	EOF

The REDPE command is almost identical to the READE command (see section 7.12.57) except that, like READP, it works backwards towards the beginning of the file.

7.12.60 REL Release Program Device

Usage: Very frequent, Frequent, Occasional, Seldom, **Very seldom**

Indicators		Fact 1	Fact 2	Result	Resulting Indicators		
7 - 8	9 - 17				54 - 55	56 - 57	58 - 59
Opt	Opt	Req	Req	Blk	Blk	Err	Blk

This command releases a device that has been acquired by means of an ACQ command (see section 7.12.1).

The device specified in Factor 1 is released from the file specified in Factor 2.

7.12.61 RETRN Return

Usage: Very frequent, Frequent, **Occasional**, Seldom, Very seldom

Indicators		Fact 1	Fact 2	Result	Resulting Indicators		
7 - 8	9 - 17				54 - 55	56 - 57	58 - 59
Opt	Opt	Blk	Blk	Blk	Blk	Blk	Blk

The use of the RETRN command is discussed fully in section 10.6.

When a return to the calling program is requested, RPG first checks the halt indicators (H1-H9), and if any are set, the program terminates abnormally.

It then checks LR. If LR is set the dynamic storage is released, files are closed, and locks released, otherwise control is simply handed to the invoking step.

7.12.62 ROLBK Roll Back

Usage: Very frequent, Frequent, **Occasional**, Seldom, Very seldom

Indicators		Fact 1	Fact 2	Result	Resulting Indicators		
7 - 8	9 - 17				54 - 55	56 - 57	58 - 59
Opt	Opt	Blk	Blk	Blk	Blk	Err	Blk

ROLBK is the converse of COMIT (see section 7.12.12). The use of COMIT and ROLBK is covered in full in Chapter 13.

There are no operands to this command apart from the error indicator. It does not affect the file pointer.

7.12.63 SETGT Set Greater Than

Usage: Very frequent, Frequent, Occasional, **Seldom**, Very seldom

Indicators		Fact 1	Fact 2	Result	Resulting Indicators		
7 - 8	9 - 17				54 - 55	56 - 57	58 - 59
Opt	Opt	Req	Req	Blk	Miss	Err	Blk

See section 7.12.64.

7.12.64 SETLL Set Lower Limit

Usage: Very frequent, **Frequent**, Occasional, Seldom, Very seldom

Indicators		Fact 1	Fact 2	Result	Resulting Indicators		
7 - 8	9 - 17				54 - 55	56 - 57	58 - 59
Opt	Opt	Req	Req	Blk	HI	Err	Hit

The SETLL and SETGT commands are used to set the file pointer – file pointers are explained in section 7.4.

SETLL positions the pointer before the requested record, in contrast with SETGT (previous section) which positions it after the record.

The following two commands will achieve exactly the same result:

```
C          'Rec-3'     SETLL FILXYZ
C          'Rec-2'     SETGT FILXYZ
```

and will set the pointer as shown:

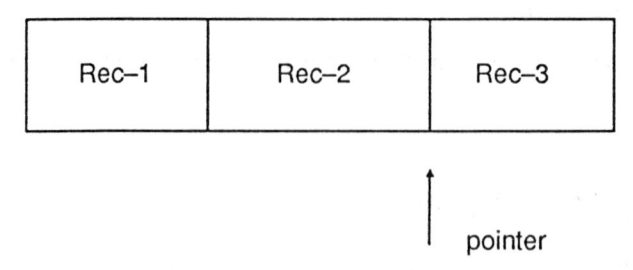

```
┌──────────┬──────────┬──────────┐
│  Rec-1   │  Rec-2   │  Rec-3   │
└──────────┴──────────┴──────────┘
                ↑
                │ pointer
```

The SETLL is particularly useful for doing existence checks. It merely interrogates the index to find out whether a record exists or not, and sets the indicator in columns 58-59 accordingly.

It is much more efficient than CHAIN (used for existence checks in most dialects of RPG II) which always reads data into the program buffer if the record is found.

The file pointer may be set to the beginning of the file by:

```
C           *LOVAL    SETLL FILXYZ
```

and to the end of the file by:

```
C           *HIVAL    SETGT FILXYZ
```

If the file is externally defined, Factor 2 may contain a format name rather than a file name.

7.12.65 SETOF Set Indicator Off

Usage: Very frequent, Frequent, **Occasional**, Seldom, Very seldom

Indicators		Fact 1	Fact 2	Result	Resulting Indicators		
7 - 8	9 - 17				54 - 55	56 - 57	58 - 59
Opt	Opt	Blk	Blk	Blk	At least 1 Req		

The indicator(s) specified in columns 54-59 are set to off.

It sometimes is clearer if one SETOF is set to off for each indicator. This, for example:

```
C           SETOF       717273
```

is not as clear as:

```
C           SETOF       71
C           SETOF       72
C           SETOF       73
```

7.12.66 SETON Set Indicator On

Usage: Very frequent, Frequent, **Occasional**, Seldom, Very seldom

Indicators		Fact 1	Fact 2	Result	Resulting Indicators		
7 - 8	9 - 17				54 - 55	56 - 57	58 - 59
Opt	Opt	Blk	Blk	Blk	At least 1 Req		

The indicator(s) specified in columns 54-59 are set to on.

It may be clearer to use one SETON per indicator set to on. This:

```
C           SETON       717273
```

is not as clear as:

```
C           SETON       71
C           SETON       72
C           SETON       73
```

7.12.67 SHTDN Shut Down

Usage: Very frequent, Frequent, Occasional, Seldom, **Very seldom**

Indicators		Fact 1	Fact 2	Result	Resulting Indicators		
7 - 8	9 - 17				54 - 55	56 - 57	58 - 59
Opt	Opt	Blk	Blk	Blk	Req	Blk	Blk

The SHTDN command is used to ask the operating system whether a controlled termination of the system, subsystem or job is in progress.

The only operand is the indicator in columns 54-55, which is set to on if a shut down is in progress.

Why should anyone want to know? A free Ford Edsel for the first correct answer!

7.12.68 SORTA Sort Array

Usage: Very frequent, Frequent, Occasional, Seldom, **Very seldom**

Indicators		Fact 1	Fact 2	Result	Resulting Indicators		
7 - 8	9 - 17				54 - 55	56 - 57	58 - 59
Opt	Opt	Blk	Req	Blk	Blk	Blk	Blk

The array specified in Factor 2 is sorted into ascending sequence.

7.12.69 SQRT Square Root

Usage: Very frequent, Frequent, Occasional, Seldom, **Very seldom**

Indicators		Fact 1	Fact 2	Result	Resulting Indicators		
7 - 8	9 - 17				54 - 55	56 - 57	58 - 59
Opt	Opt	Blk	Req	Req	Blk	Blk	Blk

The square root of the number in Factor 2 is calculated and placed in Result.

Note that this operation can be carried out on entire arrays (for what reason it is difficult to imagine) if unsubscripted array names are entered in Factor 2 and Result.

7.12.70 SUB Subtract

Usage: Very frequent, **Frequent**, Occasional, Seldom, Very seldom

Indicators		Fact 1	Fact 2	Result	Resulting Indicators		
7 - 8	9 - 17				54 - 55	56 - 57	58 - 59
Opt	Opt	Opt	Req	Req	Result +ve	Result -ve	Result zero

The SUB verb has two possible formats:

1) If Factor 1 is blank, Factor 2 is subtracted from Result and the sum placed in Result

2) If Factor 1 is not blank, Factor 2 is subtracted from Factor 1 and the sum placed in Result

In RPG III, the first format is by far the more common, but in some dialects of RPG II only the second format is available.

If one or more indicators is specified in columns 54-59 they are set according to the algebraic value of Result.

7.12.71 TAG Tag [for GO TO]

Usage: Very frequent, Frequent, Occasional, Seldom, **Very seldom**

Indicators		Fact 1	Fact 2	Result	Resulting Indicators		
7 - 8	9 - 17				54 - 55	56 - 57	58 - 59
Opt	Blk	Req	Blk	Blk	Blk	Blk	Blk

TAG is a pseudo-verb – it generates a directive to the compiler rather than executable code.

TAG is the equivalent of a COBOL paragraph name – it marks the point in a program to which control is transferred by means of a GOTO (see section 7.12.32) or CABxx (see section 7.12.7).

In RPG II, before structured commands became available, GOTO was the only way of transferring control, and so it was widely used. This excuse no longer applies in RPG III.

If there are no GOTOs and no CABs then there is no need for TAGs. The installation standards should ban them – see Chapter 17.

7.12.72 TESTB Test Bit

Usage: Very frequent, Frequent, Occasional, Seldom, **Very seldom**

Indicators		Fact 1	Fact 2	Result	Resulting Indicators		
7 - 8	9 - 17				54 - 55	56 - 57	58 - 59
Opt	Opt	Blk	Req	Req	At least 1 Req		

The TESTB command is generally used in conjunction with BITON and BITOF (see sections 7.12.5 and 7.12.6).

Bits, within the single byte field in Result, are tested asspecified in Factor 2, and resulting indicators are set to on according to the following rules:

Columns 54-55 – All specified bits are OFF.

Columns 56-57 – Some of the specified bits are ON, and some are OFF.

Columns 58-59 – All specified bits are ON.

The Factor 2 entry must number the bits from 0 to 7, rather than 1 to 8.

If field PQR in Result contains X'C1' or B'1100 0001' (which is the letter A) this instruction:

```
C                       TESTB'2'      PQR        515253
```

will set *IN51 to off, *IN52 to on, and *IN53 to off.

If that is not clear look at the following chart of bit positions:

```
B'1100 0001'
  0123 4567
```

TESTB is examining '02', and the bit position chart shows that bit 0 is on and bit 2 is off. As a result, all the specified bits are not off, so *IN51 is set off; some of the specified bits are on, and some are off, so *IN52 is set to on; and all the specified bits are not on, so *IN53 is set to off.

7.12.73 TESTN Test Numeric

Usage: Very frequent, Frequent, Occasional, **Seldom**, Very seldom

Indicators		Fact 1	Fact 2	Result	Resulting Indicators		
7 - 8	9 - 17				54 - 55	56 - 57	58 - 59
Opt	Opt	Blk	Blk	Req	At least 1 Req		

The field in Result is tested, and resulting indicators are set depending on whether or not it is found to be numeric. The following conditions set the resulting indicators to on:

Columns 54-55 – All characters are numeric.

Columns 56-57 – The field is numeric with leading blanks.

Columns 58-59 – All characters are blanks.

This apparently simple and useful instruction has a nasty trap for the unwary, which is why its usage is given as "seldom".

The letters A through I are represented by the hex values X'C1' through X'C9', which are recognised as positively signed numbers.

Similarly, the letters J through R are represented by the hex values X'D1' through X'D9', which are recognised as negatively signed numbers. TESTN therefore does *not* produce the desired results when testing a one-byte field. Use the following to test a one-byte field:

```
C          CHAR1              IFGE '0'                    B001
C          CHAR1              ANDLE'9'                    001
C                             (process numeric)           001
C                             ELSE                        X001
C                             (process not numeric)       001
C                             END                         E001
```

7.12.74 TESTZ Test Zone

Usage: Very frequent, Frequent, Occasional, Seldom, **Very seldom**

Indicators		Fact 1	Fact 2	Result	Resulting Indicators		
7 - 8	9 - 17				54 - 55	56 - 57	58 - 59
Opt	Opt	Blk	Blk	Req	At least 1 Req		

The one-byte field in Result is tested, and resulting indicators are set depending on whether the zone portion is X'C', X'D', or other. The following conditions set to indicators to on:

Columns 54-55 – The zone portion is X'C' (letters A through I, and &).

Columns 56-57 – The zone portion is X'D' (letters J through R).

Columns 58-59 – The zone portion is neither X'C' nor X'D'.

7.12.75 TIME Time and Date

Usage: Very frequent, Frequent, **Occasional**, Seldom, Very seldom

Indicators		Fact 1	Fact 2	Result	Resulting Indicators		
7 - 8	9 - 17				54 - 55	56 - 57	58 - 59
Opt	Opt	Blk	Blk	Req	Blk	Blk	Blk

Note that the TIME verb does not access only the time, as you might expect, but also the date.

Result must be specified with either a 6- or 12-digit numeric field. If a 6-digit field is specified, only the time is retrieved (in the format hhmmss). If a 12-digit field is specified, the time is retrieved in positions 1 to 6, and the date is retrieved in positions 7 to 12.

In RPG III, the date format depends on the setting of the job attribute QDATFMT, and may be ddmmyy, mmddyy, yymmdd or yyddd0 (Julian). In most dialects of RPG II the date format is mmddyy.

If the value returned by TIME is to be output in a line conditioned by 1P, the TIME verb must appear in the special subroutine *INZSR:

```
C           *INZSR        BEGSR
C                         TIME              TIMDAT  12 0
C                         ENDSR
                .
                .
OQSYSPRT H    2  1        IP
O             OR          OF
O                                           TIMDAT  22 'bb/bb/bb&&bb/bb/bb'
```

Otherwise, first pass through C-specs happens only after 1P output (see Chapter 8), and TIMDAT will therefore contain zeros when the 1P output takes place. (Note the use of ampersands to insert blanks between time and date.)

An alternative way of obtaining the date – but not the time – is by means of the figurative constants UDATE, UDAY, UMONTH and UYEAR (see section 7.3).

7.12.76 UNLCK Unlock Data Area

Usage: Very frequent, Frequent, Occasional, **Seldom**, Very seldom

Indicators		Fact 1	Fact 2	Result	Resulting Indicators		
7 - 8	9 - 17				54 - 55	56 - 57	58 - 59
Opt	Opt	Blk	Req	Blk	Blk	Err	Blk

The UNLCK command will unlock one or all of the data areas currently locked by the program. No error is raised if UNLCK is issued against a data area which is already unlocked.

Factor 2 must contain either a name specified in a *NAMVAR DEFN statement (see section 7.12.15), or the figurative constant *NAMVAR, in which case all data areas defined in the program are unlocked.

Data areas are mainly a legacy from earlier GSD machines. There is little advantage in using them on an AS/400, and they can cause problems with commitment control – see Chapter 13.

7.12.77 UPDAT Update Record

Usage: Very frequent, **Frequent**, Occasional, Seldom, Very seldom

Indicators		Fact 1	Fact 2	Result	Resulting Indicators		
7 - 8	9 - 17				54 - 55	56 - 57	58 - 59
Opt	Opt	Blk	Req	Opt	Blk	Err	Blk

The last record read for the file specified in Factor 2 is updated. If no record is being held for update, an error occurs. If the file is externally defined a record format name may be specified in Factor 2.

The read operation to the file need not necessarily have been made by a READ command. Any file input command, such as CHAIN or READC, will suffice. The file must have been specified as Update, i.e. with a U in column 15 of the F-spec, or the program will not compile. If no record is being held for update, the error indicator will be set to on. If no error indicator is specified the program will crash unless a file error subroutine (INFSR) has been specified. In practice, provided the program is intelligently structured, the error condition should never arise.

The file pointer is not affected by UPDAT.

7.12.78 WRITE Write Record

Usage: Very frequent, **Frequent**, Occasional, Seldom, Very seldom

Indicators		Fact 1	Fact 2	Result	Resulting Indicators		
7 - 8	9 - 17				54 - 55	56 - 57	58 - 59
Opt	Opt	Blk	Req	Opt	Blk	Err	EOF

A record is written to the file specified in Factor 2. If the file is externally defined, a record format name must be specified in Factor 2.

If the file is not specified as Output, Update or Combined, i.e. with an O, U or C in column 15 of the F-spec, or as Input-Add (I on column 15 and A on column 66 of the F-spec), the program will not compile.

If the WRITE does not complete successfully, the error indicator will be set to on. It will also be set on if an externally defined print file reaches overflow and no overflow indicator was specified. If no error indicator is specified, the program will crash unless a file error subroutine (INFSR) has been specified.

In practice the most likely reason for a WRITE error is that the maximum number of records for a database file, specified in the CRTPF (Create Physical File) CL command, has been exceeded.

The end-of-file indicator will be set to on if the WRITE is to a subfile and the subfile is full. See Chapter 12 for a discussion of whether or not a subfile should be of fixed length.

The file pointer is not affected by WRITE.

7.12.79 XFOOT Crossfoot (sum elements of array)

Usage: Very frequent, Frequent, **Occasional**, Seldom, Very seldom

Indicators		Fact 1	Fact 2	Result	Resulting Indicators		
7 - 8	9 - 17				54 - 55	56 - 57	58 - 59
Opt	Opt	Blk	Req	Req	Result +ve	Result -ve	Result zero

The elements of the array specified in Factor 2, are summed, and the answer placed in Result.

Result may itself be an element of an array, possibly the same array as specified in Factor 2. This is useful, for example, for calculating sales for the year to date, by providing a 13th month to hold year to date.

We might define our sales array as SLS with 13 numeric elements each 7 digits with 2 decimal places:

```
E         SLS    13    7    2
          .
          .
C         MOVE   *ZERO SLS,13
C         XFOOT  SLS   SLS,13
```

Note that SLS,13 is flushed before the XFOOT takes place. If the element in Result is a part of the array in Factor 2, the value it contains before the XFOOT is included in the XFOOT calculation.

Why not simply use a field for year to date? By including it in the array, we are able to take advantage of the special output facilities for arrays (see section 7.2 and Example 3 in Appendix D).

7.12.80 Z-ADD Zero and Add

Usage: Very frequent, **Frequent**, Occasional, Seldom, Very seldom

Indicators		Fact 1	Fact 2	Result	Resulting Indicators		
7 - 8	9 - 17				54 - 55	56 - 57	58 - 59
Opt	Opt	Blk	Req	Req	Result +ve	Result -ve	Result zero

The contents of Factor 2 are added to zero and placed in Result.

In RPG II, because of alignment problems with MOVE, (see section 7.12.42) this command was widely used for initialising counters etc.

With the arrival of RPG III and the figurative constant *ZERO this method is no longer much used. Instead of:

```
C         Z-ADD  0     XYZ
```

most RPG III programmers use:

```
C         MOVE   *ZERO XYZ
```

7.12.81 Z-SUB Zero and Subtract

Usage: Very frequent, Frequent, Occasional, Seldom, **Very seldom**

Indicators		Fact 1	Fact 2	Result	Resulting Indicators		
7 - 8	9 - 17				54 - 55	56 - 57	58 - 59
Opt	Opt	Blk	Req	Req	Result +ve	Result -ve	Result zero

The contents of Factor 2 are subtracted from zero, and placed in Result.

7.13 O Output

The use of Output Specifications (O-specs) has not declined to the same extent as that of I-specs. This is because internally defined print files remain deservedly popular for some purposes.

Right from the beginning, RPG was particularly well suited to creating printed reports (remember the name stands for *Report* Program Generator).

It is unique in defining output fields by their end positions rather than their start positions. This may appear a little clumsy at first, but in fact is most useful for setting up columns of figures.

Just as with I-specs, it is convenient to think of O-specs as comprising two basic types: header and body entries.

7.13.1 "Header" O-specs

"Header" O-specs apply only to internally defined files. For externally defined files, the compiler generates "body" O-specs and labels them with the format name it has retrieved from the external file definition.

Even with internally defined files, most entries are applicable only to print files. Disk file headers are usually quite rudimentary.

The first thing the compiler needs to know is the name of the file to which the O-specs refer, and this is provided in columns 7-14. Subsequent records may be defined without repeating the file name: it is assumed to be the same as the last file name.

The next thing needed is the type of record – whether it is a Heading, Detail or Total line, identified respectively by H, D or T on column 15.

There is a further type, called Exception, which is identified by an E. Whereas H, D and T output has to wait its turn in the cycle, Exception output is generated from within C-specs by means of the EXCPT verb (see section 7.12.26). It was originally intended as a debugging aid (hence the name) to allow snapshots of selected fields, but this use has been forgotten, and now it is merely a means of output which is sometimes more convenient than the others.

In order to understand Heading, Detail and Total output, it is necessary to look more closely at the cycle, and to do so we need to elaborate slightly on the flowchart in section 7.5.

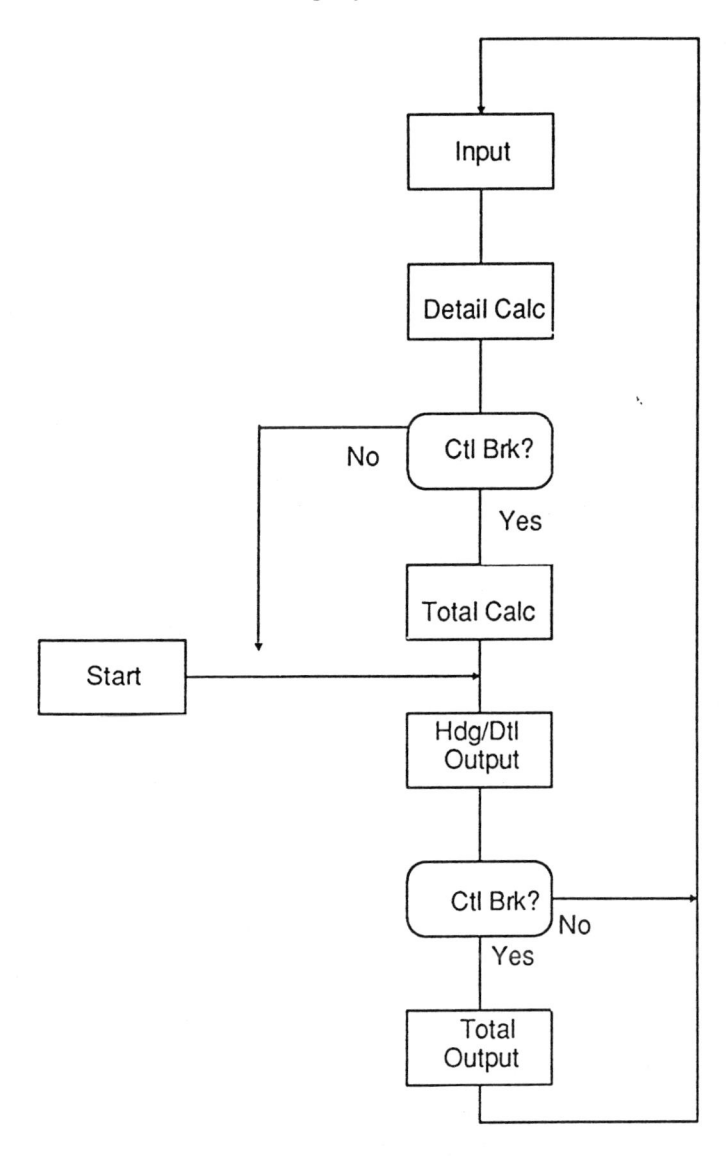

Note that processing starts not at the input of the first record, but immediately before output of H and D records. (There is only one small difference between H and D entries, which we shall cover in a moment.) Nevertheless, heading lines should be coded with an H, and detail lines with a D, just to keep the program understandable.

During the first iteration of H/D output, the 1P special indicator (see section 7.1.2) will be on, and will then be off for the remainder of the run. It is used to ensure that the first heading line is printed before the first detail line. See also section 7.12.75.

Obviously there is no control break at this point so we go round the loop to input the first record. Detail calculations are performed, then detail output, and this is repeated until there is a control break.

When a control break occurs the program goes into total calculations and then total output, and it is at total output that the T lines are processed.

Columns 16-22 are left blank for devices other than printers.

Columns 16 is for stacker selection or for "fetch overflow". A long defunct peripheral was called the MFCM, for Multi Function Card Machine. It had a range of output stackers, and stacker selection allowed the programmer to select the desired stacker for a card being punched.

"Fetch overflow" was introduced relatively late in the life of RPG II to solve a problem which was occasionally encountered. Suppose a program prints half a dozen lines for a single input record.

If the first line just happens to be very near the bottom of the page, it is possible that the last few will straddle the perforations onto the next page. The H lines are not processed until the program comes back round the cycle.

"Fetch overflow" is coded by entering an F in column 16. It causes the program to check the file overflow indicator (columns 32 and 34 of the F-spec) after writing that line, and to process immediately any H lines for which the overflow indicator was specified.

That is the difficult part. Columns 17 and 18 come next and are used to specify the number of lines that the printer should be spaced Before and After printing the line. This may be zero. Default values are zero for Before, and one for After. Similarly, columns 19-20 and 21-22 specify respectively the skipping to be done before and after printing the line.

In RPG III skipping is expressed in the form of a line number to which the program should skip before or after printing. In some dialects of RPG II, the carriage tape channel number is required.

Spacing and skipping are mutually exclusive, but it is permissible to space before and skip after, or vice versa.

Up to three conditioning indicators may be specified, and they are defined in a way very similar to record selection in the I-specs. The three indicators are AND-ed together, and a continuation line may be used if more than three are required.

Continuation lines may also be used for indicators to be OR-ed to those already specified. Continuation lines are specified by coding AND or OR as appropriate in columns 14-16.

The following shows output conditioned to indicators 01, 02 and 03 on and indicator 04 not on, or indicators 05 and 06 on:

```
O         D          01N04 02
O         AND        03
O         OR         0506
```

Note that columns 16-22 are blank, implying either that defaults are being used or that output is to a device which is not a printer.

When an EXCPT verb (see section 7.12.26) is executed all E lines are processed whose conditioning indicators are satisfied, unless an exception name is used in columns 32-37.

In a large program with numerous Exception lines it is quite difficult to get the indicators correct without using exception names. Experienced RPG II programmers tended to set the indicator to on immediately before the EXCPT verb and then to off again immediately afterwards. Their coding looked something like this:

```
        C              SETON           68
        C              EXCPT
        C              SETOF           68
                .
                .
                .
        O       E      68
        O              (body entries)
```

The modern form is much clearer:
```
        C              EXCPT  DSKOUT
                .
                .
                .
        O       E             DSKOUT
        O                     (body entries)
```

More than one E line may bear the same exception name, which is quite useful. For instance, all headings can be printed with a single EXCPT.

It is also possible to mix exception names and conditioning indicators, but it is extremely sloppy practice to do so.

7.13.2 "Body" O-specs

"Body" O-specs come in two basic forms, those with a field name in front of the end position, and those with a literal behind the end position:

```
O         FLDNAM     123
O                    123 'LITERAL'
```

Columns 7-23 are always blank. Conditioning indicators may be applied to fields in columns 23-31 in the same way as they are to records, but continuation lines and OR conditions are not supported.

If a field is to be output, its name is entered in columns 32-37, left justified; if a literal is to be output it is entered, between quotes, in columns 45-70, also left justified.

If a numeric field is to be output, an edit code may be specified in column 38. A table of these codes is printed on each O-spec form, and is reproduced below, slightly modified:

		Sign if negative		
Commas	Zeroes to Print	No sign	CR	Minus sign
Yes	Yes	1	A	J
Yes	No	2	B	K
No	Yes	3	C	L
No	No	4	D	M

By far the most frequently used of these codes are J and K, with L and M being used when space is tight. The CR codes are mainly used in accounting applications. Codes 1-4 should be avoided because there is no indication if a field contains a negative value.

Two more important codes are Z, which simply zero suppresses, and Y, the date edit. Note that Y does not verify that the field is a valid date: if a field contains X'0123456F' it will be printed as 12/34/56.

If even this selection of codes does not provide anything suitable, a custom made code may be supplied in columns 45-70, between quotes. Suppose that the above example represented a time, and that we wanted to use a more conventional time edit. An entry of 'bb:bb:bb' in columns 45-52 will yield 12:34:56. More details of custom edit codes appear below.

Column 39 may be left blank, or may contain a B, meaning that the field specified in columns 32-37 is to be set to blanks (or zeros, if numeric) after the record has been output.

This facility can be dangerous. The following will not yield the expected result:

```
OFILE1      D           68
O                             FLDXYZ B 123
  .
  .
OFILE2      D           68
O                             FLDXYZ B 123
```

By the time the program writes the record to FILE2, FLDXYZ will already have been set to blank/zero by the "blank after" for the write to FILE1. It is better to make a practice of resetting fields by means of a MOVE in C-specs – see also Chapter 8 for advice on resetting totals.

RPG is unique among programming languages in that the position of a field in an output record is described by means of the end position rather than the start position.

The end position is specified in columns 40-43, right justified, and with optional leading zeros which are better omitted.

RPG III supports relative positions, and these are coded by means of a plus or minus sign coded in column 40, i.e. left justified. The following would cause FLDB to begin 2 spaces to the right of FLDA:

```
O                         FLDA       123
O                         FLDB     +   2
```

This coding can be slightly confusing, because the DDS rules for external files call for the plus sign to be immediately adjacent to the number (an A in column 6 identifies the specification as DDS):

```
A              FLDA                 123
A              FLDB                  +2
```

Specifying end positions is occasionally inconvenient, and the facility for relative positions paves the way for a coding trick which enables us to use a start position. Suppose we wish FLDB to start in position 123. We code:

```
O                                    123 '$'
O                         FLDB     -   1
```

(The example uses '$' but since it will be overwritten by FLDB any one-byte literal will do.)

Column 44 should contain a P or B if the field is to be output in packed or binary form respectively, otherwise be left blank.

As stated above, if a literal is to be output it is entered left justified, between quotes, in columns 45-70.

Another use for relative positioning is to accommodate literals that are too long to fit on one line:

```
O                              23 'THESE ARE'
O                             + 1 'CONTINUATION'
O                             + 1 'LINES'
```

We discussed edit words briefly above. It is not often that edit words are needed, because usually edit codes are sufficient, however the rules are quite simple.

The significance start character is zero. In other words if we were to push a field containing 000123 through an edit mask of 'bb0bbb' the result would be bb0123.

Blanks may be inserted by means of ampersands. If we push a field containing 123456 through an edit mask of 'bb&bb&bb' the result will be 12b34b56.

A floating currency symbol is provided by placing the currency symbol immediately before the significance start zero. If we push a field containing 000123456 through an edit mask of 'bb,bbb,b$0.bb' the result will be bbbb$1,234.56.

The main use for this facility is to protect cheques from fraudulent alteration. Another, and perhaps easier, way of doing it is asterisk protection. Simply use the normal edit code, and put an asterisk in quotes in columns 45-47:

```
O                                   FLDA J 66 '*'
```

If FLDA contains 000123456 the result will be ****1,234.56.

This is the only exception to the rule that entries in column 38 and columns 45-70 are mutually exclusive.

External files

The body O-specs generated by the compiler for external files are very simple. There are no conditioning indicators, no edit codes or blank afters, and no literals or edit words – all the hard work is done by the DDS.

However we should note that the O-specs for an internal file will be different from the generated O-specs for an external file printing exactly the same report. This is because the spacing and editing is taken care of within DDS, and all RPG has to do is pass a buffer across to the file. The body O-specs therefore contain buffer end positions rather than print end positions.

The edit codes used within DDS are the same as those for RPG, and so are the edit words. The following two statements achieve the same result, but the first one is RPG and the second is DDS:

```
O           FLDA J        79
A           FLDA          71 EDTCDE(J)
```

Similarly, these two:

```
       O              FLDA              88 'bb:bb:bb'
       A              FLDA              81 EDTWRD('bb:bb:bb')
```

Note that DDS uses the start position, while RPG uses the end position.

7.14 ** Array content

The last statements in an RPG program are the data entries for compile-time arrays.

Unlike the specifications, which are identified by the appropriate character on column 6, compile-time array data is identified by asterisks on columns 1 and 2.

The data for each compile-time array must be preceded by a statement with asterisks on columns 1 and 2, and the array data must be presented in the same sequence as the arrays appear in the E-specs. There should be exactly the right amount of data to fill the array.

Take care that where an alternating table or array (see section 7.1.2) has been specified the data is presented in alternating format. Also be sure that the number of entries per line agrees with columns 33-35 of the relevant E-spec.

This is correct:

```
              E         ARR1 4 1 1
              I           .
              C           .
              O           .
    **
    ABCD
```

So is this:

```
              E         ARR1 1 1 1
              I           .
              C           .
              O           .
    **
    A
    B
    C
    D
```

But this is not:

```
           E        ARR1 1 1 1
           I             .
           C             .
           O             .
      **
      ABCD
```

Neither is this:

```
           E        ARR1 4 1 1
           I             .
           C             .
           O             .
      **
      A
      B
      C
      D
```

8

The RPG Cycle

8.1 RPG II and RPG III

One of DP's hardier annuals is the story that some new language is so simple to use that end-users will be able to write their own programs, so making programmers redundant.

That yarn was first heard at least 20 years ago, and RPG was the magic new language. This may surprise today's RPG programmers, particularly those who use RPG III.

The explanation appears to be that these new languages achieve simplicity only by forfeiting function. As the years pass, an increasing demand arises for the missing functions. As these are added to the language, so the simplicity is lost.

As we saw in Chapter 5, the dividing line between RPG II and RPG III is difficult to draw precisely, because RPG II is a subset of RPG III. The waters are muddied still further because some RPG III features have been retro-fitted to some dialects of RPG II. In general though, a fully procedural program (i.e. one in which the cycle is shut off – which is done simply by not declaring a Primary file) is usually regarded as RPG III.

We shall go along with this definition, though with the caveat that programmers sometimes use the cycle in programs which also use AS/400 facilities, such as external file definitions.

One sometimes encounters programmers who will not use the cycle (because they are nervous of it) and sites which ban its use (usually out of a slavish – and mindless – devotion to all that is modern). Some maintain that the object code is less efficient than for the same program written without the cycle. There may be a little truth in this, but if efficiency is that important you have no business to be using a high-level language and machine.

The cycle is used mainly for reporting programs, although it is possible to declare a Workstation file as Update Primary (UP in columns 15-16 of the F-spec).

Certainly there are cases where it is better not to use the cycle, but anyone doing so should be aware that he is forfeiting the matching and level-breaking facilities of RPG.

8.2 Primary and Secondary files

Any RPG program which uses the cycle must include one file which is designated as Primary (by a P on column 16 of the F-spec). Only one Primary file is permitted per program. When the cycle is to be used by more than one file, all the other files must be designated as Secondary (S on column 16 of the F-spec).

Full function files (F on column 16 of the F-spec) may be used in cycling programs, but are invoked by commands in the C-specs, and do not participate in the cycle.

When matching is requested (see section 8.9), each matching group is read, in the following order:

    1 all records from the Primary file;

    2 all records from the first Secondary file specified in the F-specs;

    3 all records from the second Secondary file specified in the F-specs, and so on.

When matching is not requested, the entire Primary file is read, followed by the entire first Secondary file, followed by the entire second Secondary file, and so on.

8.3 All programs read, process, output

The philosophy underlying RPG is that virtually all batch programs (the only programs that existed when RPG was conceived) have a general similarity. They read a record, do the calculations based on the data just read, optionally produce output, then go back to read the next record. Conceptually, interactive programs similarly read the screen, process, and write a fresh screen. Use of the cycle in this way was quite common on System/36, but is found on the AS/400 only where System/36 programs have been converted.

It should therefore be possible to produce a standard program, tailored by means of parameters, to suit individual requirements.

Over and above the bare bones of input/calculate/output it is desirable to handle control breaks, page headings, numbering etc., and to be able to match to or otherwise access other files.

```
I-Specs      ┌──────┐
             │ Input│◄─┐
             └──┬───┘  │
                │      │
C-specs      ┌──▼───┐  │
             │ Calc │  │
             └──┬───┘  │
                │      │
O-specs      ┌──▼───┐  │
             │Output│──┘
             └──────┘
```

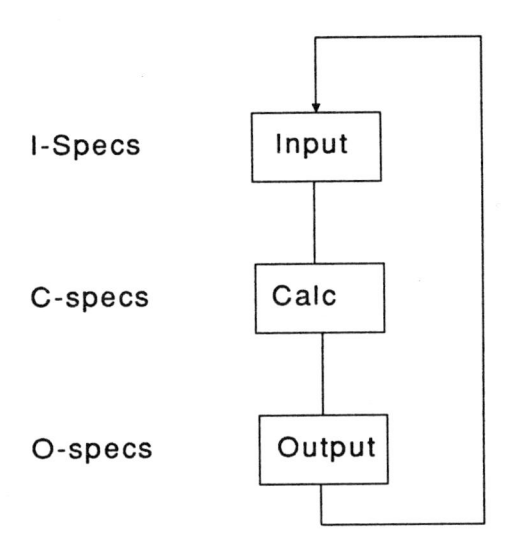

We now need to elaborate on the simple chart above. Please note that the detailed chart which fills the next page is intended to explain the concepts. It represents a trade-off between clarity and accuracy, and is *not* a definitive explanation of the internal workings of an RPG program. (A definitive flowchart is printed in the manual, but it is too detailed to use to explain basic concepts.)

8.4 Reading and "making available"

Before working through this flowchart, a word of explanation is called for as to the difference between steps C and L — in other languages a record is available as soon as it is read.

We described in section 6.4 how RPG moves each field from the input buffer to a work field. At step C, the buffer is filled, and at step L the resulting indicator is set to on and the moves are made to the work fields.

This looks complicated, but in fact makes life easier. Suppose the control break is on a field called PARTNO. The effect is that the old PARTNO will automatically be used for printing the totals etc. which refer to it.

An input file containing:

Partno.	Qty
ABC	11
ABC	12
DEF	37
DEF	13

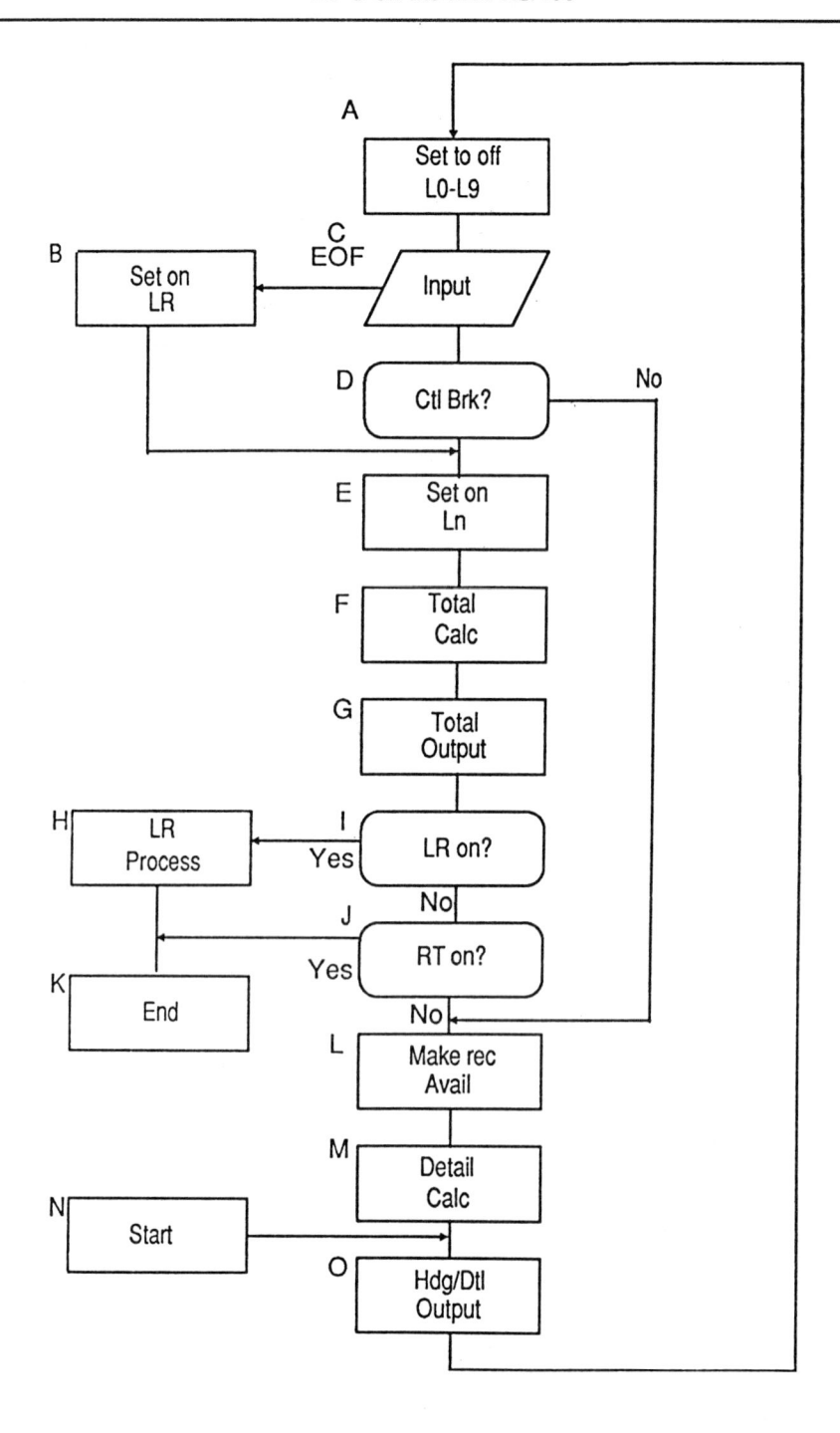

```
                          A
                    ┌───────────┐
                    │ Set to off│◄─────────────┐
                    │  L0-L9    │              │
                    └─────┬─────┘              │
          B           C   │                    │
    ┌──────────┐    EOF  ┌┴┐                   │
    │  Set on  │◄────────┤ │ Input             │
    │    LR    │         └┬┘                   │
    └────┬─────┘          │                    │
         │              D │                    │
         │         ┌───────────┐    No         │
         │         │  Ctl Brk? ├──────┐        │
         │         └─────┬─────┘      │        │
         │               │            │        │
         │             E │            │        │
         │         ┌───────────┐      │        │
         └────────►│  Set on   │      │        │
                   │    Ln     │      │        │
                   └─────┬─────┘      │        │
                       F │            │        │
                   ┌───────────┐      │        │
                   │   Total   │      │        │
                   │   Calc    │      │        │
                   └─────┬─────┘      │        │
                       G │            │        │
                   ┌───────────┐      │        │
                   │   Total   │      │        │
                   │  Output   │      │        │
                   └─────┬─────┘      │        │
    H              I     │            │        │
┌──────────┐   ┌───────────┐          │        │
│    LR    │◄──┤  LR on?   │          │        │
│ Process  │Yes└─────┬─────┘          │        │
└────┬─────┘         │ No             │        │
     │             J │                │        │
     │         ┌───────────┐          │        │
     ├─────────┤  RT on?   │          │        │
     │      Yes└─────┬─────┘          │        │
   K │               │ No             │        │
┌──────────┐         │◄───────────────┘        │
│   End    │       L │                         │
└──────────┘   ┌───────────┐                   │
               │  Make rec │                   │
               │   Avail   │                   │
               └─────┬─────┘                   │
                   M │                         │
               ┌───────────┐                   │
               │  Detail   │                   │
               │   Calc    │                   │
   N           └─────┬─────┘                   │
┌──────────┐         │                         │
│  Start   ├─────────┤                         │
└──────────┘       O │                         │
               ┌───────────┐                   │
               │  Hdg/Dtl  │                   │
               │  Output   │                   │
               └─────┬─────┘                   │
                     └───────────────────────────┘
```

should produce a report which reads:

```
                Part#              Qty
1               ABC                11
2                                  12

3        Total Part ABC            23   *

4               DEF                37
5                                  13

6        Total Part DEF            50   *

7           Grand Total            73   **
```

Lines 3 and 6 are able to contain the correct part numbers because they are printed at step G on the flowchart, i.e. before the new record has been "made available" at step L.

Although the new record has not yet been "made available", it is necessary that it should have been read, otherwise step D would not have been able to recognise that a control break had taken place.

8.5 Use of Detail-time Ln indicators

The following statements print lines 1 and 2, and 4 and 5:

```
OPRINT      D   1   01
O                   L1       PARTNO    40
O                            QTY    J  50
```

The header O-spec has a D on column 15, which means it is to be executed at Detail time — step O on the flowchart.

L1 is set to on at step E, but is not set to off until the program gets back to step A. This means it is on when lines 1 and 4 are printed, but not when lines 2 and 5 are printed.

The detail time L indicators are particularly useful in the output specs for conditioning the throw to a new page etc. In fact, they can provide a way of getting around the limitation to the use of the 1P (first page) indicator. The usual answer is to code up one's own "1P" indicator, but it is also possible to attach a (high-numbered) L indicator to a field, usually the record type, which contains a constant non-blank value throughout the file. This will be on, at detail time, for the first record only.

Indicators on output lines are always checked in the sequence in which they are written, and a common failing looks something like this:

```
OPRTXYZ      H    2 1       L4
O                 OR         OFNL4
```

The NL4 is superfluous, because the fact that the OR line is being executed, means that L4 was not on; if it was, output would have been actioned as a result of the first line's conditions being satisfied. This example shows a useful way of starting a new page for each L4 group.

The PAGEn built-in variables may be used for purposes other than the obvious. Remember that they are incremented every time they are output – this does not necessarily have to be at the beginning of a page, nor even in a print file.

If you need, for example, to number the records in a disk file, this is a satisfactory way of doing it.

8.6 The Cycle in detail

Note that processing starts at N, near the bottom of the chart. This is where indicator 1P is set to on, and any output conditioned to 1P will be processed during the first pass through O, at the end of which 1P is set to off, and remains off for the rest of the program.

Processing continues at A, where all the Level indicators are set to off, then to C to read the first record from the Primary file (see section 8.2). Assuming that the input file is not empty, the next step is D, which checks for any control breaks specified in columns 59-60 of the I-specs. RPG maintains its own internal control fields for making the necessary comparisons. They are initialised to zero if numeric, otherwise blank. Assuming that the first record contains something other than zero/blank in the control fields, the comparison will obviously yield an "unequal". That should send it through E to J, but in fact processing of the first record is E, and then L.

When the first record passes through M and O, any Ln indicators will be on. This has programming implications, which we shall look at shortly.

At E, the Ln indicators are "rippled" – RPG works backwards through the hierarchy L0-LR. If LR is on, L9 is set to on; then if L9 is on L8 is set to on etc. In other words, if any Ln indicator is on it will force all Ln indicators which are "junior" to it to on. When end of file is encountered at C, control passes to B, which sets LR to on; then to E, where all the other Ln indicators "ripple" to on.

Total calculations – step F – includes all those C-specs which have an Ln indicator coded on columns 7-8. Total output – step G – means records which have a T on column 15 of the header O-spec. When Total output at G is complete, indicator LR is tested at I (it may have been set to on in C-specs rather than at B). If LR is on, the full program termination occurs at H – files are closed, dynamic storage de-allocated etc. – and the program terminates at K. If LR is not on, indicator RT is tested, at step J. If RT is on the program terminates immediately, by-passing H.

Note that the RETRN command (see section 7.12.61) will cause control to be passed immediately from the C-spec in which it is issued to step I, with RT set to on implied.

If you are in C-specs (Detail or Total) and want an immediate full termination of the program the following will achieve it:

```
C              SETON               LR
C              RETRN
```

If neither LR nor RT is on, the new record is made available at step L, is processed at M and O, and we go back round the loop to A.

Not shown in the flowchart, is the processing of overflow indicators. If overflow is encountered by any output operation in steps G or O the appropriate overflow indicator is set to on. It is then the programmer's responsibility to test this indicator and to take the appropriate action. Usually this means using header O-specs to test the overflow indicators for each file, and to print headings if set.

The following will cause headings to be printed at the start of processing, and again whenever OF is set:

```
OPRTXYZ        H    2  1     1P
O              OR                 OF
```

Note that it is unwise to condition detail output entirely to the Not condition of one or more indicators, e.g.:

```
OPRTXYZ        D    1        N22
```

will be satisfied during the first pass through step N, when 1P is set. The resulting indicators (see section 7.11.1) are set to on at L and to off immediately after O.

You should make a point of conditioning output to a resulting indicator as well as to any Not conditions required. Assuming the resulting indicator is 01 the following will fix the problem, because 01 will not be on at 1P time:

```
OPRTXYZ        D    1        01N22
```

8.7 Structuring of programs

Structured programming, as it is understood for COBOL, for example, is virtually impossible in RPG II, but at least some attempt should be made to keep related code together, and to keep the clutter of indicators to a minimum.

Assuming the record resulting indicators are 01 and 02, the following works well:

```
C           01              EXSR    SR01
C*
C           02              EXSR    SR02
```

Other than a general requirement that total time specs (i.e. those with an Ln indicator in columns 7-8) should follow detail time specs, RPG will accept them in any sequence. However a great deal of difficulty can be avoided by arranging them in ascending sequence of L number, thus:

```
CL1                 ADD     L1VAL           L2VAL
C*
CL2                 ADD     L2VAL           L3VAL
C*
CL3                 ADD     L3VAL           LRVAL
```

8.8 Level breaks on C-specs – detail time and total time

This brings us to the use of Level indicators at detail time, i.e. as conditioning indicators when columns 7 and 8 are blank. First, let us be clear about what this means. If, for example, L2 is coded against Branch, then L2 total time represents the end of the old branch, but L2 detail time represents the beginning of the new branch.

Here too, the compiler is not particular about how you arrange the statements. However, it is good practice that they should appear before any statements conditioned to record resulting indicators, and in descending sequence of L number, so our full skeleton program appears thus:

```
C           L3              Z-ADD0          L3VAL
C*
C           L2              Z-ADD0          L2VAL
C*
C           L1              Z-ADD0          L1VAL
 *
C           01              EXSR    SR01
C*
C           02              EXSR    SR02
 *
CL1                 ADD     L1VAL           L2VAL
C*
CL2                 ADD     L2VAL           L3VAL
C*
CL3                 ADD     L3VAL           LRVAL
```

Note how the comment asterisk produces a more clear cut break when used without the C spec-type. In general, try to paragraph the code by judicious use of blank comment lines.

8.9 Matching

Matching is requested simply by entering M1 through M9 on columns 61-62 of the relevant I-specs. The least significant match field is M1, the most significant M9.

It is permitted, but not required, to use the same field name on each file specifying a given match level:

```
IEMPLEE   NS   01
I                           1    70EMP#   L1M1
I                          11    25 SURNAM
ICLCKCRD  NS   02
I                           1    70EMP#   L1M1
I                         P 8    112HRS
```

Similarly, Ln and Mn specifications may coincide – e.g. L1M1, L2M2 etc – but they are not required to do so. (In practice they nearly always do.)

For each group of matching records, the MR special indicator is set to on at the beginning of detail time for the first record, and off at the end of detail time for the last record.

Before computers came into widespread use, data processing was achieved by means of unit record machines. These comprised (card) sorters, collators, and tabulators.

RPG was designed with an eye to selling computers by providing an easy upgrade path from unit record machines, and a number of its features reflect this. Aspects of RPG which are quite baffling, not to say maddening, start to make sense when viewed against this background.

File matching is probably the area which gives the most trouble to programmers inexperienced in RPG II. The secret is to remember that it does not match in the sense that a COBOL program matches: what it is really doing, is simulating a collator or tabulator.

Consider a wages application. Punched cards containing employee information needed to be merged with those containing clock card information. When the job was converted to a computer, the employee and clock cards would be held as card images on two disk (or tape) files and matched by the RPG program. Gross pay cannot be calculated until both the employee "card" and the clock "card" have been read.

It doesn't matter which file is chosen to be Primary, but it is imperative that the calculation be conditioned to the resulting indicator for the Secondary file, not the Primary, even though the MR (matched records) indicator will be on for both. Whenever in doubt about MR simply imagine you are working with a collator, and things should fall into place.

A point to watch about MR is that it comes on only when a record from a Secondary file matches a record on the Primary file. It does *not* come on when records from two Secondaries match one another but not the Primary. Fortunately, it is not often that you need to know that this has happened, but if you do, MR will not help you and you will have to provide the code yourself.

Another little quirk, which is useful if you know about it (but can drive you insane if you don't) is that if match fields are specified on the Primary file, then any Secondary file for which match fields are not specified will be read before the Primary file.

In the bad old days before the PLIST/PARM op codes were added to the language, this feature was often used to input parameters, and a number of old systems have never been updated.

8.10 Implications with commitment control

The cycle should not be used in any program that updates under commitment control – this is discussed in Chapter 13.

When a ROLBK command (see section 7.12.62) is issued any fields which have been updated will be restored to their original state, but RPG's internal control fields, used in step D of the flowchart, will not be restored.

9

Fully Procedural Programming

9.1 What it is

Fully procedural programming is the converse of programming in the cycle, discussed in the previous chapter; and is generally thought of as "real" RPG III programming. The cycle is switched off simply by not designating a file as Primary; this implies that there also may not be any Secondary files, because the compiler will not allow Secondaries without a Primary file.

All disk input or update files are required to be fully procedural – to have an F on column 16 of their F-specs.

9.2 Programming without files

It is by no means necessary to have any files at all in a full procedural program. A program without files is usually a subprogram, which will handle its input and output via the *ENTRY PLIST – see next chapter, and sections 7.12.52 and 7.12.53.

For most practical purposes one can forget that the cycle exists. There is certainly no need to understand the cycle flowchart presented in the last chapter.

The whole feel of the thing is of writing a COBOL program, but using slightly different syntax. Indeed, it is not uncommon to have a program comprising nothing but C-specs.

That is why there is a fairly widely held view that it is easier to teach RPG III to a COBOL programmer than to an RPG II programmer.

9.3 Structuring a Fully Procedural program

Just as a good COBOL program should be properly structured, so should a fully procedural RPG program. There are many techniques available, and it really doesn't matter which you use so long as your work is clear both to you and to a maintenance programmer who comes after you.

One of the better ones is the McCracken hierarchy, presented in the next chapter in a slightly different context.

9.4 Uses of Fully Procedural programs

As we saw in the last chapter, the programmer who rejects the cycle is shutting himself off from the benefits of automatic matching and level breaking. Occasionally there are good reasons for doing so. Interactive programming on the AS/400 is invariably done in fully procedural mode. Since matching and level breaking are seldom if ever wanted in interactive programs, it does not matter that these automatic facilities are lost.

Programs which need to access only small portions of files are also good candidates for the full procedural method – again, matching and level breaking are seldom required in programs of this kind.

In general, one soon gets a feel for when the cycle is appropriate, and when not. There is only one bad reason for using full procedural programming: the programmer is too lazy to learn the cycle.

9.5 Output from Fully Procedural programs

Fully procedural programs usually use external files, although it is not compulsory to do so.

Because the cycle is switched off, Detail time output will not work, and all output should be handled by means of EXCPT commands (see section 7.12.26) for internal files, and WRITE commands (see section 7.12.78) for external files.

For all but the most trivial print layouts, external print files are an attractive option. The print layout is built into the file definition, and the program is left with nothing more to do than to pass a buffer (for which the compiler creates the O-specs). The only drawback is that it is necessary to create and maintain a second object, the print file.

Print file DDS is very similar to workstation file DDS, and it is possible to create your print layout on the screen, using SDA (Screen Design Aid), and then to convert the resulting DDS to print file DDS.

The conversion may be done manually, but that is very tedious and time consuming. It is much better to use a program. Reinventing the wheel is seldom profitable, and such a program may be bought more cheaply than it may be written. Conversion programs are available from a number of sources – see Appendix B.

9.6 Terminating a Fully Procedural program

In an old-style, cycling RPG II program, indicator LR was always set to on automatically – see step B of the flowchart in the previous chapter.

Because a fully procedural program has no Primary or Secondary files, it also does not set indicator LR to on automatically, and it is therefore up to the programmer to provide some way of terminating the program. If he fails to do so the program will not compile. The easiest solution is to ensure that the last executable instruction in the program is SETON LR. It must be the last executable instruction because LR is not tested until the calculations are complete. In the following example:

```
C           SETON              LR
C           ADD   1      COUNT
```

COUNT will be incremented even though LR is set. This is where the RETRN verb (see section 7.12.61) is useful, and the following will ensure immediate termination (i.e. before COUNT is incremented:

```
C           SETON              LR
C           RETRN
C           ADD   1      COUNT
```

Using the RETRN verb on its own, without LR, has a number of implications, which are discussed in section 10.6. Unless you are using modular programming it is nearly always sufficient simply to set LR to on.

10

Modular Programming

10.1 Principles and reasons

Modular programming was one of those fads that hit the computer industry from time to time. Usually the buzzword is on everyone's lips for a year or two, then it quietly disappears. The difference between modular programming and some of the other fads was that modular programming actually was – and is – a good idea. Indeed, for really large software projects, such as compilers, it is quite difficult to go any other way.

Large projects often require 100 man-years and more of programmer effort. Since it is obviously impractical to sit one man down for 100 years, a more usual approach is to use 100 programmers for one year. This immediately raises the question: how is the work to be shared out?

For applications software there is an almost instinctive answer: the system generally consists of numerous discrete and relatively small programs, and these become the natural unit of work sharing.

But what about compilers and the like? Frequently they comprise many more lines of source code than the biggest applications system, but they have to work as a single giant program. Because they are intended to be used in thousands of installations all over the world, performance is much more critical than for an applications system, and the financial consequences of bugs are similarly greater.

The solution is modular programming, with the subprogram module becoming the unit of work sharing, and there is no reason whatever why these principles should not also be used in applications programming.

What is modular programming? It is simply structured programming in which the subroutines are replaced by subprograms, invoked by means of CALLs rather than PERFORMs (COBOL) or EXSRs (RPG).

Most readers will have been taught not to use the COBOL GO TO, and its equivalents in other languages, but frequently not the reason. Some years ago a statistical analysis of program bugs revealed that about 75% were caused by faulty GO TO instructions – the obvious cure was to find some other way of achieving the same result.

The answer was structured code, and it has the useful by-product of being very much easier for a maintenance programmer to follow. There are a number of methodologies around, and the adherents of some – notably Jackson – have an almost religious fanaticism. (Before Mr. Jackson's lawyers reach for their writ-pads, I am sure he is a very nice man, in no way responsible for the inanity of some of his followers.)

It really doesn't matter very much which you use, as long as there is some sort of formal organisation to your work, and as long as your method is reasonably intelligible to the maintenance programmer who comes after you.

One of the best is the McCracken* hierarchy chart, if only because its meaning is completely obvious even to a maintenance programmer who has never heard of McCracken – now try springing a Nassi-Schneidermann diagram on him!

The following shows the general principle of a McCracken hierarchy:

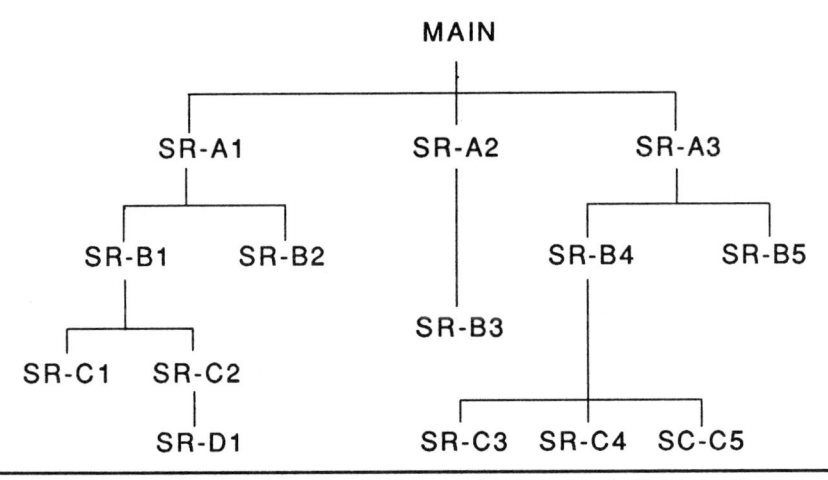

```
                          MAIN
            ┌───────────────┼───────────────┐
          SR-A1           SR-A2           SR-A3
         ┌──┴──┐            │            ┌──┴──┐
       SR-B1 SR-B2        SR-B3        SR-B4 SR-B5
         │                              ┌──┴──┐
      ┌──┴──┐                         SR-C3 SR-C4 SC-C5
    SR-C1 SR-C2
            │
          SR-D1
```

*For a detailed discussion see page 299 et seq of "A Simplified Guide to Structured COBOL Programming" by D. D. McCracken. See Appendix C.

The main program invokes subroutines SR-A1, SR-A2 and SR-A3; SR-A1 invokes SR-B1 and SR-B2, and so on. There is no compulsion about naming the subroutines A1, B1 etc. to indicate their levels in the hierarchy, but doing so helps in the general aim of making the program intelligible.

There is, of course, nothing to prevent the person programming a module from producing an internal structure chart, McCracken or other. Software is available to "reverse engineer" a McCracken hierarchy from an existing system – see Figure below (the R or C preceding the text denotes whether the module is written in RPG or CL). Similarly, a McCracken hierarchy may be "reverse engineered" from an existing RPG program. See Appendix B.

```
UPATHFFR1                                    FORWARD FLOW BEGINNING WITH MAIN              3/12/92

   MAIN
      SRA1                                       R  This is the program text for SRA1
         SRB1                                    R  This is the program text for SRB1
            SRC1                                 R  This is the program text for SRC1
            SRC2                                 R  This is the program text for SRC2
               SRD1                              C  This is the program text for SRD1
         SRB2                                    R  This is the program text for SRB2
      SRA2                                       R  This is the program text for SRA2
         SRB3                                    C  This is the program text for SRB3
      SRA3                                       R  This is the program text for SRA3
         SRB4                                    R  This is the program text for SRB4
            SRC3                                 R  This is the program text for SRC3
            SRC4                                 R  This is the program text for SRC4
            SRC5                                 R  This is the program text for SRC5
         SRB5                                    R  This is the program text for SRB5
```

10.2 Coding the links – passing parameters

Coding the links is simplicity itself. Suppose three fields, X, Y, and Z are to be passed. In the calling program we would code:

```
              CALL  'SRA1'
              PARM  'JKL'   X
              PARM          Y
              PARM          Z
```

In the called program we would code:

```
     *ENTRY   PLIST
              PARM          A
              PARM          B
              PARM          C
```

The value JKL is loaded into field X before it is passed.

Note that the fields are called A,B,C in the called program, but X,Y,Z in the calling program. This was done to illustrate that there is no compulsion to use the same names (though in practice it is usually better to do so as it makes the program easier to understand).

How does the operating system know that A in the called program is the same field as X in the calling program? It all works on position and length, and in fact what happens behind the scenes is that it is the *addresses* of the three fields within the calling program which are passed. This implies that while the names do not matter, it is vitally important that the fields are of the same length and type, and appear in the same sequence in both parameter lists.

The same convention is used in COBOL on all machines, and on all languages used on the AS/400.

If a numeric field is passed, it must be packed in both lists or zoned in both lists, which can be more difficult than it sounds. The RPG compiler has something of a mind of its own when deciding whether a numeric field is to be zoned or packed.

When testing a program, it is often useful to call it from the programmer's command entry screen, using literals as parameters. This can be awkward with zoned fields and is impossible with packed fields. Bearing these considerations in mind, a practical programming tip is to avoid passing numeric fields at all: convert them to alpha before passing, and convert back to numeric after receiving. The extra effort is trivial.

Note how easily some, or all, of the subroutines could be replaced by subprograms, invoked by means of CALLs rather than PERFORMs or EXSRs, without in any way altering the concept. However, trying to split up an existing program in this way is about as easy as unscrambling an egg. There is some help available – see Appendix B.

At first sight there does not appear to be much point in SR-B3, as it is simply called by SR-A2. Apart from size considerations, it seems that it might as well be incorporated in SR-A2. This could well be true in a structured program but, as we shall see below, the designer of a modular program may have good reasons for setting it up as shown.

Pure McCracken theory requires that each module be called once and once only. In practice this may be awkward, however it is nothing that cannot be overcome by judicious application of common sense. One possibility is to introduce a Z-level. Modules called more than once would be named SR-Z1, SR-Z2 etc.

Modular programming has many advantages in addition to facilitating the sharing of work. It imposes a discipline early in the design process, because the writer of each subprogram needs to be told exactly what input he is to expect, and exactly what output is required of him. If he is to call further subprograms he will similarly need to be told exactly what parameters to supply, and what data to expect in return.

This is a great help when debugging. The very existence of formalised interfaces between the modules makes it easy to isolate the module which is receiving the proper input but not providing correct output, and thus to locate the cause of a bug.

Once the bug has been found and fixed, the relevant piece of code has to be recompiled, and it is much quicker and easier to recompile small programs than big ones.

10.3 Multi-language programming

Modular programming makes multi-lingual programming possible. Each programming language has its own strengths and weaknesses, and modular programming enables the designer to adopt a "horses for courses" approach.

Suppose that we have surname and forename fields each of 30 bytes, and a title field of 10 bytes, and we are required to output the name in the form "SMITH, MR. JOHN".

To do this in RPG (or COBOL) would require redefining each of the fields as arrays having single byte elements, followed by some fairly complex scanning and moving.

The AS/400 Control Language (CL) command CHGVAR (Change Variable) – essentially a move command – provides the operators *TCAT (Truncate and Concatenate) and *BCAT (Truncate, insert a Blank, and Concatenate).

Our problem could therefore be handled in CL by a single instruction:

```
          CHGVAR  VAR(OUTNAM)                              +
                  VALUE(SURNAM                             +
                  *TCAT ','                                +
                  *BCAT TITLE                              +
                  *BCAT FORNAM)
```

If, in the example above, SR-B3 was to be a CL program containing this instruction, then it could not be integrated with RPG module SR-A2.

There can be all sorts of other reasons for wanting to split a function into a number of modules. If it is known that a certain aspect of the business is likely to be in a state of change, then it is prudent to isolate the sensitive part of the program into a module of its own.

Mainframe Assembler programmers who find themselves needing to re-use hardware registers may well find it expedient to call a new module instead.

Designing modular programs offers more opportunity for flair and creativity than almost any other aspect of DP, and enables a good designer to be a hundredfold more productive than a mediocre one.

10.4 Effects of single-level storage
and why AS/400 needs no link editor

Modular programming sounds too good to be true. What are its drawbacks?

A potential problem is that various aspects may have to be re-coded for each module which uses them – for example, file definitions, data structures, and so on. In practice modern text editors and/or judicious use of the /COPY command relegate this to a minor irritation.

More serious is the possible impact on performance. Suppose each record of a disk file is to be read, calculations performed on its contents, and the result printed. If we use a sub-program to do the calculations the flowchart will look like this:

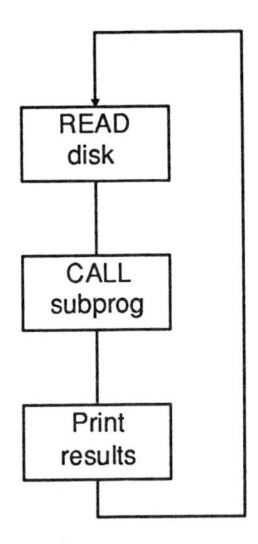

```
      ┌──────────┐
      │   READ   │
      │   disk   │
      └──────────┘
           │
      ┌──────────┐
      │   CALL   │
      │  subprog │
      └──────────┘
           │
      ┌──────────┐
      │   Print  │
      │  results │
      └──────────┘
```

Each time we go round the loop, not one but two disk accesses will be required – one to read the record, and another to pull in the subprogram. The effect on performance would be disastrous and, if solutions had not been found, modular programming would have been still-born.

Fortunately, solutions were found. The first was to make compilation into a two-stage process. Each source module is compiled into an object module, and then the object modules are linked together into a "run-program" by means of utility called a "link-editor" (IBM), or "binder" (Burroughs).

No such facility exists on the AS/400. It depends instead on a natural consequence of single-level storage, which works by dividing the contents of the disks into 512-byte blocks, called pages. Clearly large records will span more than one page, and small records may fit more than one to a page, while even a very small record may happen to straddle a page boundary. The operating system keeps track of which pages are in core by means of a table, and each entry in this table has a corresponding usage entry. The usage entries are regularly incremented from the system clock, but each time a page is referenced, the usage entry is re-initialised. The operating system is thereby able to answer the question "Which page was last used longest ago?".

All requests for records (or programs) are translated by the operating system into requests for the relevant pages, and checked against the table of loaded pages. Obviously, if a requested page is already loaded it is passed to the requester without further ado.

If a requested page is not already loaded, it is read in from disk to an empty page in core. If there are no free pages in core a condition called a "page fault" is raised, and one of the pages already loaded is written out to disk to make way for the newcomer. Which one? The one "last used longest ago". [I must stress that this is a grossly simplified explanation of the paging algorithm, but it is adequate for our present purpose.]

In the light of all this let us walk through the above flowchart on the assumption that it is running on an AS/400.

  1 The read to the first record will be resolved into page requests. Assuming that the pages are not in core (and there is no reason why they should be) they will be loaded.

  2 Next the CALL to the subprogram will generate some more page requests, again these will probably not be in core and will have to be loaded.

  3 The results will be printed, and a read issued for the second record. Once more the requested pages will probably not be in core, and will have to be loaded.

  4 Now we come to the interesting bit, the second CALL. The operating system will check its table of pages, and will find that the sub-program's pages are already in core, having been brought in a few nanoseconds ago, for the first CALL. (If they have already been paged out the machine is in a state called "thrashing", which is beyond the scope of this book. Fortunately it doesn't happen very often.)

  It will re-initialise their usage entries, and proceed through the printing operation to the third record and the third CALL. Again, the subprogram's pages will already be in core, and again their usage entries will be re-initialised.

  Because the usage entries are continually being re-initialised, the sub-program's pages will never become the ones "last used longest ago", and so will never be in line for deletion when a page fault occurs. Consequently our sub-program will be read in from disk only once, no matter how many records are processed.

There is a further twist to this which can be quite important from a programming point of view. On almost every other machine it is very poor programming practice to read a record and then, nanoseconds later, to read the same record again. Although a program that does this may well produce correct results, the effect on performance will be dire. However, not on an AS/400. Why? Because when the second read is issued the operating system will find the relevant pages still in core, and so will be able to satisfy the read request without further disk access.

10.5 Multi-threading

Very few AS/400 programmers realise that the programs they write are "multi-threadable". Multi-threading was pioneered on the PL/I compiler on IBM mainframes about 25 years ago, and works like this:

Suppose that two users are using the same program at the same time. The operating system will load only one copy of the program to service both of them. Each user's path through the program is called a "thread". (Observant users – both programmers and end-users – of the AS/400 may notice that they get a quicker initial response if somebody else is already using the program they require. The explanation is that it is already loaded for the first thread, and so the disk read(s) necessary to bring it into core are avoided.)

If the program uses a field called PARTNO it is highly unlikely that both users will have the same value in that field: how does the operating system distinguish between the two versions of PARTNO? The answer is a device called "dynamic storage allocation". Instead of core for variables being allocated at compile time, it is allocated when the program is loaded or, more precisely, when a thread is activated. Unless you do something to prevent it, that core will be de-allocated when the thread terminates. This can have a substantial impact on efficiency.

Look at the small flowchart above. Each time we come round the loop, the dynamic storage allocator will have to allocate storage for each variable in the CALLed subprogram.

10.6 Reclaiming resources
RT and LR indicators and the RETRN verb

The solution is that de-allocation takes place only if indicator LR is on. To prevent de-allocation, terminate the program by setting the RT indicator to on, or by using the RETRN verb.

The difference between the two is that RETRN passes control back to the CALLing program immediately, whereas setting RT to on does not take effect until the logical end of the calculation statements is reached.

Sometimes we need to de-allocate and to return control immediately. This is done in the following way:

```
            SETON          LR
            RETRN
```

The operating system will always check to see if LR is set before handing control back to the invoking program.

There is a danger when using RT and RETRN of leaving storage allocated after the need for it has passed, although the impact is less than might at first appear, because the pages involved will soon be paged out.

To some extent, the operating system cleans up automatically. When a program terminates any core still belonging to its sub-threads is automatically de-allocated, e.g. in the example in section 10.1 above, when SR-B4 terminates any core still belonging to SR-C3, SR-C4 and SR-C5 will be de-allocated.

It is also possible to clean up explicitly, by means of the CL command RCLRSC (Reclaim Resources). The easy way to use this, assuming that your installation follows the usual practice of writing menus in CL, is to follow each menu CALL by a RCLRSC.

If you particularly wish to clean up from within an RPG program, then the following code will do it:

```
CALL  'QCMDEXC'
PARM  'RCLRSC'   CMD       6
PARM  6          LENGTH    155
```

(On System/38 substitute QCAEXEC for QCMDEXC.)

11

Workstation Programming

11.1 The screen

The AS/400 sees the terminal as a file of device type WORKSTN, as does its predecessor, the System/36. Other teleprocessing monitors, notably CICS, have the screens talking direct to the TP monitor, which calls application programs on request.

Whereas an interactive program on an AS/400 or System/36 accesses database files in exactly the same way as a batch program, CICS programs do so by means of a call to the appropriate service module of CICS.

11.2 Screen files

CICS, AS/400 and System/36 all use compiled screen maps. This means that literals, the layout of the screen, etc. are built into the screen map, and all the application program has to do is send and receive data in the form of buffers.

The buffers must conform to the layout that the screen map is expecting, and in CICS and System/36 it is the programmer's responsibility to ensure that they do.

The AS/400 takes the next logical step and generates the buffer layouts in the program from the expected buffer layouts in the screen map. This means that the program buffers can never be out of step with the maps. Or does it?

What happens if the program is compiled, then the screen map is changed and recompiled, and then an attempt is made to run the program? Obviously it is at least possible that the expected buffer format will have changed. When this occurs, OS/400 will raise a "level check" as soon as an attempt is made to open the file. This applies to all external files — not only to display files. (It is able to recognise a level check because it maintains an internal hash number calculated from various attributes of the file. The hash number is stored in the object program, and when the file is opened the stored hash number is checked against the number in the file.)

OS/400 does support internally described display files, but only to provide upward compatibility with System/36. It is quite pointless to use an internal display file in a newly written RPG III program.

11.3 DDS and SDA

All external files on the AS/400 are described by means of DDS (Data Description Specifications). DDS is broadly similar for all types of files, but there are some variations depending on file type. For example, form spacing would be meaningless for a disk file, and display attributes would be meaningless for a printer file.

It is beyond the scope of this book to present DDS in detail, but here is a brief example of a very simple display file (known by the figurative constant *DSPF). Although DDS is not a part of RPG, DDS specifications are also identified by an entry on column 6 — in this case an A.

```
  1.00 A                                        CHGINPDFT
  2.00 A                                        DSPSIZ(24 80 *DS3)
  3.00 A                                        REF(FRF *LIBL)
  4.00 A                                        PRINT
  5.00 A                                        HELP(60 'Help Key')
  6.00 A                                        CF02(02 'Delete')
  7.00 A          R FORMAT1
  8.00 A                                        CA13(13 'Add')
  9.00 A                                    10  22'Literal'
 10.00 A     22    FLDXYZ    R     B        11  33
 11.00 A                                        EDTCDE(J)
 12.00 A           FLDABC    R     B        12  33REFFLD(PQR DSKFIL)
 13.00 A           FLDZYX         9A B          +3
 14.00 A    N23                                 DSPATR(HI BL)
```

The keyword CHGINPDFT is recommended for all *DSPFs, even if used as shown, without operands. If it is not used, all fields will be underlined.

The display size shown in line 2 is the default, but larger screens are available.

Line 3 will be discussed with lines 10 and 12.

Line 4 enables the PRINT key. If the user presses this key the display before him will be dumped to the default printer. Without the keyword he would simply get an "Invalid command key" message".

Line 5 enables the HELP key, and associates indicator 60 with it. If the user presses HELP control will be returned to the program with indicator 60 set to on. The text "Help key" will be printed alongside the generated I-spec in the program listing. Without the keyword the user would simply get an "Invalid command key" message".

Line 6 enables command key 2, and associates indicator 02 with it. If the user presses command key 2 control will be returned to the program with indicator 02 set to on. The text "Delete" will be printed alongside the generated I-spec in the program listing. (Special indicator KB will be set to on automatically – see section 7.1.2). Without the keyword the user would simply get an "Invalid command key" message".

Line 7 defines the format name – note the R on column 18.

Line 8 is subtly different from line 6. It enables command key 13 but, because it appears below the first format name, enables it only while FORMAT1 is displayed. The difference between CF (Command Function) and CA (Command Attention) is that CF causes a normal return of input capable fields, whereas CA merely sets on the associated indicator.

Line 9 shows how to display a literal on the screen. Note that changes to literals do not affect the level check hash number.

Line 10 displays field FLDXYZ if indicator 22 is on. The R in column 29 (immediately following FLDXYZ) indicates that the field is defined by reference to another. Line 3 defined the default reference file as FRF in *LIBL, and the DDS compilation will fail if FRF does not contain a field called FLDXYZ. The B stands for both; other options are I for Input and O for Output. FLDXYZ will be displayed on column 33 of line 11.

Line 11 is a continuation of line 10, and supplies an edit code for it. Note that this edit code is the same as the edit codes presented in section 7.13.2.

Line 12 displays field FLDABC on column 33 of line 12. As in line 10, the R in column 29 indicates that the field is defined by reference to another. This time the REFFLD keyword is used, to refer to field PQR in file DSKFIL. It over-rides the REF keyword on line 3.

Line 13 displays field FLDZYX 3 positions beyond the end of FLDABC. It also defines FLDZYX as 9 alphanumeric characters.

Line 14 will cause FLDZYX to be highlighted and to blink if indicator 23 is not on.

Display files usually contain many formats. Unless there is a good reason to do otherwise each panel – each screenful of information – is provided by a single format. Naturally, each format must have a unique name. Probably the most common reason for having more than one format on the screen at a time is to support subfiles, to which the next chapter is devoted.

It is not unknown for two or more programs to share a single *DSPF, and when this happens they may not all use all the formats. Any unwanted formats should be ignored by means of the IGNORE keyword on columns 54-59 of the kontinuation F-spec (see section 7.7.2).

There are basically two ways of creating *DSPF DDS: it may be coded directly using SEU (the Source Edit Utility), or it may be generated with the aid of SDA (the Screen Design Aid). In practice the two methods are usually intermixed.

SDA offers access to database field definitions, which may be copied into the display file. These are copied in full, i.e. the REFFLD DDS keyword is created incorporating the format name in which the field resides, and the library name in which the file resides (or the figurative constant *LIBL).

All this tends to make the REFFLD occupy more than one line, and readability is greatly improved by removing format and library names wherever the defaults will serve. This may be done using the global change facility in SEU.

If the file is a Physical File there will be only one format, and the default for the library is *LIBL – i.e. the first occurrence of the file in the library list – see section 1.7.

If a set of DDS has been created directly using SEU then it should be viewed, checked and corrected using SDA. SDA will allow you to view the screen with selected indicators set.

11.4 EXFMT, WRITE and READ

The EXFMT (Execute Format) command – see section 7.12.27 – is equivalent to a WRITE immediately followed by a READ.

RPG programmers usually use EXFMT unless there is a particular reason for using a WRITE followed by a READ. (AS/400 COBOL programmers have no choice: they must use a WRITE followed by a READ.) Because the READ command is allowed to specify a file name, instead of a format name, some programmers use the WRITE/READ method, and then inspect the result of the READ to see which format was returned to them. This is very much a System/36 technique, and is better not used on the AS/400.

Sometimes we wish to put more than one format on a screen at once, and some new keywords are needed, for example:

```
     A                                                LOCK
     A                                                FRCDTA
     A                                                OVERLAY
```

LOCK simply locks the keyboard until the next buffer is received from the CPU, which may or may not unlock it.

FRCDTA causes the data which has been sent to be displayed immediately, rather than to wait until the end of the I/O sequence.

OVERLAY tells OS/400 that this new format is permitted to overlay other formats already on the screen. If this format overlaps any existing format and the keyword is not present, the screen will be cleared before the new format is displayed.

The WRITE command should be used rather than EXFMT, because once a READ or EXFMT command is issued the program will stop processing until a response is received from the screen.

11.5 Response times

When you use SEU, you will notice that the first thing you see on the screen is a message telling you that the member you requested is being loaded into the SEU work space. This is done by means of a format containing a literal and the LOCK and FRCDTA keywords, which is written to the screen using a WRITE command. It is followed by another WRITE, using a format which does not have OVERLAY specified.

Why bother? Because SEU sometimes takes quite a while to load up the requested member, particularly if it is large. The appearance of the message on the screen is a form of activity, and creates an illusion that response is quicker than it really is.

Slow response is a chronic problem with large computers, and particularly with database systems, and it is well worth borrowing this leaf from IBM's book.

Sometimes a complex screen will contain data from a dozen or more database files. It takes time to access all these files, and there is not much anyone can do to speed it up. What can be done is to divide the screen into a number of small formats, which are written as soon as their data becomes available, rather than waiting until it is all available and then using an EXFMT to send a single large format. To make sense, this means ordering the reads from the database so that the fields most frequently looked at are read first.

Heated meetings over response times are an occupational hazard for database programmers. Depending on the complainant's position in the corporate pecking order, you can sometimes send him off with a flea in his ear if you can put a stop-watch on the screen, preferably in the presence of his boss, and "prove" he is talking nonsense.

Here is a sneaky way to rig the evidence. Insist that you want the average of half a dozen responses, to even out fluctuations caused by extraneous factors. This sounds plausible, and has the further merit of being partly true. Make sure that all the tests enquire upon the *same* data. The second and subsequent tests will be very much quicker than the first, and will do great things for your average. But only because of the effects of single level storage . . .

Having won the battle, do not assume you have won the war. All you have won is breathing space to get back to the drawing board to figure out a way of improving response.

Remember, "acceptable response" is whatever it takes to mollify an angry, irrational and influential user – *not* an objective measure made with a stop-watch.

11.6 PUTOVR (Put Over-ride)

Computer performance is only one component of response times. Another is line time – the time the data takes to travel between the CPU and the screen.

Obviously the less data you send, the quicker the operation will be over. It seldom matters for locally attached screens, but can be a real headache on remote screens.

There is an easy way to reduce considerably the amount of line traffic. Suppose a user is making repeated enquiries, using the same screen format. There is no need to keep sending the literals each time; it is sufficient to send the changed data.

On the AS/400 this can be achieved by using the PUTOVR (Put Over-ride) OVRDTA (Over-ride Data) and OVRATR (Over-ride Attribute) family of keywords. PUTOVR must be specified at format level, the others at field level.

PUTOVR enables the whole process for the format in question. Any field which has OVRDTA specified against it will be updated only when its contents change.

OVRATR should be specified only against attributes which are conditioned by indicators. If the attributes are to be changed then only the relevant indicator(s) are transmitted.

Suppose a format for a data capture application looks like this:

```
A              R FORMATA
A                                              PUTOVR
A*
A                FLD1       R       B    11 33
A                                              OVRDTA
A      21                                      DSPATR(RI BL)
A                                              OVRATR
A                FLD2       R       B    +3
A                                              OVRDTA
A      22                                      DSPATR(RI BL)
A                                              OVRATR
```

When the entered data is validated, indicators 21 and 22 respectively are set to on if errors are detected in FLD1 and FLD2. They cause the field(s) in error to be displayed in reverse image and to blink, calling the user's attention to the error. Now picture what happens when an error is detected in FLD2. Indicator 22 is set to on, but only that one byte is sent back to the screen, and FLD2 switches to reverse image and starts blinking. The user corrects the error and presses [ENTER]. FLD1 has not changed, and so only FLD2 is sent back to the CPU. Obviously this will only work if the screen has not changed. If some other format has been sent to the screen in the interim it will be necessary to send the whole of FORMATA.

There is one slight complication. PUTOVR does not work with conditioned fields and literals. This will not work:

```
A            R FORMATB
A                                              PUTOVR
A*
A       31                           10  22'Literal'
A                                              OVRDTA
A       32   FLD      R      B       11  33
A                                              OVRDTA
```

Instead use:

```
A            R FORMATB
A                                              PUTOVR
A*
A                                    10  22'Literal'
A                                              OVRATR
A       N31                                    DSPATR(ND)
A            FLD      R      B       11  33
A                                              OVRATR
A       N32                                    DSPATR(ND PR)
```

The display attribute ND stands for Non Display, and means that the field will be displayed in "dark". PR means that the field will be protected.

Note particularly that the sense of the indicators has changed. Rather than displaying FLD if indicator 32 is set, we blank it out if indicator 32 is not set.

PUTOVR does not work with subfiles.

11.7 Error Messages

Do not use the old System/36 technique of treating messages as conditionally displayed literals.

On the AS/400 messages may be displayed using the ERRMSG keyword, or may be picked up from an *MSGF (Message File), in which case the best technique by far is to use a message subfile, as explained in the next chapter.

For very simple applications the ERRMSG keyword is adequate. It is coded like this:

```
A            FLD      R      B       11  33
A       32                                     ERRMSG('FLD invalid')
```

12

Subfile Programming

Part 1: The Basics

12.1 What is a subfile?

One of the most useful features of the AS/400 is the concept of the subfile, yet it is one which is approached with some diffidence by those migrating to the AS/400 family from other types of machines.

What is a subfile? Imagine that you need to display something on the screen which has a certain amount of fixed information followed by *n* occurrences of subsidiary information. For example, an invoice will have header information – the customer's name and so on – plus an unpredictable number of line items.

Other machines would require you to load up a screenful of data, directing each line item to its proper place on the screen. In COBOL you might simplify the task by means of a two-dimensional array. When the user presses the [Roll Up] key the code is invoked again to load another screenful of data.

With the subfile concept, each invoice line item is written away to a subfile record when it is read, and the subfile format is then displayed. When the user presses the [Roll Up] key it is not even necessary for the application program to know that this has happened. Instead, the operating system intercepts the request and displays the next panel.

12.2 Format names

The formats within a display file should be given meaningful names; and it is much easier to maintain programs if all programmers within an installation use the same naming convention.

Here is one that works, though it is certainly not the only satisfactory convention. We shall use it for the remainder of this chapter.

The first four characters are DSPR, for **DiSP**lay **R**ecord. The fifth character is n, where n is the panel number as seen by the user (more than one format may appear on the screen at a time). The sixth character is left blank if the format does not involve a subfile, unless it is to share the panel with other formats. In this case, it is "numbered" A through Z. The second format on the third panel would be DSPR3B. If the format involves a subfile the sixth character is either C for control format, or S for subfile format, and the seventh character is a numeric digit which gives the subfile number within the panel (as seen by the user).

The convention is extended to encompass the naming of the field which contains the subfile relative record number. The first three characters are RRN, the fourth is the panel number and the fifth gives the subfile number within the panel.

For example, the second subfile within the third panel of the display file would be DSPR3S2, its controlling format would be DSPR3C2, and its relative record number would be contained in field RRN32. The attributes of this field should always be declared as *four* digits (numeric) even though this is not a syntactic requirement, because less than four may cause problems for a maintenance programmer who comes after you. The system will not allow more than four digits, even though normal good programming practice would be to declare a packed field with an odd number of digits.

Each subfile format is required to have a controlling format, which may (and usually does) contain fields and literals of its own. In the invoice example, the customer's name and address would be fields within the controlling format.

12.3 Keywords

All subfile related keywords in DDS are prefixed by SFL. The subfile is identified by the keyword SFL within the DDS (Data Description Specifications).

The controlling format is described by the keyword SFLCTL, which has as its operand the name of the subfile to be controlled.

An example of a subfile and its controlling format follows (note that the subfile definition must precede the definition of its control format, which seems unnatural):

```
A          R DSPR1S1                       SFL
A             .
A             .
A          R DSPR1C1                       SFLCTL(DSPR1S1)
A             .
A             .
```

When a subfile is displayed, and there is not enough room on the screen to show the entire subfile, this condition can be notified to the user by means of a plus sign (System/38) or the word "more.." (AS/400) at the bottom right of the subfile display area. If this facility is required it is activated by means of the SFLEND keyword.

A quirk of the SFLEND keyword is that a conditioning indicator is required. Choose an indicator that is not used in the program, and condition SFLEND to the not-state of that indicator, thus:

```
A  N88                                     SFLEND
```

(The GSD dialects of COBOL have language extensions to allow RPG indicators to be tested and set. AS/400 COBOL programmers do not need a detailed understanding of indicators, but need to know enough about them to understand the uses within DDS.)

The subfile control format may be displayed without the attached subfile being displayed, but the subfile may not be displayed unless its control format is also displayed. The DDS keywords, which require conditioning indicators, are SFLDSP and SFLDSPCTL.

They would typically be coded (with arbitrary choice of indicators) as follows:

```
A  21                                      SFLDSPCTL
A  22                                      SFLDSP
```

and the code within RPG to display the subfile would be (note that the command is always issued to the control format):

```
C              SETON              21
C              SETON              22
C              EXFMT DSPR1C1
C              SETOF              21
C              SETOF              22
```

(The EXFMT verb is equivalent to a WRITE immediately followed by a READ, and some programmers prefer to use the latter form; COBOL programmers have no choice as there is no equivalent to EXFMT in COBOL).

Two further important keywords are SFLDLT, which deletes all records currently within the subfile, and SFLCLR which blanks out existing subfile records, but does not remove them. Conditioning indicators are mandatory here too.

The coding is very similar to that for SFLDSPCTL (again with arbitrary choice of indicators) as follows:

```
A  23                              SFLDLT
A  24                              SFLCLR
```

and within RPG the code to delete the subfile would be:

```
C           SETON                  23
C           WRITE DSPR1C1
C           SETOF                  23
```

It can now be seen why an indicator is mandatory for the SFLDSPCTL. Situations can arise, such as the last example, where a write is issued to the control format without any screen I/O being intended.

Early releases of CPF, the System/38's operating system, restricted the number of subfiles which could be active at any one time to three. This restriction has since been eased, so SFLDLT is not as important as it used to be, however there are possible performance implications, which will be discussed in Part 2 of this Chapter.

Another pair of linked keywords is SFLPAG and SFLSIZ. SFLPAG gives the number of subfile records which may be fitted onto a single page (i.e. screen) after leaving room for any other formats needed.

SFLSIZ gives the total number of records permitted in the subfile. But, and it is a very important but, if SFLSIZ = SFLPAG + 1 then SFLSIZ is treated as unlimited, although the general restriction that a subfile may not contain more than 9999 records still applies.

A subfile may be initialised with the number of records specified by SFLPAG. The fields will be blank if alphanumeric, and zero if numeric, and this is achieved by means of the SFLINZ keyword.

Closely related to SFLPAG is SFLLIN, which permits small subfile records to be displayed side-by-side, so showing more records on a screen. This is the only exception to the rule of (at least) one line per record.

What the keyword actually specifies is the number of spaces to be left between subfile records displayed side-by-side. If it is omitted or set to zero OS/400 assumes that subfile records are to be displayed one per line.

The format is:

```
A                                  SFLLIN(5)
```

meaning that five spaces must be left between the columns of displayed output.

The opposite situation, of records that are too big to fit on one line, is catered for by the SFLDROP keyword. While there is no restriction on the number of lines that each record of a subfile may occupy, multi-line records often require excessive scrolling by the user.

Using SFLDROP, only the first line of each record is displayed, and the user toggles between the first line and all lines by pressing the designated command key.

The format is:

```
     A                                          SFLDROP(CF03)
```

where CF03 denotes that toggling is to be done by command-key 3.

12.4 Identifying subfiles to RPG

Subfiles are made known to the RPG compiler by means of kontinuation lines to the File Specification, which link each subfile to the fields which are to contain their relative record numbers, thus:

```
FXYZFILE    CF    E              WORKSTN
F                                     RRN11 KSFILE DSPR1S1
F                                     RRN21 KSFILE DSPR2S1
```

The familiar RPG CHAIN command (similar in function to the random READ construct in COBOL) may be used to retrieve a specific record from the subfile using its relative record number.

The AS/400 offers the facility to specify fields as "hidden" within the screen formats. The current relative record number may be written to each subfile record just like any other field, hidden or visible.

One easy way of setting up an impromptu menu is to write the relative record number visibly to each subfile record, then invite the user to specify his choice by a number keyed into a field in a page-footing format. The DDS code is:

```
     A          R DSPR1S1                  SFL
     A             .
     A             .
     A          R DSPR1C1                  SFLCTL(DSPR1S1)
     A             .
     A             .
     A          R DSPR1A
     A             REQ         4S 0B
```

The corresponding RPG code is as follows:

```
C           SETON               21
C           SETON               22
C           EXFMT  DSPR1C1
C           SETOF               21
C           SETOF               22
C           READ   DSPR1A              71
C           CALL   AR,REQ
```

Note that the implied read in EXFMT applies only to format DSPR1C1. A READ is required to access the contents of DSPR1A.

The relative record number is used also in DDS, in conjunction with the SFLRCDNBR keyword, to specify which subfile record is to appear at the top of the screen when the subfile is first displayed, and the two are tied together through DDS as follows:

```
A           RECNO          4S 0H                 SFLRCDNBR
```

By default, the screen is rolled one page at a time, however this may be overridden by the SFLROLVAL keyword, which specifies a field to contain a value which stipulates the number of records to roll.

12.5 The RPG READC (Read Changed) command

All the foregoing keywords, except SFL, are specified in the control format; however there is one other keyword, SFLNXTCHG, which is specified in the subfile format.

Some people find the use of this keyword a little puzzling, and it is best explained by means of an example. Suppose you are writing a data capture program, with field validation, using a subfile.

If the user enters invalid data you need to flag it, but you also need to validate his correction.

SFLNXTCHG, which usually makes sense only if used with a conditioning indicator, forces the entire subfile record to be treated as "changed" on the next read to the subfile.

It would typically be coded as follows (with arbitrary choice of indicators):

```
A    41                              SFLNXTCHG
```

SFLNXTCHG is used in conjunction with the RPG verb READC – Read Changed – or its equivalent in other languages (there is an extension to COBOL), which retrieves only changed records from the subfile.

The RPG coding would look something like this:

```
C                       MOVE  'YES'    DSPLY
C           DSPLY       DOWEQ 'YES'
C                       MOVE  'NO'     DSPLY
C
C                       EXFMT DSPR1C1
C
C                       READC DSPR1S1                71
C           *IN71       DOWEQ '1'
C                         .
C                         .
C                       validate (set ERRORS)
C                         .
C                         .
C           ERRORS      IFEQ  'YES'
C                       MOVE  'YES'    DSPLY
C                       SETON                        41
C                       UPDAT DSPR1S1
C                       SETOF                        41
C                       END
C                       READC DSPR1S1                71
C                         .
C                       END
C                       END
```

Note that a READC to an empty subfile will result in a program crash not, as you might reasonably expect, in an end of file condition.

Subfiles can appear in unexpected places. For example, the text editors on the AS/400 are simply subfile programs, and some command prompts are also implemented by means of subfiles.

The first part of this chapter has described the raw materials of subfile programming. The second part discusses programming technique, with particular reference to performance considerations.

Now and again it is desirable that succeeding lines of a subfile should have totally different layouts. There is no direct way of achieving this, but it can be done indirectly by defining the subfile record as a single field 79 bytes long, then moving to it appropriate data structures which have been set up elsewhere.

Part 2: Performance

12.6 Basics of hardware cost vs programmers' time

Twenty years ago, when COBOL was hot from the laboratories, its protagonists admitted that it was less efficient than the assembler languages which went before, but claimed that the benefits – easier to write code, and improved maintainability – justified the extra hardware costs involved.

The validity of this argument is taken for granted today, but only because of the huge change in the ratio between the cost of hardware and the cost of programmers. And of course, history repeats itself. There are numerous instances today where there is similarly a trade-off between two ways of achieving an objective, the first involving spending less on hardware but more on programmers' salaries, and the second the other way round. It should be obvious (though often it is not) that the *total* cost is what matters. However it is not necessarily the deciding factor.

Other considerations include the availability of suitably skilled programmers and, where time is of the essence, the fact that spending the money on hardware will usually get results sooner. Such thoughts are what make programming a craft rather than an exact science, and should be borne firmly in mind when tackling subfiles on an AS/400.

Before proceeding let us briefly review two important concepts from the first part of this chapter. Firstly, subfiles are somewhat misnamed, because they are in fact not files at all, but are implemented as arrays.

12.7 Indefinite length subfiles

Secondly, if the subfile size is equal to page size plus one (i.e. SFLSIZ = SFLPAG + 1) then the subfile will be treated as being of variable length. In other words, the array will be created somewhat as if the COBOL OCCURS DEPENDING ON construct had been used.

The implications for performance are obvious: if every user is continuously creating large subfiles the available main storage will rapidly be used up, and the machine will start "thrashing" to accommodate the demand for virtual storage.

12.8 Handling of ROLLUP/ROLLDOWN – auto vs manual

Some sites try to avoid this storage problem by imposing an installation standard prohibiting the use of variable length subfiles. However, doing so implies that the programs will handle the [Roll Up] and [Roll Down] keys, rather than leaving them to OS/400.

This means that these keys have to be "enabled": the operating system is told not to handle them, but instead to pass the request on to the application program. The application program in turn has to contain considerable additional code in order to handle loading the data to the subfile a portion at a time.

Is there not a sense of *dêja vu* in this? We are back in the position of a programmer contending that a job should be done in assembler even though this requires more work than doing it in COBOL, out of consideration for the machine resources saved.

While machine resources are unquestionably saved, we are flying in the face of overwhelming experience that the high-level way is nearly always better. Note *nearly* always. One can easily think of applications which mainframers to this day tackle in Assembler rather than COBOL, but they are very much the exception – usually programs which are in continuous and widespread use – for example the programs which drive ATMs.

It is worth pointing out that when we opt to handle the roll keys ourselves we are, in effect, rewriting in a high level language that which the IBM laboratory has already written in a low level language, and that our code is likely to be less efficient than theirs, probably by a factor of at least ten.

This then, is the first key question when planning a subfile program: do we use a fixed or variable length subfile? (Of course, if you work for an installation whose standards prohibit variable length subfiles then the decision is made for you, unless you are willing to risk the wrath of the development manager.)

Assuming that the choice is left to you, consider first how often the program is likely to be used, and whether it will be used during the computer's busy periods.

There is very little point in going to great lengths to ensure efficiency in a program which is to be used only once a year, on the Saturday following the financial year end; or in one-off programs.

12.9 Search keys

The next thing to look at is whether it is possible to restrict the search keys more stringently. (Arguably this has more to do with systems design than with program design, but anyone who insists that there should be no interaction between these two functions should rejoin the real world.)

We should consider the best case, the worst case, and the average case.

Suppose we are writing a program for an insurance company to search its file of policy holders by name. This would typically be required where a policy holder has come in to make an inquiry but has forgotten his number.

If the surname is Snodgrass we probably won't have a problem, but if it is Smith, we probably will. Obvious ways of tightening the search argument are to call for any or all of sex, initial, and date of birth though such filters should, of course, be optional.

This example is drawn from a real life investigation, which turned up exactly one Snodgrass, and 17 Goodalls irrespective of initial, but 742 Smiths with the initial J alone.

Clearly Snodgrass is no problem, and the Goodalls can be accommodated without difficulty but, even with further filtering by sex and date of birth, the Smiths appear to present an impassable stumbling block. Or do they?

This is where a dash of common sense is called for. People with the surname Smith and initial J are very well aware that theirs is a common name. They are well used to being confused with others, and consequently are most unlikely to demand that an insurance company recognise them without a policy number.

And suppose that, once a year or so, a particularly "difficult" member of the clan makes this demand. Certainly we shall have to create an unacceptably large subfile but, remembering that it is only once a year, does it matter?

Users are generally quite receptive to suggestions as to how to improve their response times. It is worth explaining to them during user education that lengthy subfiles will damage everybody's responses, including their own.

They tend to forget this once the training sessions are over, and need to be reminded. A good way is to display the subfile record count every time the subfile is displayed. After all, you have to keep track of the subfile relative record number anyway, and the extra effort to display it is negligible.

12.10 Variable record lengths

There is one other difficulty that sometimes keeps programmers from using variable length subfiles, and that is that they do not support optional fields – i.e. fields whose display is conditioned by indicators.

This is easily circumvented by displaying the fields unconditionally but conditioning display attributes of **PR**otect and **N**on-**D**isplay (i.e. dark) to the not state of the required indicator.

In other words, instead of this:

```
          A    33         FLDXYZ    R     B    14   14
```

code this:

```
          A               FLDXYZ    R     B    14   14
          A    N33                                       DSPATR(PR ND)
```

12.11 Multiple active subfiles

Remember that the size of a subfile means, in this context, its size in bytes, not the number of records in it. If it looks as though there is a risk of a subfile growing unacceptably large, consider whether it is possible to reduce the amount of information carried in the subfile record, and display this instead, upon demand, in a following screen.

Remember also that hidden fields must be included when calculating the subfile record size, and so must those which are displayed only when a subfile drop (keyword SFLDROP) is in effect.

In the first part of this chapter we learned that early releases of CPF restricted the programmer to three active subfiles at any given moment, but that this restriction has now been lifted, and of course does not apply to OS/400 at all.

Presumably the purpose behind the original restriction was to prevent programmers from having several active subfiles hanging off each program in a long invocation stack.

Just because we are no longer forbidden to do this sort of thing, does not mean that it is now a good idea! At the earliest possible opportunity get rid of any subfiles which are no longer needed, (by means of a write to the controlling format, having set to on the indicator which governs the SFLDLT keyword).

12.12 Importance of field naming

In RPG, but not in COBOL or PL/I, the use of MOVE instructions, to transfer the data from the input database file to the subfile, can be avoided provided that the same field names are used in both.

This drastically reduces the size of the object program, the complexity of writing it, and the number of machine instructions needing to be executed when it is invoked.

Every time the screen is rolled a substantial amount of both line and CPU activity is generated, and this is equally true whether the roll is handled by the application or by the operating system. Use the SFLLIN keyword wherever reasonably possible, to keep rolling to a minimum.

12.13 Message subfiles

The message subfile is a special case within the general subfile concept. The idea is that messages are sent to a designated part of the screen, identified by the MSGLOC keyword.

Very possibly, there will be more messages than are able to fit into the MSGLOC area. By treating them as a subfile, it is possible to have as many messages as you like.

The user simply places his cursor on any message and presses [Roll Up] or [Roll Down].

The details of how this is done owe much more to CL than to RPG. It is beyond the scope of this book to go into a detailed account of how message queues and the associated CL commands work, but Appendix D contains an example of how to use a message subfile.

13

Journalling and Commitment Control

13.1 Problems with a corrupted database

One of the major practical difficulties with database technology is what to do if the database becomes corrupted. Under the old-fashioned flat file system it was easy: you simply restored the file from the back-up copy, corrected the error, and re-ran.

Because a database is shared amongst many users, an attempt to correct an error in this way would be likely to have the undesired effect of removing other user's transactions, as well as the desired one of correcting your own.

13.2 Journalling the changes

The first part of the solution to restoring the database, is to maintain a journal of changes, but this too raises a query. Suppose the problem is a program crash: how do you know whether the crash happened before or after the program changed data?

The answer is that you don't, and the only way you can be sure is to journal both before and after images of each record changed.

If the faulty program changes record(s) before writing the journal(s) it may have gone down after writing to the database, but before recording the change in the journal; if after, there may be a record in the journal, but no corresponding change to the file.

These problems are common to all databases, whether hierarchical, networked or relational, and any DBMS software worth its rental will offer some such means of recovery.

13.3 Applying journal changes

A moment's thought will tell you that even if you have a journal there is a massive amount of work in unpicking and re-creating, for example, a day's workings of a large database.

And it is important that you do. Imagine a banking installation, where a defective program allowed a spurious client record to be created. Subsequently, another program might permit a cash withdrawal on the strength of that spurious record.

13.4 Reason for commitment control

So in the correction process, it is not enough to remove the bad record; we must also remove all transactions posted to the database subsequent to the addition of the bad record, and then re-enter them.

During re-entry, the invalid cash withdrawal will be picked up, because this time the existence check against the client file will fail.

13.5 Commitment control

There are various ways of at least partially automating the recovery process, and on AS/400 this takes the form of Commitment Control.

The idea is that a batch of changes – a "transaction" – is written to the database as a single entity when, and only when, a commit command is issued.

13.6 Rollback

If one decides half way through a transaction to abort it, a rollback command is issued, and all updates and writes performed since the previous commit are reversed. A transaction is defined as the total activity embraced by a single COMIT statement.

Journalling may be run without commitment control, and basic journalling offers the choice of logging after-image only, or before- and-after images. However, as soon as commitment control is invoked, OS/400 forces before-and-after images.

Note that use of before-and-after images will not double the space required, because OS/400 makes some entries to the journal for its own internal purposes, and these will not be affected.

13.7 Creating your own journal entries

All journals are time-stamped by OS/400, and it is possible to write your own journal entries in addition to the before-and-after images, and those created by OS/400. This is done using the SNDJRNE (Send Journal Entry) CL command, which may be accessed from RPG or COBOL by means of QCMDEXC on the AS/400, or QCAEXEC on the System/38.

Logging OPEN and CLOSE operations is optional. This saves a fair amount of journal activity – especially in a largely on-line environment – but removes the facility for a history of file access. If they are used, and provided all files are closed at the same invocation level as they are opened, it is relatively easy to identify abnormal terminations.

IBM supplies a library called JRNAID which contains a number of useful tools, including a program which checks journal receivers for "incomplete file operations". (It assumes open/close at the same invocation level.)

Commitment control involves the use of two new verbs in the high level language – in RPG III they are COMIT and ROLBK (see sections 7.12.12 and 7.12.62); in COBOL these same verbs are spelt with rather more regard for the English tongue, and of course, become reserved words.

13.8 BGN/ENDCMTCTL

Commitment control itself is started by the BGNCMTCTL CL command in the invoking CL, and ended by an ENDCMTCTL, after control is returned from the application program(s).

These two commands are heavy on the machine, and should be issued sparingly.

It is unfortunately possible to have a given file being used under commitment control by some programs, but not by others. The potential problems should be obvious, and data added by those not under commitment control is referred to as "dirty data".

Users not under commitment control can read records locked by users who are, so a subsequent rollback can create havoc.

13.9 Journals and receivers

Two AS/400 objects are involved in journalling (whether or not under commitment control). They are:

> 1) The journal itself, which may be thought of as a funnel,
>
> to
>
> 2) The journal receiver, which contains the journalled data.

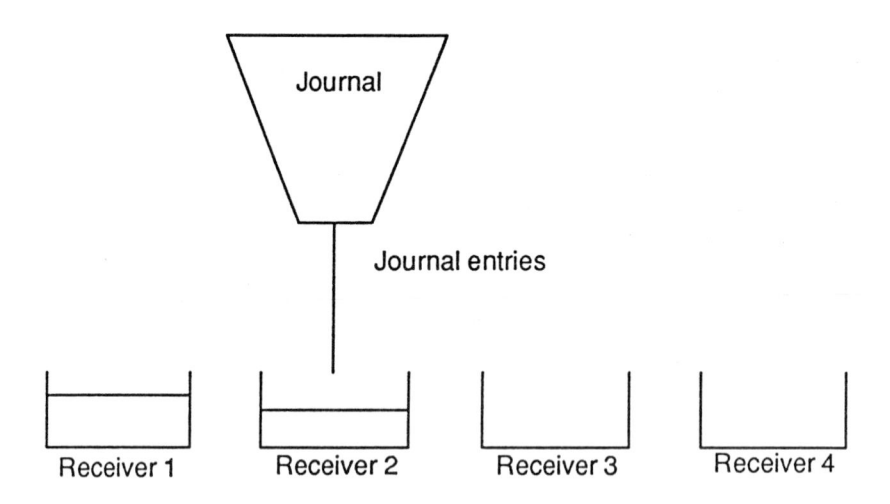

```
        Journal
          |
          |
     Journal entries
   |      |      |      |
   |      |      |      |
Receiver 1  Receiver 2  Receiver 3  Receiver 4
```

If you are the sort of person who wears a belt and braces, and still worries that they might both snap at the same moment, then consider using dual receivers.

Realistically, the only likely need for these is if there is a head crash or similar failure on the drive on which the journals are resident, so if you decide to use dual receivers, be sure to put them on different spindles. Similarly, journal receivers and database files should be placed on different spindles.

Obviously two journal receivers will require twice as much disk space as one, but the CPU overhead is not doubled.

13.10 Flip-flop logging

It is possible to detach a receiver from a journal and substitute another (not to be confused with dual receivers), which makes possible "flip-flop" logging.

The idea behind "flip-flop" logging is to avoid having to dedicate a tape drive. Instead the available disk area is divided into two sections, call them A and B. The log is written to A until A is full, then it immediately switches to B and starts a job to copy A to tape. When B is full, A is checked to make sure the copy is complete, whereupon a job is released to copy B to tape, while logging continues to A.

This works well provided that the available tape drive can write data considerably quicker than the data is written to the logging mechanism; if not, the entire database will hang while the copying operation is completed.

If the tape drive has the necessary capacity, but is not available again the database will hang – the level of user annoyance in this situation has to be experienced to be believed.

Two common causes are:

1) The drive is being used for something else

2) The operator is not "on the ball"

In general, flip-flop logging is more hassle than it is worth, and if the volume of journals is too great to be accommodated on disk, it is worth making a great fuss to get your management to buy you a dedicated tape drive.

13.11 Sizing of logical transactions

Both excessively large and excessively small transactions are undesirable, and it is important to strike a happy medium. This is difficult to define, and is really mostly a matter for experience and common sense. Here are some suggestions which may be helpful.

First examine the application to see if a logical transaction presents itself. If not, consider the impact of a rollback on the terminal user. For example, if invoices were being captured, it would not be sensible to have the user capture 99 of 100 line items, then be rolled back to the beginning.

On the other hand, one would not wish to COMIT after each line item. Probably a sensible compromise would be 10 line items per transaction with, obviously, some additional check to ensure that half-captured invoices did not enter the system.

13.12 Recording successful completions

automatic ROLBK rather than COMIT

Recovery operations are made very much easier if the successful completion of each transaction is recorded, and the SNDJRNE CL command offers an excellent way of doing this.

If an application program terminates abnormally, for example, due to an invalid index, it will close the files; consequently it will not be immediately obvious that an abnormal termination has occurred – i.e. there will be no difference between the opening and closing invocation levels – whereas if successful completions are journalled it is relatively simple to back out to the last one.

Note that, unlike most 4GLs, if a commitment control group (i.e. the interval between BGNCMTCTL and ENDCMTCTL) terminates without explicitly ending the transaction, an automatic ROLBK rather than an automatic COMIT will be generated. Similarly, if ENDCMTCTL is issued following a series of updates and/or outputs, but without a COMIT being issued first, again an automatic ROLBK rather than an automatic COMIT will be generated.

13.13 Record locking

The database is updated by the UPDAT command, not – as in most other DBMS's – by the subsequent COMIT. This implies that whenever ROLBK is invoked a physical rollback is performed, rather than merely omitting to write to disk the data being held in an intermediate buffer.

Record locking is an area where there are some major deviations from normal programming expectations. If more than one record is read from a single update file all – not only the last one – are locked until a COMIT or ROLBK is issued.

13.14 RPG cycle and commitment control

The RPG cycle should not be used under commitment control because indicators such as L1-L9 and MR are not updated by a ROLBK. Data areas likewise are not updated, and so should be avoided or used with circumspection.

The DSPJOB (Display Job) CL command has an option which enables one to display the commitment control status.

A maximum of 1024 records may be locked within one COMIT cycle (i.e. transaction), which is another reason why common sense should be used in setting transaction lengths. If the limit is exceeded message CPF5079 will be issued and may be monitored.

13.15 Locking levels: *CHG and *ALL

Locking may be invoked at two levels, *CHG and *ALL.

If *ALL is used, other programs may not access a locked record even on a read-only basis until a COMIT or ROLBK is issued. This suggests that *CHG should be used unless there is a cast iron reason to do otherwise.

13.16 Locked records

If a record has been locked by program A, and program B attempts to access it, program B will hang for the period defined in the WAITRCD parameter of the file creation command (default value, 60 seconds), then B's read will fail with the error indicator set – if no error indicator is specified B will crash. This does not apply if the file is designated as input (I on column 15 of the F-spec).

This raises the question of what to do if this indicator is set to on.

One possibility would be to ask the user if he wishes to wait, or to cancel his transaction. The latter would lead to a rollback, the former to a retry with the potential to repeat the question.

13.17 The WAITRCD parameter

Note that WAITRCD offers the options *IMMED and *NOMAX in addition to specific periods: *NOMAX would theoretically cause the waiting program to wait for ever, and should thus be used with circumspection.

Note also that the use of *NOMAX will obstruct the AS/400's mechanism for dealing with "deadly embraces".

In general, the WAITRCD default value should not be tampered with other than by those who are familiar enough with its implications that they do not need to read this book.

13.18 "Think time" and locking records

It is highly desirable that records should not be locked during the terminal operator's "think time", which implies that records should be read for the initial display, released, then reread for update.

The data retrieved by the initial read should be stored in a data area, then compared with the data read by the second read to ensure that there have been no (significant) updates of the record between the two reads.

Beware that updated screen fields may be overwritten by the re-read if they have the same name in the display file (*DSPF) as in the database file.

13.19 Impact on CPU load

Obviously all this activity consumes a certain amount of the machine's resources. The additional CPU load is very roughly 20%, but generally there is a bigger risk of bottle-necks because of increased disk load.

13.20 Journals versus back-ups

When the database needs to be restored, the usual procedure is to restore from the last back-up and then apply the journals. Obviously the more time has elapsed since the last back-up, the more journals will have to be applied, and the longer the whole process will take.

He who relies on the journals rather than taking nightly back-ups is living dangerously.

13.21 Running batch without commitment control

Commitment control is particularly heavy on the system when batch runs are taking place, and it is therefore sometimes suggested that the database should be backed up before batch runs, and commitment control then turned off.

This does have the advantage that it enforces frequent back-ups; on the other hand, batch is normally run at night, when CPU loading is typically a third of what it is in prime time, so a certain amount of extra CPU activity will not matter very much.

13.22   Whip-round programs
what they are – false sense of security

It is worth having what are sometimes called "whip-round" programs. These are programs which check the consistency of the database.

They can take the form of:

1) Comparatively small programs run quite frequently during normal processing, checking batch totals etc. and/or

2) Larger programs run to verify the success of disaster recovery procedures. However, since the nature of a disaster cannot be predicted it is difficult to know in advance what to check.

In either case, the danger of whip round programs is that they may lull people into a sense of false security. The uneventful ending of a whip round program merely means that it hasn't found any errors; it is *not*, repeat not, a guarantee that there is nothing wrong in the database.

13.23 Synchronised checkpoints
how to implement them

Recovery is simplified if the database is periodically synchronised – i.e. brought to a point where there are no half-completed transactions. Once all programs are at this point, the fact is logged by means of a SNDJRNE CL command, and processing may continue.

Synchronised checkpoints may be created by setting up two data areas, one counting active transactions, and the other holding a Yes/No flag indicating whether or not a synchronised checkpoint is impending.

Before commencing a transaction, each application program would check the flag, and if it is set to "yes", the application would go into a wait state (implemented on AS/400 by the DLYJOB CL command). For each transaction started the count would be incremented, and for each one finished, decremented.

A small program would be released whenever a checkpoint was to be taken – perhaps hourly. It would set the flag, then check the count and go into a wait state if it was greater than zero, looping until the count reached zero. It would then issue the checkpoint by means of a SNDJRNE CL command, reset the flag, and terminate.

All the foregoing represents a considerable use of both human and machine resources, and is only of any value if disaster recovery becomes necessary.

13.24 Recovery from hardware failure and database corruption

Recovery may be considered under two broad headings:

❑ Recovery from a power or hardware failure

❑ Restoring the integrity of the database following its corruption, probably by an erroneous program.

The former is fairly straightforward, and consists simply of applying the journals forward from the last back-up.

The latter is not only much more difficult, it is much more difficult to advise on, simply because it is almost impossible to predict what might go wrong. Most installations – AS/400 and other – handle these situations on an *ad hoc* basis.

I personally have only once been involved in a major disaster recovery "for real" (not on an AS/400), and I can assure you that was one of the longest nights of my life!

13.25 Audit trails

An option to the (Display Journal) CL command allows output in the form of a database file, containing details of what was done to any given record, when, where, by whom, and using which program.

Using this as raw material, it is possible to create audit trails sufficient to satisfy the most suspicious auditor. In practice the limits are imposed not so much by the programmer's imagination as by the snowstorm of paper generated. One solution is microfiche output.

The ability to discover the exact history of a given record has obvious applications to trouble shooting, and this is covered in Chapter 14.

13.26 Mirror databases

No account of AS/400 journalling and commitment control would be complete without mention of mirror databases.

Essentially this is a way of guaranteeing that even if the machine room is destroyed by a bomb, the database will be up and running for online users within about five minutes. Which sounds impossible.

Two CPUs are required for this seemingly magic trick, and common sense suggests they should be at least a mile apart. Naturally, modems, switching equipment etc. has to be in place so that the network of terminals may be connected to either CPU.

The CPUs are linked by the aptly nicknamed "golden cable" – golden because it costs so much – which is simply a very high speed data link.

Machine A is used for production, and runs under commitment control. Machine B contains a copy of the database; journals are passed along the golden cable, and used to update the database on B, which thus runs in sync with A.

Apart from providing protection against such improbable events as a bomb in the machine room, mirror data bases make it possible to continue processing the database even while it is being backed up. The only practical use that springs to mind is for providing a 24 hour service from Automatic Teller Machines, rather than shutting them down between 1 a.m. and 2 a.m. for back-ups.

But when did you last want an ATM at that hour ?

14

Debugging

14.1 Older systems – with the DEBUG verb

A powerful and sophisticated array of debugging tools is one of the main reasons why the AS/400 offers such a high level of programmer productivity.

As with so many aspects of this remarkable machine's architecture, it seems that IBM distilled the best from its own and its competitors past endeavours and combined it all into one machine.

For example, the ability to stop an executing program and manipulate fields within it was first seen on the PL/I Checkout Compiler on IBM's mainframes, around 1970. The trace facility had a remarkably effective progenitor on Burroughs' long-defunct B200-B300 range, which came into service in the early Sixties.

As mentioned previously, RPG is an old language, and many of the facilities found in it are vestiges, provided only for compatibility with earlier versions.

A prime example of this is the DEBUG verb. DEBUG statements inserted in the C-specs cause the program to produce a list of the contents of fields at the time the DEBUG in question was encountered and, optionally, the statement number.

Many an RPG II programmer blessed DEBUG, even though it had the drawback of requiring the program to be recompiled twice, once to insert the DEBUG statements, and again to remove them when they had served their purpose.

14.2 AS/400 debug system – STRDBG

The RPG III programmer is well advised to forget DEBUG: there are much, much better ways of achieving the same effects, and without the recompiling hassle.

The key to the AS/400's Aladdin's cave of debugging tools is the STRDBG (Start Debug) command. On System/38 this was called ENTDBG (Enter Debug), but the parameters have not changed.

Note that it is a CL command, *not* an RPG verb. In theory it can be used in batch mode, but in practice is invariably used interactively.

Simply type STRDBG and hit [CF4], to prompt for parameters – see Figure 14.1 for an example of the prompt display. The first of these is the name of the program to be placed under the microscope.

```
                          Start Debug (STRDBG)

      Type choices, press Enter.

      Program  . . . . . . . . . . . PGM              *NONE
        Library  . . . . . . . . . .
                                   + for more values

      Default program  . . . . . . . DFTPGM           *PGM
      Maximum trace statements . . . MAXTRC           200
      Trace full . . . . . . . . . . TRCFULL          *STOPTRC
      Update production files  . . . UPDPROD          *NO
```

Figure 14.1

Again, theoretically, more than one program can be placed in debug mode at a time, and the debugging environment can be used without a program. In practice these latter facilities are very seldom used.

If you issue a STRDBG command while already in debug mode, the operating system will give an error message, similarly if you issue an ENDDBG while not in debug mode.

The DFTPGM parameter may safely be ignored, and the next important parameter is MAXTRC, which stipulates the maximum number of statements to be traced if the trace (see section 14.4) is invoked, of which more anon. The default value is 200.

What happens once you have traced 200 statements (or whatever number you request), depends on the option you choose for the TRCFULL parameter, either *STOPTRC or *WRAP, (the default being *STOPTRC). Before explaining the meaning of these it is necessary to understand that the trace is implemented as a subfile. (For a discussion of subfiles see Chapter 12). Because a subfile is in fact an array, there are performance implications in making it too large, while if it is too small it may not be able to do the job. The default value of 200 is a sensible compromise; by all means use more if you have to – just be aware of the implications.

There is a special case in which MAXTRC should be set to 1 – this is discussed below, where we look at tracing in more detail.

If *WRAP was specified for the TRCFULL parameter, any further statements traced will overwrite the subfile, starting at the beginning.

If *STOPTRC was specified then the trace will stop, but it will do so on a screen identical to that for breakpoints – see section 14.3.

The last parameter on the STRDBG command is UPDPROD (Update Production [Files]), and the options are *YES and *NO, *NO being the default. The intention is to prevent accidental updating of production files but, in practice, this safety device tends to cause more problems than it avoids, and most experienced programmers use *YES.

A close cousin of STRDBG is CHGDBG (Change Debug), which offers exactly the same parameters and options as STRDBG, plus the *SAME option, which is self explanatory. CHGDBG may be used only when in debug mode (else what would it change?).

As hinted above, a debugging session is terminated with an ENDDBG (End Debug) command, which has no parameters. The only points to watch on ENDDBG are the performance aspects, and the fact that it destroys the trace subfile – so do not issue it prematurely.

Debug mode is heavy on machine resources, so issue your ENDDBG as early as possible. (Making a point of issuing it as early as possible also helps to prevent forgetting that you are in debug mode.)

14.3 Breakpoints
DSPPGMVAR and CHGPGMVAR, hex or char

Apart from the trace, the main use of debug mode is to provide for breakpoints. A breakpoint is a stipulated point in a program – invariably the program specified in the STRDBG command – at which you wish the machine to cease processing and to refer back to you.

It is specified by means of the ADDBKP (Add Breakpoint) command – see Figure 14.2, and may be removed by means of the RMVBKP (Remove Breakpoint) command, otherwise all breakpoints are removed automatically by an ENDDBG.

Breakpoints may be modified while active by means of the CHGBKP (Change Breakpoint) command.

Multiple breakpoints may be specified for a single program, though in practice specifying more than about half a dozen confuses more than it helps.

```
                              Add Breakpoint (ADDBKP)
          Type choices, press Enter.
          Statement identifier . . . . . . STMT          > 3000
                              + for more values
          Program variables:              PGMVAR
            Program variable . . . . . . .              *NONE
            Basing pointer variable  . . .
                              + for more values
                              + for more values
          Output format  . . . . . . . . . OUTFMT        *CHAR
          Program  . . . . . . . . . . . . PGM           *DFTPGM

                                    Additional Parameters
          Char output start position . . . START         1
          Characters to display  . . . . . LEN           *DCL
          Skip value . . . . . . . . . . . SKIP          0
          Breakpoint condition:            BKPCOND
            Variable . . . . . . . . . . .               *NONE
            Operator . . . . . . . . . . .
            Compare value or variable  . .
          Breakpoint program to call . . . BKPPGM        *NONE
            Library  . . . . . . . . . . .
```

Figure 14.2

Like any other command, ADDBKP may be prompted by means of [CF4]. The first thing to be entered is the number of the statement at which you wish the program to stop, or "break".

This *must* be specified using the full statement number, but without the decimal point displayed by SEU (the Source Edit Utility).

For example, statement 38 will be shown by SEU as 38.00, and must be entered in the ADDBKP command as 3800. Any deviation will lead to what IBM manuals call "unpredictable results".

Having stopped the program, it is more often than not desirable to look at the contents of one or more fields, which can be specified on the ADDBKP command.

By placing a plus sign against "+ for more", a break may be specified to occur at more than one statement. The difference between doing this and issuing multiple ADDBKPs is that this will cause the specified field(s) to be displayed each time. Of course, if different fields are required at different breakpoints, then multiple ADDBKP commands will be needed.

The programmer is further invited to specify whether the field(s) are to be displayed in character or hex, the default mode being character. Note, however, that an invalid value encountered in a numeric field will cause the display to be in hex, even if character was specified.

The number of characters to be displayed defaults to the length of the field, but this may be over-ridden – a facility not often used, but sometimes useful, especially when displaying a very long field.

The BKPCOND (Breakpoint Condition) parameter enables the programmer to specify that this breakpoint is to be activated only when a stipulated field contains a given value.

For example, if the breakpoint was placed immediately following a READ command, it could be stipulated that the break would occur only when a specific claim had been read.

This is a tempting facility, but use it with caution – it can be very heavy on machine resources.

```
                        Display Breakpoint

    Statement/Instruction . . . . . . . . . : 3000 /005A
    Program . . . . . . . . . . . . . . . . : UDDSR1
    Recursion level . . . . . . . . . . . . : 1
    Start position  . . . . . . . . . . . . : 1
    Format  . . . . . . . . . . . . . . . . : *CHAR
    Length  . . . . . . . . . . . . . . . . : *DCL

    Variable  . . . . . . . . . . . . . . . : FLDTYP
      Type  . . . . . . . . . . . . . . . . :     CHARACTER
      Length  . . . . . . . . . . . . . . . :     1
      *...+....1....+....2....+....3....+....4....+....5
      'A'




    Press Enter to continue.

    F3=Exit program    F10=Command entry
```

Figure 14.3

When the breakpoint occurs, a screen will appear – see Figure 14.3 – displaying any fields which were specified. Along the bottom will be the advice that [CF03] will cancel the run, [ENTER] will cause processing to continue, and [CF10] will call the command entry screen. (On System/38 the run is cancelled by [CF1] and command entry is called by [CF3].)

The call to the command entry screen is the really useful option, because it enables you to run any command or program you wish, while the program being debugged is held at the breakpoint.

The possibilities thus made available are limited only by your imagination. Some of the more commonly used facilities would be a database interrogation utility such as VIEW, the CHGDBG, CHGBKP and CHGTRC commands, and the various trace-related commands discussed below.

Also important are DSPPGMVAR (Display Program Variable) and CHGPGMVAR (Change Program Variable). The former allows you to look at any field(s) you may have omitted to specify in the original ADDBKP command, and the latter enables you to change the contents of a field before proceeding.

```
UPRTRPG

                                       Add Trace (ADDTRC)
 Type choices, press Enter.
 Statements to trace:            STMT
   Starting statement identifier                    *ALL
   Ending statement identifier  .
                                 + for more values
 Program variables:              PGMVAR
   Program variable . . . . . . .                   *NONE
   Basing pointer variable  . . .
                                 + for more values
                                 + for more values
 Output format  . . . . . . . . . OUTFMT            *CHAR

                                 Additional Parameters
 Char output start position . . . START             1
 Characters to display  . . . . . LEN               *DCL
 When output  . . . . . . . . . . OUTVAR            *CHG
```

Figure 14.4

For example, an indicator may have been set to on when it was intended to set it to off; this may be rectified, and testing may then proceed without the need to recompile. Or an error flag may be set to off if it is not relevant to the problem at hand.

14.4 The Trace

how to single step. TRCDTA implemented as an array – performance implications; augmenting the trace

The trace may be used on its own, or in conjunction with breakpoints. A useful technique is to run the program up to a specified statement, where it is stopped by means of a breakpoint. The user then hits [CF10] ([CF3] on System/38) to get a command screen, from which the trace is invoked.

What does the trace do? It provides a list of all the statements executed with, optionally, a display of the contents of one or more variables. These contents may be displayed only when they change (the default) or after each statement. (You have to be really desperate to use this last option!)

The trace is invoked by means of the ADDTRC (Add Trace) command. Again, [CF4] provides a prompt – see Figure 14.4 – if required. An ADDTRC command may be used to select one or more variables, and also one or more blocks of statement numbers. The rules for ADDTRC parameters are very similar to those for the ADDBKP command. Statement numbers must be provided in the same way (i.e. statement 38 must be coded 3800, not 38 or 38.00), and the variable(s) to be displayed are also specified in the same way.

The default situation is that all executed statements are displayed. In many cases this will lead to the display of vast numbers of superfluous statements: each line on the input specs, i.e. each field in each file being read or written, will be displayed. A situation rapidly arises in which you cannot see the wood for the trees.

This may be avoided by using the STMT parameter to specify that only C-specs are to be traced. A useful tip is to code any subroutine(s) which do a substantial amount of looping at the end of the program, so that they may easily be omitted from the trace. Otherwise it becomes necessary to specify several blocks of statements to be traced.

Just as there is a CHGBKP command, so there is a CHGTRC command, though this tends to be used less frequently.

A common mistake made by newcomers to the machine is to attempt to change the MAXTRC value by means of the CHGTRC command, when what is required is the CHGDBG command.

Having generated a trace – see Figure 14.5a – we now need to look at it, and we do this using the DSPTRCDTA (Display Trace Data) command. This has two output options: output may be printed, or it may be viewed on the screen, which is the default situation. Remember that if output is printed it is first sent to a spool file, which itself may be viewed on the screen. For a large trace, this is an attractive option, for two reasons.

1) All the normal spool file options are available, i.e. scanning, top and bottom commands etc.

2) Once the trace subfile has been output to a spool file, the subfile may be destroyed, which implies that it is now safe to issue an ENDDBG command.

As stated, the raw trace output provides a list of the statement numbers of all statements executed (plus, optionally, a display of the contents of one or more variables). This is a great deal better than nothing, but does involve much to-ing and fro-ing to the program listing to discover what each statement is doing.

A trace augmentor utility is available which converts the raw trace output into a spool file in which the RPG statements are listed alongside the statement numbers. Not only does this greatly simplify the use of the trace, it also provides many more targets for scanning if the spool file is displayed on the screen, (which the utility does automatically).

Compare the two Trace Data Display examples – see Figures 14.5a and 14.5b. The raw trace output (Figure 14.5a) repetitively tells us the program name and invocation level, plus providing

```
              Statement/
Program       Instruction        Recursion Level      Sequence Number
MG01CMT       5700                     1                     1

Start position . . . . . . . . . . . . : 1
Length . . . . . . . . . . . . . . . . : *DCL
Format . . . . . . . . . . . . . . . . : *CHAR
Variable . . . . . . . . . . . . . . . : EXIT
  Type . . . . . . . . . . . . . . . . :   CHARACTER
  Length . . . . . . . . . . . . . . . :   1
  *...+....1....+....2....+....3....+....4....+....5
  ' '

              Statement/
Program       Instruction        Recursion Level      Sequence Number
MG01CMT       3700                     1                     2
MG01CMT       3900                     1                     3
MG01CMT       4400                     1                     4
MG01CMT       5300                     1                     5
MG01CMT       5600                     1                     6
MG01CMT       5700                     1                     7
MG01CMT       3700                     1                     8
MG01CMT       3900                     1                     9
MG01CMT       4400                     1                    10
MG01CMT       5300                     1                    11
MG01CMT       5600                     1                    12
MG01CMT       5700                     1                    13
MG01CMT       3700                     1                    14
MG01CMT       3900                     1                    15
MG01CMT       4400                     1                    16
MG01CMT       5300                     1                    17
MG01CMT       5600                     1                    18
MG01CMT       5700                     1                    19
MG01CMT       3700                     1                    20
MG01CMT       3900                     1                    21
MG01CMT       4400                     1                    22
MG01CMT       5300                     1                    23
MG01CMT       5600                     1                    24
MG01CMT       5700                     1                    25
MG01CMT       3700                     1                    26
MG01CMT       3900                     1                    27
MG01CMT       4400                     1                    28
MG01CMT       4500                     1                    29
MG01CMT       4600                     1                    30
MG01CMT       4700                     1                    31
MG01CMT       4800                     1                    32
MG01CMT       6100                     1                    33
MG01CMT       6200                     1                    34
MG01CMT       6400                     1                    35
MG01CMT       6500                     1                    36

Start position . . . . . . . . . . . . : 1
Length . . . . . . . . . . . . . . . . : *DCL
Format . . . . . . . . . . . . . . . . : *CHAR
*Variable  . . . . . . . . . . . . . . : EXIT
  Type . . . . . . . . . . . . . . . . :   CHARACTER
  Length . . . . . . . . . . . . . . . :   1
  *...+....1....+....2....+....3....+....4....+....5
  'N'

              Statement/
Program       Instruction        Recursion Level      Sequence Number
MG01CMT       6600                     1                    37
MG01CMT       6700                     1                    38
MG01CMT       6900                     1                    39
MG01CMT       7000                     1                    40
MG01CMT       7100                     1                    41
MG01CMT       7200                     1                    42

Start position . . . . . . . . . . . . : 1
Length . . . . . . . . . . . . . . . . : *DCL
Format . . . . . . . . . . . . . . . . : *CHAR
*Variable  . . . . . . . . . . . . . . : EXIT
  Type . . . . . . . . . . . . . . . . :   CHARACTER
  Length . . . . . . . . . . . . . . . :   1
  *...+....1....+....2....+....3....+....4....+....5
  'Y'
```

Figure 14.5a

Debugging

```
       5700  C              END                                    1
             Variable . . . . . . . . . . . . . : EXIT
             *...+....1....+....2....+....3....+....4....+....5
             ' '
       3700  C              *IN81    DOWNE '1'                     2
       3900  C              SRCSEQ   IFGE  5561         EO LIVE SRC 3
       4400  C              OPCD     IFEQ  'BEGSR'                  4
       5300  C                       EXCPT OUT1                     5
       5600  C                       READ  X@MG01           81      6
       5700  C                       END                            7
       3700  C              *IN81    DOWNE '1'                     8
       3900  C              SRCSEQ   IFGE  5561         EO LIVE SRC 9
       4400  C              OPCD     IFEQ  'BEGSR'                 10
       5300  C                       EXCPT OUT1                    11
       5600  C                       READ  X@MG01           81     12
       5700  C                       END                           13
       3700  C              *IN81    DOWNE '1'                    14
       3900  C              SRCSEQ   IFGE  5561         EO LIVE SRC 15
       4400  C              OPCD     IFEQ  'BEGSR'                 16
       5300  C                       EXCPT OUT1                    17
       5600  C                       READ  X@MG01           81     18
       5700  C                       END                           19
       3700  C              *IN81    DOWNE '1'                    20
       3900  C              SRCSEQ   IFGE  5561         EO LIVE SRC 21
       4400  C              OPCD     IFEQ  'BEGSR'                 22
       5300  C                       EXCPT OUT1                    23
       5600  C                       READ  X@MG01           81     24
       5700  C                       END                           25
       3700  C              *IN81    DOWNE '1'                    26
       3900  C              SRCSEQ   IFGE  5561         EO LIVE SRC 27
       4400  C              OPCD     IFEQ  'BEGSR'                 28
       4500  C                       Z-ADD 1          X            29
       4600  C              FACT1    LOKUP AR,X             82     30
       4700  C              *IN82    IFEQ  '1'                    31
       4800  C                       EXSR  SRBEG                   32
SRBEG  6100  C                       MOVE  SRCDTA HLDSRC           33
SRBEG  6200  C                       MOVE  SRCSEQ HLDSEQ           34
SRBEG  6400  C                       MOVE  'N'    EXIT   1         35
SRBEG  6500  C                       READ  X@MG01           81     36
             *Variable . . . . . . . . . . . . . : EXIT
             *...+....1....+....2....+....3....+....4....+....5
             'N'
SRBEG  6600  C              *IN81    DOWNE '1'                    37
SRBEG  6700  C              EXIT     ANDNE 'Y'                    38
SRBEG  6900  C              COMENT   IFEQ  '*'                    39
SRBEG  7000  C              C10#20   ANDNE *ALL'*'                40
SRBEG  7100  C                       MOVE  'Y'    EXIT            41
SRBEG  7200  C                       EXSR  SR2                    42
             *Variable . . . . . . . . . . . . . : EXIT
             *...+....1....+....2....+....3....+....4....+....5
             'Y'
SR2    8200  C              HLDSEQ   SUB   .01    COMSEQ          43
SR2    8300  C                       EXCPT OUT2                    44
SR2    8400  C                       EXCPT OUT3                    45
SR2    8500  C                       ENDSR                         46
SRBEG  7700  C                       READ  X@MG01           81     47
SRBEG  7800  C                       END                           48
SRBEG  6600  C              *IN81    DOWNE '1'                    49
SRBEG  6700  C              EXIT     ANDNE 'Y'                    50
SRBEG  7900  C                       ENDSR                         51
       4900  C                       ELSE                          52
       5200  C                       ELSE                          53
       5600  C                       READ  X@MG01           81     54
       5700  C                       END                           55
       3700  C              *IN81    DOWNE '1'                    56
       3900  C              SRCSEQ   IFGE  5561         EO LIVE SRC 57
       4400  C              OPCD     IFEQ  'BEGSR'                 58
       5300  C                       EXCPT OUT1                    59
       5600  C                       READ  X@MG01           81     60
                                 * * * * * END OF LISTING * * * * *
```

Figure 14.5b

the literal "Stmt/Inst:" on each line.

The augmented version (Figure 14.5b) has replaced all this with the actual RPG statements (it works with other languages too), and note that on the extreme left it also shows the names of any subroutines which are executed. Any lines which cannot be resolved are passed through unchanged. The augmentor is called UTRC and is available in the UK from Waspforce Ltd. – see Appendix B.

Before leaving the subject of traces we should look at "single stepping".

The first computers to have operating systems were the IBM 360 and its competitors. Earlier machines – so-called second generation machines such as the IBM 1401 and Burroughs B200 had no operating systems. Consequently all the services we now take for granted from an operating system had to be provided either by the operators or from inside the application program.

This was not all bad, however, and these machines had buttons on their consoles which enabled one to execute one machine instruction at a time (in those days all programming was in Assembler, so there was a one to one correspondence between source instructions and machine instructions).

Debugging of particularly knotty problems was greatly facilitated, even though the use of machine resources was horrendous.

On the AS/400 this facility has effectively been restored, working one RPG (or COBOL etc.) statement at a time, and without any machine overhead greater than that for normal tracing.

It works simply by setting MAXTRC to 1, while leaving TRCFULL at the default of *STOPTRC. The net result is that the trace stops on a trace-full breakpoint after each instruction.

14.5 AS/400 Dump

Interpretation. File data. Scan for field names.

Dumps are much less important today than they were on earlier machines, largely because the power of the debugging environment is so great that there is seldom any need to pore over dumps any more. (And the manufacturers of white sticks have lost their programmer market...)

Nevertheless, a great deal of useful information may be obtained from a dump, and it is particularly handy if it is a live program which has blown up, because the data is frequently available automatically without the need to re-create the whole situation in debug mode.

Indeed, if it does become necessary to re-create the whole situation in debug mode, then the information from the trace provides the information needed to set up "test data" consisting of only the offending record(s).

Consider the tiny example program in Figure 14.6, which was deliberately run against an empty file, to raise an end of file condition on statement 2 and a divide by zero on statement 3.

```
SOURCE FILE . . . . . . .  QTEMP/QRPGSRC
MEMBER . . . . . . . . .   QQQ

SEQNBR*...+... 1 ...+... 2 ...+... 3 ...+... 4 ...+... 5 ...+... 6 ...+... 7 ...+... 8 ...+... 9 ...+... 0
   100     FQQQ    IF  E                    DISK
   200     C                       READ QQQ                              01
   300     C            QQQFLD     DIV  QQQFLD    QQQFLD
   400     C                       SETON                    LR

                       * * * *  E N D   O F   S O U R C E  * * * *
```

Figure 14.6

The dump – see Figure 14.7 – begins with program status information, including the number of the statement which blew, the name of the last file used and, towards the end, the date and time the program was compiled, and the source file from which it was compiled – all useful for checking that the correct version of the program has been used.

Next comes a block of information for each file. The entries are self-explanatory, and each block is followed by a dump of the file buffer. In the example no record has been read, so the dump is all blanks.

At the end of the dump is an alphabetic list of program variables and their contents. Even though the list is in alphabetic order, it is frequently useful to pick out a required field by means of the spool file scanning facility.

Note that the indicators are treated as fields whose names begin with *IN, and also as an array whose name is *IN. At the end of the dump are some fields whose names begin with Z, including ZPGMSTUS which does no more than repeat the program status information, in an unformatted fashion.

File and program status information may also be obtained and acted upon from within the program, by means of the file and program status data structures.

14.6 Messages

monitoring, second-level messages

Monitoring for messages is a subject more associated with CL programming, however it is worth noting that the number and text of a message may be obtained from the program status area – from the dump, or within the program by means of a program status data structure.

Many messages have "second level text". The message itself is a single line, and the second level text is a screenful of further explanation. It is accessed by placing the cursor on the message line and pressing HELP.

RPG III FORMATTED DUMP

Program Status Area:
Program Name . . . . : QTEMP/QQQ
Program Status . . . . : 00102
         tried to divide by zero (factor 2) (C G S D F).
Previous Status . . . . : 00000
Statement in Error . . . . : 300
RPG Routine . . . . : *DETC
Number of Parameters . . . . : 000
Message Type . . . . :
MI Statement Number . . . . :
Additional Message Info . . . . :
Message Data . . . . :
Last File Used . . . . : QQQ
Last File Status . . . . : 00011
         RPG0011 End of file (input).
Last File Operation . . . . : READ F
Last File Routine . . . . : *DETC
Last File Statement . . . . : 200
Last File Record Name . . . . :
Job Name . . . . : DSP03
User Name . . . . : B_TOMLINS0
Job Number . . . . : 084498
Date Entered System . . . . : 061792
Date Started . . . . : 061792
Time Started . . . . : 125512
Compile Date . . . . : 061792
Compile Time . . . . : 125438
Compiler Level . . . . : 0001
Source File . . . . : QRPGSRC
  Library . . . . : QTEMP
Member . . . . : QQQ

RPG III FORMATTED DUMP

File . . . . : QQQ
File Open . . . . : YES
File at EOF . . . . : YES
Commit Active . . . . : NO
File Status . . . . : 00011
         RPG0011 End of file (input).
File Operation . . . . : READ F
File Routine . . . . : *DETC
Statement Number . . . . : 200
Record Name . . . . :
Message Identifier . . . . :
MI Instruction Number . . . . :
ODP type . . . . : DB
File Name . . . . : QQQ
  Library . . . . : QTEMP
Member . . . . : QQQ
Record Format . . . . :
Primary Record Length . . . . : 5
Secondary Record Length . . . . : 0
Input Block Length . . . . : 4112
Output Block Length . . . . : 0
Device Class . . . . : '0015'X
Lines per Page . . . . : 0
Columns per Line . . . . : 0
Number of Records in File . . . . : 0
Access Type . . . . : ARRIVAL SEQ
Allow Duplicate Keys . . . . : NO
Source File . . . . : NO
UFCB Parameters . . . . : 'A20000000000500000'X
UFCB Overrides . . . . : '000000000000000000'X
Records to Transfer . . . . : 256
Number of Puts . . . . : 0
Number of Gets . . . . : 0
Number of Put/Gets . . . . : 0
Number of other I/O . . . . : 0
Current Operation . . . . :
Device Class . . . . : '4040'X
Device Name . . . . : '4040'X
Length of Last Record . . . . : 0
DDS Information . . . . :
Relative Record Number . . . . : 0
Records Transferred . . . . : 0
Current Line Number . . . . : 0

Figure 14.7 (part 1)

Debugging

RPG III FORMATTED DUMP

NAME	OFFSET	ATTRIBUTES	VALUE
*IN	005471	CHAR(1)	DIMENSION(99)
	005471	(1)	'1'
	0054D3	(2-99)	'0'
*INIT	05046E	CHAR(1)	'0'
*INLR	005470	CHAR(1)	'0'
*INXX	00546F	CHAR(1)	'1'
*IN01	005471	CHAR(1)	'1'
M.UDATE	005630	ZONED(6,0)	61792
M.UDAY	005632	ZONED(2,0)	17
M.UMONTH	005630	ZONED(2,0)	6
M.UYEAR	005634	ZONED(2,0)	92
QQQFLD	0054D4	PACKED(5,0)	0
UDATE	005630	ZONED(6,0)	61792
UDAY	005632	ZONED(2,0)	17
UMONTH	005630	ZONED(2,0)	6
UYEAR	005634	ZONED(2,0)	92
WORK.	0054D8	CHAR(124)	' '
	0054D8	VALUE IN HEX	'00000000004040404040404040404040404040'X
			'4040404040404040404040404040404040404040'X
	005505	+46	'4040404040404040404040404040404040404040'X
	005532	+91	' '
ZIGNDECD	006001	CHAR(1)	'0'
ZPGMSTUS	005636	CHAR(400)	'QQQ 001020000300 *DETC 000'
	005695	+96	'QQQ 00011READ F*DETC 200 QTEMP'
	0056F4	+191	'120617921254380001QRPGSRC QTEMP 0102'
	005753	+286	'B_TOMLINSO00844980617920617921255'
ZZ01BIN	000640	CHAR(5)	'8000000000'X
ZZ01BOUT	005A10	CHAR(5)	'0000000000'X

STATIC STORAGE FOR PROGRAM QQQ   BEGINS AT OFFSET 0053C0 IN THE PROGRAM STATIC STORAGE AREA (PSSA)
AUTOMATIC STORAGE FOR PROGRAM QQQ   BEGINS AT OFFSET 001F90 IN THE PROGRAM AUTOMATIC STORAGE AREA (PASA)

RPG III FORMATTED DUMP
    * * * * *   E N D   O F   R P G   D U M P   * * * * *

Figure 14.7 (part 2)

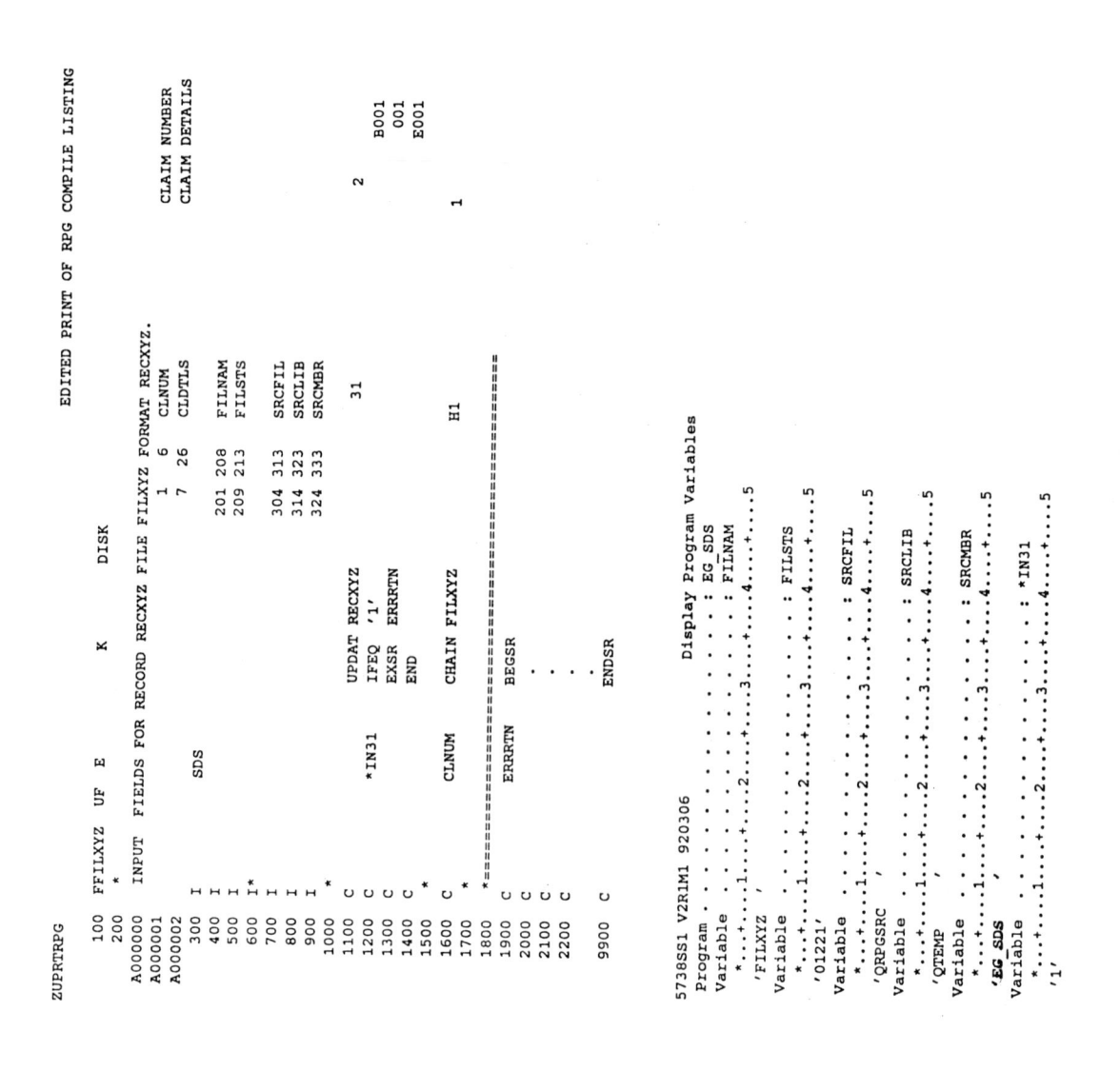

```
ZUPRTRPG                                    EDITED PRINT OF RPG COMPILE LISTING

    100  FFILXYZ  UF  E           K        DISK
    200  *
A000000      INPUT FIELDS FOR RECORD RECXYZ FILE FILXYZ FORMAT RECXYZ.
A000001                                     1    6  CLNUM         CLAIM NUMBER
A000002                                     7   26  CLDTLS        CLAIM DETAILS
    300  I              SDS
    400  I                                201 208  FILNAM
    500  I                                209 213  FILSTS
    600  I*
    700  I                                304 313  SRCFIL
    800  I                                314 323  SRCLIB
    900  I                                324 333  SRCMBR
   1000  *
   1100  C                     UPDAT RECXYZ
   1200  C           *IN31     IFEQ  '1'                                31
   1300  C                     EXSR  ERRRTN
   1400  C                     END
   1500  *
   1600  C           CLNUM     CHAIN FILXYZ                              H1
   1700  *
   1800  C           ==========================================================
   1900  C           ERRRTN    BEGSR
   2000  C                     .
   2100  C                     .
   2200  C                     .
   9900  C                     ENDSR


5738SS1 V2R1M1 920306                     Display Program Variables
 Program  . . . . . . . . . . . . . . :   EG SDS
 Variable . . . . . . . . . . . . . . :   FILNAM
   *...+....1....+....2....+....3....+....4....+....5
  'FILXYZ   '
 Variable . . . . . . . . . . . . . . :   FILSTS
   *...+....1....+....2....+....3....+....4....+....5
  '01221'
 Variable . . . . . . . . . . . . . . :   SRCFIL
   *...+....1....+....2....+....3....+....4....+....5
  'QRPGSRC   '
 Variable . . . . . . . . . . . . . . :   SRCLIB
   *...+....1....+....2....+....3....+....4....+....5
  'QTEMP     '
 Variable . . . . . . . . . . . . . . :   SRCMBR
   *...+....1....+....2....+....3....+....4....+....5
  'EG SDS    '
 Variable . . . . . . . . . . . . . . :   *IN31
   *...+....1....+....2....+....3....+....4....+....5
  '1'
```

Figure 14.8

Debugging

Errors are monitored by providing an indicator in the error indicator position – if no indicator is provided the program falls over. The monitoring process is illustrated in Figure 14.8.

The program issues an UPDATe of record RECXYZ, and if an error is encountered, then indicator 31 (the choice is arbitrary) is set to on. Indicator 31 is coded in positions 56-57. The following lines test indicator 31, and execute the error handling subroutine ERRRTN if it is on.

Suppose that these statements are executed without there having been a READ executed first. Clearly there is a problem – the program does not know which record is to be updated.

```
UPRTRPG                                    EDITED PRINT OF RPG COMPILE LISTING
   OUTPUT FILE FOR DSPJRN COMMAND

       100    FQADSPJRNIF  E           K        DISK
              RECORD FORMAT(S): LIBRARY QSYS FILE QADSPJRN.
                        EXTERNAL FORMAT QJORDJE RPG NAME QJORDJE
   A000000    INPUT  FIELDS FOR RECORD QJORDJE FILE QADSPJRN FORMAT QJORDJE.
   A000000             Journal Entries
   A000001                                        1    5 0 JOENTL       Length of entry
   A000002                                        6   15 0 JOSEQN       Sequence number
   A000003                                       16   16   JOCODE       Journal Code
   A000004                                       17   18   JOENTT       Entry Type
   A000005                                       19   24   JODATE       Date of entry
   A000006                                       25   30 0 JOTIME       Time of entry
   A000007                                       31   40   JOJOB        Name of Job
   A000008                                       41   50   JOUSER       Name of User
   A000009                                       51   56 0 JONBR        Number of Job
   A000010                                       57   66   JOPGM        Name of Program
   A000011                                       67   76   JOOBJ        Name of Object
   A000012                                       77   86   JOLIB        Objects Library
   A000013                                       87   96   JOMBR        Name of Member
   A000014                                       97  106 0 JOCTRR       Count or relative record number changed
   A000015                                      107  107   JOFLAG       Flag: 1 or 0
   A000016                                      108  117 0 JOCCID       Commit cycle identifier
   A000017                                      118  125   JORES        Not used
   A000018                                      126  225   JOESD        Entry Specific Data - Variable contents
       200   C                      READ    QADSPJRN              01         3
       300   C                      SETON                         LR         1
                 * * * *  E N D   O F   S O U R C E  * * * *
                             C r o s s   R e f e r e n c e
   Field References:
          FIELD        ATTR     REFERENCES (M=MODIFIED D=DEFINED)
   * 7031 JOCCID       P(10,0)  A000016D
   * 7031 JOCODE       A(1)     A000003D
   * 7031 JOCTRR       P(10,0)  A000014D
   * 7031 JODATE       A(6)     A000005D
   * 7031 JOENTL       P(5,0)   A000001D
   * 7031 JOENTT       A(2)     A000004D
   * 7031 JOESD        A(100)   A000018D
   * 7031 JOFLAG       A(1)     A000015D
   * 7031 JOJOB        A(10)    A000007D
   * 7031 JOLIB        A(10)    A000012D
   * 7031 JOMBR        A(10)    A000013D
   * 7031 JONBR        P(6,0)   A000009D
   * 7031 JOOBJ        A(10)    A000011D
   * 7031 JOPGM        A(10)    A000010D
   * 7031 JORES        A(8)     A000017D
   * 7031 JOSEQN       P(10,0)  A000002D
   * 7031 JOTIME       P(6,0)   A000006D
   * 7031 JOUSER       A(10)    A000008D
```

Figure 14.9

14.7 System-supplied data structures

If no indicator had been specified in positions 56-57, then the program would simply have fallen over. As it is, the program continues, giving the programmer the opportunity to find out what was wrong, by interrogating the program status data structure (see section 7.11.1)

The program was stopped at the beginning of ERRRTN, and various fields were displayed using the DSPPGMVAR command, as shown on the lower half of Figure 14.8.

Statements 3 through 9 declare the program status data structure, and make a selection of the fields within it, available to the program. The DSPPGMVAR output tells us that the file in error was FILXYZ, and that it went down with an error code of 01221.

The next few lines show the name of the source member, file and library from which the program was created – very useful for confirming that the correct version of the program is in use.

Finally, the last few lines show that Indicator 31 was set to '1' (on).

14.8 Use of journals for debugging

All these useful tools are a great help if we are chasing after a specific, known bug. But what about those nebulous intermittent problems that users sometimes encounter?

Here is an example drawn from real life. A clerk in an insurance company stated that a claim she had closed "about two months ago" had mysteriously been re-opened – she was adamant that she had closed it but could offer no proof.

This is where the journalling facilities on the AS/400 are useful (described in detail in Chapter 13). The DSPJRN (Display Journal) command allows one to make extracts from the journal receivers using almost any conceivable criteria – workstation, program, date, time, physical file etc., or any permutations thereof.

The first step in tracking down her problem was to use DSPJRN to extract all movements for the file in question for the past three months, which resulted in a very large extract file. So how to find the needle in the haystack?

The DSPJRN command produces a file named QADSPJRN (easier to remember as QA-DSP-JRN), the model for which lives in library QSYS. The layout is given by Figure 14.9. (Incidentally, a tiny program like this, which does nothing but declare a file, issue a read to it, and set on LR, is the easiest way to obtain a file layout.) This file consists of header information – the selectable criteria listed above plus various other odds and ends – followed by before and after images of the record in question. The default length of such images is 100 bytes, but this may, and should, be over-ridden to the actual record length. Unfortunately these before and after images are presented as a single field, named JOESD (the last one on Figure 14.9).

The next step was to obtain a set of DDS for QADSPJRN. This may be done manually, alternatively a physical file decompiler is available from the same company as the trace augmentor – see Appendix B.

This DDS was copied to a work member, field JOESD was deleted, and the actual DDS for the file in question substituted for it – this was done simply by browsing it in through the SEU split screen facility. A suitable key was provided – in this case the Claim number field.

The DDS thus created was compiled and the DSPJRN output copied to the new file by means of the CPYF (Copy File) command, with the FMTOPT parameter set to *NOCHK (No Check) to avoid level check problems – see Appendix A.

Once this had been done, the VIEW utility was used to locate all transactions for the claim in question, and to discover when the Closed flag had been updated, by whom, and using which program.

VIEW is an excellent product for this purpose because it offers facilities to tailor the presentation of data to exactly what is required. It hails from California, and is available in the UK from Galois Computers – see Appendix B.

It turned out that the clerk was quite right in stating that she had closed the claim.

It had been re-opened because the company has a policy that if a letter is written about a closed claim then that claim is re-activated. Another clerk had entered a letter which had been written years previously, but somehow had not been notified to the computer.

15

Conversion from older, RPG II, machines

15.1 S/36 Environment on the AS/400

System/36 installations make up the vast majority of RPG II sites contemplating a move to RPG III. As with any conversion, the immediate problem is job controls, and IBM has provided help in the form of the so-called "System/36 environment". (There is also a "System/38 environment", which handles the relatively simple task of emulating System/38's "filename.libname" format.)

New AS/400 users wishing to migrate from other types of machines are on their own as regards converting job controls. They will have to write their own CL, and will have to decide whether or not it is worth automating the task.

The System/36 environment was not the most successful part of the introduction of the AS/400. It works by means of an IBM-supplied library which is placed near the top of the library list (see section 1.7).

All OCL commands are trapped in this library before they reach the CL interpreter. One consequence is that it is possible to mix OCL and CL in the jobstream: CL statements drop unrecognised through the System/36 environment, to be interpreted like any other CL statement.

Before the AS/400 came out, IBM supplied a converter from OCL to (System/38) CL. It worked fairly well; certainly one did not hear the horror stories that one hears about the System/36 environment.

Much of the code it created was redundant, and it was advisable to have it pruned by a CL expert. This underlines the desirability of having an AS/400 expert on hand: if the budget will not allow for one to be hired onto permanent staff, at least engage a contractor for a minimum of six months.

One way of avoiding the problems with the System/36 environment would be to convert the OCL to System/38 CL, and then run it via the System/38 environment. This sounds like a messy, stop gap measure, and much depends on how the RPG itself is to be converted (to be discussed in the next section). If the RPG is to be retained indefinitely it is probably better to write fresh AS/400 CL from scratch.

15.2 The existing system

The existing RPG is likely to be flawed on two accounts. First, it is likely to be rife with GOTOs, conditioning indicators, etc. But, as long as the programs were working on the old machine, there is no reason why they should not continue to do so on the AS/400.

There may be a maintenance problem but, again, it will be no worse than that already encountered for the same reason on the old machine. The authors of those programs will presumably still be available to tackle any bugs.

Much more serious is that the systems will have been designed around flat file principles. Any reader in doubt as to what this might imply should review Chapter 2.

We need to ask ourselves how well the existing systems serve the organisation's needs. If the answer is that they serve very well indeed, then we may be justified in treating the AS/400 as little more than a go-fast System/36.

However, if we are continually tripping over the limitations of non-normalised data, we should consider very seriously re-designing the systems, which implies re-writing the programs.

Even if the systems are to be re-written, they cannot all be done at once – not in-house anyway. Quite apart from staff availability, we must consider the capacity of the machine to support development – programmers are heavy users of machine resources.

The chances are that we shall have to spend some time – possibly as much as two years – running with a mix of old and new systems.

15.3 A compromise approach

Much depends on the levels of discipline imposed with the old machine. If standardised field names within files were enforced, there should be little problem in converting to externally described disk files.

Unfortunately, not many RPG II installations are that disciplined. The best we can hope for is to find the most commonly used name for each field. We have three choices for the remaining names: we can

1) leave some programs with field names internally described

2) generate renaming I-specs – see section 7.11.2 – where appropriate. This is simply a matter of entering the external name in columns 21-30 and the existing RPG name in columns 53-58.

3) rename the fields everywhere they appear in the program

Option 3 is not recommended. The choice between options 1 and 2 is largely a matter of individual preference. Either way, it is necessary to identify the most commonly used names.

This is a big job to do manually, and it is better to use a program. In the UK, a service is available – see Appendix B.

15.4 The transition – use of joined logical files

Assuming that you decide against "freezing" your old systems, there are two basic ways of going about the conversion. Either convert bit by bit as the new programs are released, or hold back until all the new programs are ready and have a "sudden death" overnight conversion.

Either way has drawbacks. The sudden death approach is likely to swamp you with teething troubles, while the alternative means a transitionary period when part of the organisation's data is in a normalised database, and part of it is in flat files. During that transitionary period it is necessary to ensure that both sets of data are updated, or to make interim arrangements for new programs to obtain data from old files and vice versa. The situation is analogous to the decision whether to switch over from the new machine to the old in one fell swoop, or to do it piecemeal.

One approach is to move the data into the new normalised files, and then to use the AS/400's powerful logical file facilities to mimic the old flat files. This is one of the few occasions when renaming of fields and the use of logical joins can be recommended. Remember, though, that it is not possible to update a joined logical file.

16

Conversion from Mainframe: CICS Implications

16.1 Why go from mainframe to AS/400?

There are two main operating systems on IBM mainframes, VSE and MVS, plus an optional "hypervisor" called VM.

VSE, originally called DOS (not to be confused with PC-DOS), was introduced because the early 360s lacked the power to drive OS, the predecessor to MVS. As core size and mip-ratings exploded in the early 1980s, the original justification for VSE rather than MVS disappeared.

IBM would of course have us believe that the costs of maintaining two mainframe operating systems (plus VM) is crippling them. Since the installed VSE customer base is probably larger than any other manufacturer's total revenue, we can leave the tears to our crocodile.

The vast increase in main storage size also brought a problem with addressability. A solution was provided by means of an enhancement to MVS, making it MVS/XA, and VSE users were "encouraged" to migrate.

From the user's point of view, the snag is that converting from VSE to MVS is almost like converting to another machine. The job controls are completely different. Vast amounts of software, both IBM and third party, come in VSE and MVS versions – and the MVS versions are frequently much more expensive.

While all this was going on, System/38 was developing into AS/400 and growing to a size where it might challenge the smaller mainframes.

The VSE DP Manager might well say to himself that if his arm was going to be twisted into a conversion anyway, why not get the benefit of the AS/400's modern architecture? As a further bonus, he would save the salaries of the army of systems programmers who seem inevitably to accompany mainframes.

From IBM's point of view, the possibility of small mainframe customers moving to AS/400 is a mixed blessing. It is widely believed that IBM's gross margin on the AS/400 is only 60 per cent, against 80 per cent for mainframes, so at first glance it would seem logical for Armonk to put VSE accounts off limits to GSD salesmen.

On the other hand, the plug compatibles have recently been making substantial inroads into IBM's customer base, and top management at Big Blue might calculate that 60 per cent is better than nothing.

16.2 Teleprocessing considerations

Any VSE DP Manager tempted to go AS/400 is faced with a daunting conversion task. He has to deal with all the issues addressed in Chapter 15, and also has to contend with a completely different philosophy of teleprocessing. The problem, in a word, is CICS, almost universally used by mainframe sites as their teleprocessing monitor.

The System/38 and AS/400 (and System/36 for that matter) see the invoking user's screen as an input-output file for a device of type Workstation, and I/O is handled by normal READ and WRITE verbs. See Chapter 11. Disk I/O is handled exactly as for batch programs.

There is a powerful screen design aid, or screens may be coded directly in DDS (Data Description Specifications), which roughly correspond to CICS BMS (Basic Mapping Support).

The IBM mainframe was designed before teleprocessing was more than a twinkle in somebody's eye, and consequently TP monitors, including CICS, were an afterthought. CICS therefore runs in an application partition (VSE) or virtual space (MVS). Partitions and virtual spaces correspond roughly to an AS/400 subsystem (SBS).

All I/O, screen and disk, is handled by means of COBOL CALLs to CICS (or the equivalents in other host languages). An expert programmer with time on his hands can analyse the incoming screen buffers to ascertain exactly which fields have been sent back. He can organise output so as to send only necessary fields. Line traffic is kept to the absolute minimum. Unfortunately CICS experts with time on their hands are a bit thin on the ground. So most programs end up being written with their MDTs (Modified Data Tags) forced on, and all modifiable fields are sent back and forth, whether changed or not. This greatly simplifies programming, but keeps the electrons buzzing in the comms lines.

The AS/400, on the other hand, offers a simple high-level mechanism to ensure that lines are not clogged with unnecessary traffic. A similarly simple high-level mechanism lets the program know which fields have been changed.

16.3 Pseudo-conversational CICS and its implications

Generations of CICS programmers have been taught "pseudo-conversational" programming.

What this means is that the equivalent of an RPG III EXFMT command (see section 7.12.27) goes something like this: program A001 writes a screen containing the literal A002 in non-display in the first four bytes (i.e. at top left), and then terminates.

When the user hits [ENTER], CICS receives the screen, and uses this literal to determine that A002 is the program to call to handle the response. The idea is that programs are kept small and, more important, do not occupy space in core during the user's "think time".

Since 370 took over from 360, virtual storage has meant that it no longer matters if programs do remain in (virtual) core while the user wanders off for a coffee: they will simply be paged out. But the tradition of pseudo-conversational programming continues.

The implication of all this is that conversion of a CICS system to AS/400 is virtually impossible. It is easy enough to convert BMS to DDS, but program logic is so different that rewriting is almost inevitable – a dauntingly huge task considering that installations with 15,000 CICS programs are not uncommon.

16.4 CICS on the AS/400?

Shortly after the introduction of the AS/400, IBM announced that it was to develop an AS/400 version of CICS. At first sight this was a strange move indeed. Why should any AS/400 user want to spend a lot of money and effort on the cumbersome and archaic CICS methodology? Surely half the point of going AS/400 is simply to get away from that sort of thing? And why should IBM put itself to enormous expense for what amounts to a retrograde step? Surely not merely to make a handful of CICS-based packages available to the AS/400 market?

IBM's mainframe customers have untold millions invested in CICS programs and, until they are offered a convincing conversion path, AS/400 is unlikely to win many of them over.

17

Standards and Conventions

17.1 Introduction – reasons for standards

Standards are one of those things that irritate some people, yet they are necessary to the orderly running of a computer installation. Of course, standards which are ignored may as well not exist and, in practice, the easiest and best way to see that this does not happen is to enlist the willing co-operation of all concerned. Easier said than done. Democracy is all very well, but not really appropriate to this situation – your senior programmers' good ideas may well be voted down by those who are less experienced. Nevertheless, a meeting where everybody gets a chance to express a view is useful, if only because it offers an opportunity to explain the purpose behind seemingly arcane and arbitrary requirements.

This raises another point: do not impose standards and conventions which do not have a sound underlying purpose – and that means that if you are challenged you had better be ready and able to explain the thinking behind any requirement. Nothing is more calculated to bring the installation's standards into disrepute than a conviction that they are hand-me-downs from a machine which became obsolete ten years ago. (Especially if the junior programmers privately believe that to be the last machine the DPM actually understood. . . .)

Standards may conveniently be considered under three headings: operations, systems design and programming.

Operations standards are broadly similar for all computers, and boil down to imagining every conceivable catastrophe – and having a plan for each. At the very least, that means saving all files, programs etc. to tape at regular intervals, and ensuring that the tapes are stored off-site. For some types of machines, or combinations of machine and software, including the AS/400, there is also the question of journalling. Should journalling be used? If so, should the journals be saved? If so, are less frequent system saves acceptable? The answers to these questions will vary from site to site, and will depend on the answers to questions such as: how much down time can be tolerated? Those who rely on journalling to avoid daily saves will burn a great deal of midnight oil if they ever need to recover in anger.

It is amazing how some people cannot grasp that a chain is only as strong as its weakest link. I once worked at a bank where the requirements specification laid down a maximum downtime of five minutes even for the nearly unthinkable – a bomb in the computer room.

Two big System/38s were installed; journals from the live database were applied immediately to a mirror database on the standby machine, and there was some fancy hardware so that the comms could be switched quickly from one CPU to the other.

Such a pity the two CPUs were only ten feet apart!

System design standards are much more machine-specific. Standards which work for a CODASYL network database will be nearly useless in an AS/400 environment, and vice versa.

17.2   PFs equivalent to entities

The fundamental rule for a relational database is that the data must be properly normalised – i.e. rendered into Third Normal Form (3NF). For those (myself included) who have trouble remembering the formal definition of 3NF, the following may be helpful:

Data should be described by:

the key	1NF
the whole key	2NF
and nothing but the key	3NF

The "entities" thus formed correspond handily to Physical Files on the AS/400 or, to put it the other way round, if you can truthfully say that the keys in your Physical Files describe their data in this way, then you will not go far wrong.

17.3   Intersection files

A slight complication occurs with intersection data, which is information pertaining to a particular combination of two entities.

For example, in an insurance database, a claimant may have multiple claims against a given policy: the incident dates and particulars of injury would be data at the intersections of the claimant and policy entities.

This would be handled by a further Physical file whose key would be the combined keys from each of the two intersecting entities.

17.4 UNIQUE keyword and Physical Files

All Physical Files should be described as keyed and given the attribute UNIQUE, however some authorities prefer to leave the Physical File itself unkeyed and instead to build a Logical File, keyed as described.

The important thing is that it should be done – by whatever method is preferred. Naming conventions raise their head at this point.

Entities should be given names as meaningful as possible within the constraints of being allowed only ten characters by the system rules for object names.

If the site uses RPG, then the RPG rule of a maximum of eight characters for a file name comes into play. It is possible to use an OVRDBF (Override Database File) command to link a 10-character external name to an RPG name – but scarcely worth the bother.

17.5 Naming and number of Logical Files

The position is further complicated by the need for a naming convention for Logical Files. Most sites use the name of the underlying Physical File suffixed by the letter L and a serial number, thus the first Logical File over the Physical File POLICY would be POLICYL1.

The L serves no discernible purpose, and the file could equally well be called POLICY1. All sorts of nonsense is talked about the number of Logical Files which may be built over a Physical File, but the fact is that it all depends on the volatility of the Physical File.

The oft-quoted IBM rule-of-thumb of ten logical files is just that: a rule-of-thumb, not Holy Writ. Every time a record is changed the operating system has to update all relevant access paths, so for an extremely volatile file ten may be too many; on the other hand a dormant file may happily have as many Logical Files as you like.

17.6 Work files

Work files are not a part of the database, and it is as well that they should be clearly distinguished. One way of naming them is to use the name of the program which creates them, suffixed by a W and, if necessary, by a serial number. Thus, the second work file created by program ABC123 would be ABC123W2. Similarly, printer files would take a P suffix (or R, for report), and screen files a D suffix, for Display.

17.7 Program names

position in hierarchy chart, language identification

The alert reader will notice that programs are assumed to be named by a combination of three letters and three numbers. This works well, but clearly is not the only possibility.

It is useful to have a system of suffixes which permit quick identification of a program module's language, and position in the hierarchy.

A program which has no suffix will be the main module, a C suffix means it is a calling CL program, Kn means a called program where n is the position in the hierarchy (McCracken) chart, and Rn means a called RPG program where n is the position in the hierarchy chart. An S suffix means it is the CL module which submits the calling CL to batch.

Thus:

```
CSC110     is the main program

CSC110C    is the calling CL

CSC110K1   is the 1st CL service module to the main program

CSC110R3   is the 3rd RPG service module to the main program
```

and

```
CSC110S    is the submitting CL
```

17.8 Library conventions

All these objects have to be stored in libraries, and at least two environments are needed, Live and Test. If space permits there is a great deal to be said for a third environment – Development.

The use of the service facilities to SEU is simplified if these environments are differentiated by means of prefixes – common sense suggests L, T and D – rather than suffixes. Libraries which are too large may be a pain to work with, so it is usually a good idea to give each major system its own set of libraries.

There is some scope for ingenuity in how the libraries are set up. Some things are obvious: a separate library for database files means you can save them all with a SAVLIB command rather than specifying them individually with a list of SAVOBJ commands – and avoids having to remember to update the list every time a file is added or deleted.

Some like to have their logical files in a separate library, which can be a help when restoring. (If you attempt to restore a logical file before restoring its underlying physical file, you will get into difficulty.)

Alternatively, ensure that logical files have names which always follow in the collating sequence the names of the physical files on which they are based. Logical files based on more than one physical file present a problem, which may be overcome by prefixing them with a Z.

Source code is usually kept in a separate library from anything else, mainly because the action of a number of commonly used commands, particularly DSPOBJD (Display Object Description), is greatly slowed by a need to wade through numerous source file members.

Sundry objects such as printer files and display files are usually lumped together with programs, but a separate miscellaneous library is better.

There is no significant overhead in having an additional library, and it is good to be able to look at programs without being bothered with all the other bits and pieces. The principal difficulty is thinking of a suitable name.

The libraries for the live environment of a claims system might therefore be named something like this:

```
LCLAIMSRC      Source

LCLAIMPGM      (Object) programs

LCLAIMFILE     Database files

LCLAIMOBJ      Work files, display files, printer files, etc.
```

17.9 Library names

Library names should never be hard-coded. Instead, the *LIBL construct, explicit or implied, should be used.

Within the source library one would expect to find the usual source files: QCLSRC, QDDSSRC, and QRPGSRC (and/or QCBLSRC etc.). The prevailing habit of including change notes as comment lines within source code is most unsatisfactory.

17.10 Program amendment notes

The notes tend to be terse to the point of being meaningless, and/or clutter the listing to an irritating degree. One also has to flick backwards and forwards between the change notes and the actual amendments.

One way to resolve the dilemma is to create another source file, QLOGSRC (or whatever you prefer), to contain the change notes. This would have a member for each member in QRPGSRC and QCLSRC, which could be displayed with the actual source member on a split screen. Having a separate member seems to encourage programmers to write more expansively.

17.11 Format naming conventions

Format names within files depend on the type of file. The syntax requires that formats do not have the same names as their files, and for database files most installations prefix or suffix the file name with an R. Not much to quarrel with there.

Display files are a thornier question. There is a school of thought that says one should have only one display file for an entire system, for performance reasons. There may be some merit to this argument, but any benefit would surely be outweighed by the overhead of having to recompile the file every time a screen format had to be changed.

Most installations therefore have one display file per on-line program, naming the file by the program name suffixed by a D. Should the formats follow the convention of suffixing the file name with a number (e.g. ABC123D1)? This makes it more difficult to cannibalise code from one program to another, so DSPR1, DSPR2 etc. is better. It is worth emphasising that the number refers to the screen number as seen by the user, thus if the second screen seen by the user contains multiple formats then they would be named DSPR2A, DSPR2B etc.

For subfile formats and their controlling formats substitute S and C respectively for the R, thus DSPR1S1/DSPR1C1 etc.

All but the simplest print files should be externally defined, using a convention of Hn for heading lines, Dnn for detail lines (note D01 not D1), and Tn for total lines.

In order to facilitate testing, print files should always be compiled using default parameters. If the defaults are not what is required, the appropriate values should be provided by means of an OVRPRTF in the calling CL.

Note that if you want to use a distinctive file name for an internally defined print file (and you should), but do not wish to clutter the system with unnecessary objects, it is quicker to do a CRTDUPOBJ of QSYSPRT into QTEMP, rather than a CRTPRTF without DDS. This has the further advantage that any change to QSYSPRT will "ripple" automatically.

17.12 Data areas

Data areas tend to open a number of cans of worms, and should be avoided. In particular, they do not work with commitment control (a ROLBK will not reset data areas). You may not wish to have commitment control now, but it is folly to bar your way from ever doing so.

17.13 The FRF (Field Reference File)

The fields in all database files should be declared by reference to one Field Reference File – which is the equivalent of a Data Dictionary in an orthodox DBMS. It is often a good idea to have an FRF per major system.

"Root fields" should be defined at the beginning of the FRF, with subsequent iterations referred back to the root definition. Thus:

```
     A          CLAMNO              7S 0      COLHDG('CLAIM' 'NO')
                  .
                  .
                  .
     A          SCCLAM       R
     A                                        REFFLD(CLAMNO *SRC)
```

An ingenious system used by one well-known software house may be of interest. They have a live FRF, and each team has a development FRF where additions are made. A logical file is declared over both of these, and it is this logical file which is used as the FRF by the programmers.

Some installations specify that numeric fields should be declared as packed. This seems penny-wise and pound-foolish: the saving in disk space and processor cycles is negligible, and is made at the cost of reducing readability of dumps etc.

17.14 Use of PUTOVR in DSPFs

Display files should normally use PUTOVR. It is sometimes objected that this does not work with literals; the solution is to give the literal a display attribute of non-display (DSPATR(ND)), and to condition the display attribute rather than the literal itself.

17.15 Indicator conventions

Programming standards are almost a subject on their own, and for this chapter we shall confine ourselves to RPG standards.

It is usually worth standardising on the use of indicators – but remembering that it may not always be practical to follow the standard. Indicators 1 through 24 should be used for the corresponding command keys, which of course means that they will be free for other purposes in batch programs.

In general, use of indicators should be kept to the minimum imposed by the need to condition fields and attributes within files. In all other cases use flag fields set to Y or N.

Some installations like their programmers to use a /EJECT statement before each subroutine – a good idea in theory, which creates unwieldy listings in practice. It is sufficient to put a row of asterisks (or = signs) between subroutines.

17.16 The GOTO command

The GOTO command and its close cousins, the TAG pseudo-command and the CABxx construct, should be forbidden. This is not mere pedantry. A survey in the United States some years ago found that about 75 per cent of all program bugs were rooted in GOTOs.

Admittedly this referred to COBOL programs, but it is doubtful that RPG would be much different.

17.17 Indicators

A similar source of trouble is the use of indicators to the left of the first operand – do not use this construction except in those very rare cases where they are unavoidable – mainly programs using the logic cycle.

17.18 Logic cycle and commitment control

Remember that the logic cycle will preclude the use of commitment control. A ROLBK across an Ln boundary will *not* cause appropriate resetting of Ln indicators.

17.19 Use of OPNQRYF

Files should be opened by the calling CL rather than individually and repeatedly, by RPG programs. OPNQRYF generally causes confusion which outweighs the very small benefits it brings; debugging becomes tricky when the access path has already disappeared.

17.20 Multiple definition of a file in a single program

If it is desired for whatever reason to define a given file twice to a program, do not create a separate logical for this purpose. Instead, use a different name, and compile by means of a SBMDBJOB stream which includes an OVRDBF.

17.21 Comments and paragraphing

Paragraphing of statements, by means of blank comment lines, is even more important than comments. Some installations have a convention whereby actual comments – as distinct from blank comments – are identified by an asterisk on column 8 as well as column 7. They never use the comment field on the right of the C-spec. This facilitates extracting comments if it is ever desired to do so.

Comments should be used only when they tell us something that is not self-evident. The following is one of my pet irritations:

```
C*       Read Customer Master
C                      READ CUSTMST                    71
```

Comments should be in lower case so that they stand out from statements. (If code is "commented out" (a dubious practice) it should be moved two positions to the right so that it stands out from the live code.)

All subroutine names should be prefixed by SR unless it is quite obvious without doing so that the name in question refers to a subroutine.

17.22 Use of CASEQ rather than multiple IF/ELSE

Make use of the facilities of CASEQ. This:

```
C           OPTION    CASEQ'1'       SROPT1
C           OPTION    CASEQ'2'       SROPT2
C           OPTION    CASEQ'3'       SROPT3
C                     END
```

is far more intelligible than this:

```
C           OPTION    IFEQ  '1'
C                     EXSR  SROPT1
C                     ELSE
C           OPTION    IFEQ  '2'
C                     EXSR  SROPT2
C                     ELSE
C           OPTION    IFEQ  '3'
C                     EXSR  SROPT3
C                     END
C                     END
C                     END
```

17.23 Using *LIKE DEFN

Any work field which is related to a database field should be declared by means of the *LIKE DEFN construct, rather than explicitly.

e.g.

```
     C            *LIKE      DEFN CMCLM     WRKCLM
     C                       MOVE CMCLM     WRKCLM
```

not:

```
     C                       MOVE CMCLM     WRKCLM    6
```

This ensures that a change to (say) the length of the database field CMCLM will automatically be applied to WRKCLM when the program is recompiled.

The *LIKE DEFN statements should be the first C-specs, and should be followed immediately by the *ENTRY PLIST statements (if any), then any KLISTs.

Subprograms should terminate with RETRN or SETON RT, unless there is no chance that they will be re-used.

A North London installation has a program which vets RPG source for transgressions of rules such as the foregoing. It is an idea worth imitating.

17.24 Costs/benefits of monitoring

In both RPG and CL some thought should be given to the cost/benefit tradeoff of monitoring for every conceivable eventuality.

For example, record locking tests are of value only if there is a realistic possibility of two users attempting to update a given record at a given moment.

A completely tidy system never falls over, but it is wasteful to expend expensive programming resources on catering for a situation which is unlikely to arise.

Many of the "conventions" recommended will be things that the better programmers are already doing. If all the others can be brought into the fold, a more reliable and easier to maintain system will result, with fewer sleepless nights for DP staff, and happier users.

APPENDIX A

The Versatile AS/400 copy command

Strictly speaking, CPYF (Copy File) is a CL command, and has nothing to do with RPG. But it is an invaluable addition to any AS/400 programmer's toolbox, and this book would be incomplete without a mention of it.

It is one of the most complicated commands on the AS/400 and System/38, and some programmers seem nervous to progress beyond its basic uses. In so doing, they deprive themselves of a powerful and versatile tool.

The CPYF command has a number of close cousins:

```
CPYFRMDKT    -    Copy From Diskette

CPYFRMTAP    -    Copy From Tape

CPYTODKT     -    Copy To Diskette

CPYTOTAP     -    Copy To Tape
```

Most of these are seldom used – except perhaps by operations staff – and it is sufficient to refer to the manual on those rare occasions when they are needed.

This discussion does not attempt to address every nuance of CPYF – here too the manual should be consulted for rarely used options – instead it attempts to explain and illustrate the more commonly useful features.

Appendix A - The Versatile AS/400 Copy Command

At its simplest, CPYF does exactly what you would expect; copies one disk file to another, e.g.:

```
CPYF    MYFILE    YOURFILE
```

In this case the qualifier *LIBL (Library List) is assumed. That means that the job will look through its library list until it finds the first occurrence of a file named MYFILE, then repeat the process for YOURFILE.

If we were in any doubt as to whether this process would yield the desired result we might amplify the command thus:

```
CPYF    LIB_A/MYFILE    LIB_B/YOURFILE        (AS/400)
```

or

```
CPYF    MYFILE.LIB_A    YOURFILE.LIB_B        (System/38)
```

When using the command interactively it is safer to specify library names explicitly unless absolutely certain that the files to which you wish to refer do not have namesakes higher up the library list. This is particularly true of the TOFILE parameter.

When used in batch, the considerations for using the library list are exactly the same as for a program which produces database output. It is perhaps advisable to specify *LIBL if that is what is wanted, so that a maintenance programmer can be immediately certain that you have not merely forgotten the library entry.

The parameters may be coded with or without brackets, and trailing blanks are permitted within the brackets, this is valid:

```
CPYF    (LIB_A/MYFILEbbb)    LIB_B/YOURFILE
```

The figurative constant *PRINT (*LIST on System/38) is valid for TOFILE, and causes the specified records (see below) to be dumped to a printer spool file. If PRTFMT(*HEX) is specified a hex dump will be produced, almost identical in appearance to that produced by the VSE utility DITTO.

*PRINT is not used as much as it used to be, now that sophisticated (third party) database interrogation utilities such as VIEW have become available.

The easiest way to familiarise oneself with the numerous parameters available is to make a point of using the prompt key, which is, as usual, [CF4].

Not every possible permutation of parameters is allowed, but this is no big problem as the operating system will not allow you to do anything silly. In general, let common sense be your guide and you will not go far wrong.

There is one exception to this: CPYF will not allow you to copy *to* a logical file (though there is no restriction on copying *from* a logical file).

The prompt requires more than one panel, and further panels are accessed by means of the ROLL (up) key. On System/38 the [ENTER] key is used unless requesting further iterations of repeatable parameters. You may back up to the previous panel using [CF12] on the AS/400 or [CF2] on the System/38.

On both AS/400 and System/38, pressing [CF16] will terminate the prompt, and execute the command with those parameters so far provided.

Just as there are FROMFILE and TOFILE parameters, so there are FROMMBR and TOMBR parameters, the main use of these being for copying members of source files – ordinary physical files with more than one member are not very often encountered.

It is important to realise that a source file is basically just a special physical file containing three set fields: SRCSEQ (the sequence number), SRCDAT (the date the record was last modified) and SRCDTA, the data.

SRCSEQ and SRCDAT are always six digit numeric fields, SRCSEQ has two decimals, SRCDAT none. SRCDTA is a character field of the length specified when the source file was created, the default length being 80 bytes, and the maximum 256 bytes.

The default value for FROMMBR and TOMBR is *FIRST, presumably in recognition of the fact that multi-member Physical Files are uncommon. Other possible values for FROMMBR are: a member name, a generic member name, and the figurative constant *ALL.

Other possible values for TOMBR are: a member name, and the figurative constant *FROMMBR. The latter makes sense principally when FROMMBR is coded with a generic value of *ALL. For example

```
CPYF    LIB_A/QRPGSRC    QTEMP/QRPGSRC
        FROMMBR(CCST*)   TOMBR(*FROMMBR)
```

will copy to QRPGSRC in QTEMP all source members in QRPGSRC in LIB_A whose names begin CCST. CCST123 in LIB_A will be CCST123 in QTEMP also.

A significant difference between creating a duplicate source member this way, and doing it by means of the browse facility in SEU, is that this way preserves the values of SRCSEQ and SRCDAT.

It is possible to create the TOFILE within CPYF, by specifying CRTFILE(*YES), which makes the command equivalent to a CRTDUPOBJ. The only real advantage in doing it by CPYF is if the FROMFILE is a DDM (Distributed Data Management) file. A DDM file is a file on another CPU where multiple AS/400s and/or System/38s are networked together. CRTDUPOBJ does not work with DDM files; CPYF does.

CPYF allows you to select records by key, by RRN (Relative Record Number), or by field content, and by sensible permutations of these.

If you need to select a few records from a large file then there are obvious advantages in using the keys. If the FROMFILE's own keys are not suitable it is worth checking to see if it has a dependent logical whose keys are suitable.

Where a keyed copy is required, it is necessary to stipulate the number of key fields required – partial keys are allowed – in the FROMKEY parameter.

Copies by RRN are specified by entering the required starting record number in the FROMRCD parameter.

Such copies are terminated using the TOKEY and TORCD parameters respectively. Alternatively, if you are quite sure how many records you want, you may save a few keystrokes by using the NBRRCDS (Number of Records) parameter.

The main use of NBRRCDS, apart from the above, is to extract a small sample for testing purposes. It is also useful if a CRTDUPOBJ with DATA(*NO) is required for a DDM file (see above): CPYF will not allow NBRRCDS to be specified as zero, so specify 1, then immediately do a CLRPFM (Clear Physical File Member) on the TOFILE.

The INCCHAR and INCREL parameters are useful for making selections by field values. INCCHAR permits only one entry, but allows you to start at a point within a field, and to use the operator *CT (Contains).

INCCHAR allows the figurative constant *RCD, which is mainly useful when copying from a file created without DDS.

Here is an example of selecting the first three lines containing the word EVELYN after column 11 from member XYZ in source file QTXTSRC in LIB_A, and copying it to the equivalent member and file in QTEMP:

```
CPYF    FROMFILE(LIB_A/QTXTSRC)          +
          TOFILE(QTEMP/QTXTSRC)          +
        FROMMBR(XYZ)                     +
          TOMBR(*FROMMBR)                +
        NBRRCDS(3)                       +
        INCCHAR(SRCDTA 11 *CT EVELYN)
```

Note that this is presented as if in a CL program. (The plus signs are CL continuation symbols.) It is not obligatory to arrange parameters neatly in matching sets in CL programs, but it certainly makes them more readable.

INCREL permits multiple entries, with and/or relationships. The first entry is always IF, written as the figurative constant *IF. The ANDs and ORs are similarly written as figurative constants. All entries must refer to field names within the file.

Here is an example of copying all records in the STAFF file for people with the forename EVELYN, not female, and older than 33. A new file, also called STAFF, is created in QTEMP to hold the copied records.

```
CPYF   FROMFILE(LIB_A/STAFF)          +
         TOFILE(QTEMP/STAFF)          +
         CRTFILE(*YES)                +
         INCREL((*IF   FORNAM *EQ EVELYN)   +
               (*AND  SEX    *NE F    )    +
               (*AND  AGE    *GT 33   ))   +
```

This too is presented as if in a CL program.

Essentially these facilities work in an interpretive mode, and execution is therefore slower than if the same selections had been made by means of a logical file or an OPNQRYF (Open Query File).

On the other hand, the coding is much simpler and more natural than that for the alternatives. There is a tradeoff between programmer time and CPU time.

Consider this example:

```
CPYF   FROMFILE(LIB_A/STAFFL1)        +
         TOFILE(QTEMP/STAFF)          +
         MBROPT(*ADD)                 +
         FROMKEY(1 M)                      +
         TOKEY(1 M)                        +
         INCCHAR(ADDRESS  1  *CT 'NEW YORK')   +
         INCREL((*IF   FORNAM *EQ EVELYN)   +
               (*AND  AGE    *GT 33   ))   +
```

It is assumed that STAFFL1 is a logical file built over STAFF and keyed by sex (and possibly having minor keys as well). By using this key rather than an INCREL entry only half the number of records are tested – assuming STAFF contains equal numbers of males and females – with dramatic effect on run time.

Why is NEW YORK in quotes, but EVELYN not? Because NEW YORK contains an embedded blank. The MBROPT of *ADD taken in conjunction with the implied (default) CRTFILE option of *NO, means than any records copied will be added on to the end of an existing file.

Alert readers may have noticed that the field name ADDRESS, used in the INCCHAR parameter, violates the RPG length restriction of 6 characters. It is however within the DDS limit of 10 characters, so the command will work, but in an RPG shop much unnecessary renaming of fields is caused by this sort of thing.

The CPYF command performs standard level checking by default, i.e. it checks that the fields and their lengths, numbers of decimal positions etc. are the same in both the sending and receiving files. This may be switched off by taking the option *NOCHK for the parameter FMTOPT, and the sending record is then simply copied byte-by-byte to the receiving record.

This is principally useful for moving data from a file created without DDS to one created with DDS, a situation frequently encountered during conversions from older machines.

The FMTOPT entry *CVTSRC also switches off level checking but in addition, as the name implies, it converts data from a normal physical file to a source file, inserting the usual 12-byte prefix (see above), or vice versa.

If any of the field names in the sending file do not exist in the receiving file then FMTOPT *DROP must be specified (unless *NOCHK or *CVTSRC are being used).

FMTOPT *MAP ensures that fields with similar names and attributes are correctly copied irrespective of their positions in the files. Any fields in the receiving file that do not exist in the sending file are set to the value specified in the DFT keyword in the DDS, failing which they are set to zero if numeric and blank if alpha.

FMTOPTs *MAP and *DROP are invariably used as a pair. They are chiefly used when fields have been added to an existing database file and it is necessary to copy the data from the old version to the new one.

A close relative of CPYF is CPYSPLF (Copy Spooled File). It copies a spooled print file to a physical file, and does so with what may be thought of as an implied FMTOPT of *NOCHK.

It will *not* copy to a source file, and getting the contents of a spooled file into a source file is therefore a two-stage operation; first copy it to a scratch physical file (usually 133 bytes long and created in QTEMP without DDS), then copy this to the required source file member using FMTOPT(*CVTSRC).

The command also has some sophisticated options for dealing with the skipping and spacing entries on the spooled file, but these will not be dealt with here as they are very seldom needed in practice.

APPENDIX B

Useful addresses

For Trace Augmenter (section 14.4 and Figures 14.5a and 14.5b), File Decompiler (section 1.12), print file DDS converter (section 9.5), McCracken hierarchy generators and assistance with modularising large programs.

Waspforce Ltd.
13 Hawthorne Close
Woking GU22 0BT
ENGLAND

For the VIEW database interrogation utility (Chapter 14)

Within the United States

Questcomp Inc.
19800 MacArthur Blvd.
Suite 720
Irvine
California CA92715-2421

Outside the United States

Galois Computers Ltd
2 The Mount
Rickmansworth
Herts WD3 4DW
ENGLAND

For an emulator of RPG III and the AS/400 which runs on IBM-compatible PCs under MS-DOS, PS/2 or Unix

Native Software
9210 Arboretum Parkway, Suite 200
Richmond
Virginia 23236
U.S.A.

The UK agents are:

9380 Systems Ltd
Unit 8
Surrey Technology Centre
40 Occam Rd
Guildford GU2 5YS

APPENDIX C

Bibliography

Details of Daniel McCracken's method of program structuring may be found in:

A Simplified Guide to Structured Cobol Programming

by

Daniel D McCracken
published by John Wiley & Sons
ISBN 0-471-58284-0

APPENDIX D

Examples

Example 1

Statements 36.00 to 41.01 on Figure D-1a load an array with a well known limerick. Statements 42.00 to 46.00 load a second array with another.

The object of the program is to display the two limericks one after the other as message subfiles. While your manager may not thank you for displaying this sort of message to his users, the principles are the same for any message.

Statement 1 simply declares a workstation file for the purpose. It is a Combined, Full function file, and is externally defined. The DDS to create the file is given in Figure D-1b.

Statement 1 of Figure D-1b sets the screen size, though it is doubly redundant because *DS3 means 24 x 80, and is the default. All fields would be underlined if statement 2, a CHGINPDFT (Change Input Default) without parameters, were not present.

Statement 5 defines a format called MAIN, and statement 6 provides that it may overlay other formats. Statement 7 provides the literal 'DUMMY SCREEN' starting on line 8 column 41.

Statement 8 declares a format called MSGSFL and tells us that it is a subfile. See Chapter 12. It is controlled by the control format MSGCTL, defined on statement 12 – the SFLCTL keyword on statement 12 links the two.

The SFLMSGRCD parameter on statement 9 specifies where the message area is to begin on the

```
SOURCE FILE . . . . . . .     WJTLIB/QRPGSRC
MEMBER . . . . . . . . .      MSFL_EG

SEQNBR*...+... 1 ...+... 2 ...+... 3 ...+... 4 ...+... 5 ...+... 6 ...+... 7 ...+... 8 ...+... 9 ...+... 0
   100      FMSFLEGD CF  E                  WORKSTN
   200      *
   300      E                    NR1       1   5 50         Limerick 1
   400      E                    NR2       1   5 50         Limerick 2
   500      *
   600      I         SDS
   700      I                                       1  10 @@@PGM
   800      *
   900      C* Initialise program message queue variable with program name
  1000      C                    MOVEL@@@PGM    PGMQ
  1100      C*
  1200      C                    EXFMTMAIN
  1300      C*
  1400      C           1        DO   5         X       10
  1500      C                    CALL 'MSFL_EG1'                Send message
  1600      C                    PARM NR1,X       MSG   50
  1700      C                    END
  1800      C*
  1900      C                    WRITEMSGCTL
  2000      C                    EXFMTMAIN
  2100      C*
  2200      C                    CALL 'MSFL_EG2'                Clear messages
  2300      C*
  2400      C                    WRITEMSGCTL
  2500      C                    EXFMTMAIN
  2600      C*
  2700      C           1        DO   5         X       10
  2800      C                    CALL 'MSFL_EG1'                Send message
  2900      C                    PARM NR2,X       MSG   50
  3000      C                    END
  3100      C*
  3200      C                    WRITEMSGCTL
  3300      C                    EXFMTMAIN
  3400      C*
  3500      C                    SETON                  LR
  3600   **
  3700   There was a young man from Darjeeling
  3800   Who got on a bus bound for Ealing
  3900   It said on the door
  4000   "Don't spit on the floor"
  4001   So he carefully spat on the ceiling
  4100   **
  4200   Said an eminent erudite ermine
  4300   There's one thing I cannot determine
  4400   When a dame wears my coat
  4500   She's a lady of note
  4600   When I wear it I'm said to be vermin

                    * * * *  E N D   O F   S O U R C E  * * * *
```

Figure D-1a

screen, in this case on line 22. Note that SFLSIZ on statement 13 is 4, or 1 greater than SFLPAG, on statement 14, so this is an indeterminate length subfile.

The SFLPGMQ parameter at statements 11 and 21 tells the compiler that the name of the program message queue is to be found in a variable called PGMQ (which is loaded at statement 10 on Figure D-1a). Message queues are beyond the scope of this book – details of what they are and how they work may be found in the OS/400 manuals.

```
SOURCE FILE . . . . . . .   WJTLIB/QDDSSRC
MEMBER  . . . . . . . . .   MSFLEGD

SEQNBR*...+... 1 ...+... 2 ...+... 3 ...+... 4 ...+... 5 ...+... 6 ...+... 7 ...+... 8 ...+... 9 ...+... 0
  100     A                                   DSPSIZ(24 80 *DS3)
  200     A                                   CHGINPDFT
  300     A                                   PRINT(QSYSPRT.*LIBL)
  400     A*
  500     A          R MAIN
  600     A                                   OVERLAY
  700     A                                 8 41'DUMMY SCREEN'
  800     A          R MSGSFL                 SFL
  900     A                                   SFLMSGRCD(22)
 1000     A            MSGKEY                 SFLMSGKEY
 1100     A            PGMQ                   SFLPGMQ
 1200     A          R MSGCTL                 SFLCTL(MSGSFL)
 1300     A                                   SFLSIZ(0004)
 1400     A                                   SFLPAG(0003)
 1500     A                                   OVERLAY
 1600     A                                   LOCK
 1700     A N88                               SFLEND
 1800     A                                   SFLINZ
 1900     A                                   SFLDSP
 2000     A                                   SFLDSPCTL
 2100     A            PGMQ                   SFLPGMQ

                          * * * *  E N D  O F  S O U R C E  * * * *
```

Figure D-1b

Before looking in detail at the operation of the RPG program, we must consider briefly the two small CL programs in Figures D-1c and D-1d. Program MSFL_EG2 simply clears the program message queue.

```
SOURCE FILE . . . . . . .   WJTLIB/QCLSRC
MEMBER  . . . . . . . . .   MSFL_EG1

SEQNBR*...+... 1 ...+... 2 ...+... 3 ...+... 4 ...+... 5 ...+... 6 ...+... 7 ...+... 8 ...+... 9 ...+... 0
  100  PGM   PARM(&MSG)
  200        DCL         VAR(&MSG) TYPE(*CHAR) LEN(50)
  300
  400        SNDPGMMSG   MSGID(CPF9898) MSGF(QCPFMSG) +
  500                      MSGDTA(&MSG)                +
  600                      TOPGMQ(*PRV)
  700
  800        RETURN
  900  ENDPGM

                          * * * *  E N D  O F  S O U R C E  * * * *
```

Figure D-1c

```
SOURCE FILE  . . . . . . .   WJTLIB/QCLSRC
MEMBER  . . . . . . . . .    MSFL_EG2

SEQNBR*...+... 1 ...+... 2 ...+... 3 ...+... 4 ...+... 5 ...+... 6 ...+... 7 ...+... 8 ...+... 9 ...+... 0
    100 PGM
    200             RMVMSG      PGMQ(*PRV) CLEAR(*ALL)
    300
    400             RETURN
    500 ENDPGM

                       * * * *  E N D  O F  S O U R C E  * * * *
```

Figure D-1d

Program MSFL_EG1 is used to send messages to the queue. Note that the SNDPGMMSG command (in statement 4) may <u>NOT</u> be executed from within an RPG program using the QCMDEXC or QCAEXEC facilities.

The message is passed to MSFL_EG1 in the field &MSG, which is defined in statement 2 as a character variable 50 bytes long. The PARM parameter in statement 1 declares that it is an incoming parameter.

Message CPF9898 is an IBM-provided general purpose message. Statement 5, which is a continuation statement for the SNDPGMMSG command on statement 4, provides that the text for CPF9898 is to come from &MSG.

Returning to the RPG program in Figure D-1a, we find our two limericks declared on lines 3 and 4 as arrays NR1 and NR2, each 5 elements of 50 bytes each. They are to be loaded at compile time, 1 element per record.

The program status data structure is defined at line 6 – the DS means Data Structure, and the preceding S tells us that it is the program Status data structure.

The only reason it is there is to obtain the name of the program (which we need because the message queue has the same name). RPG will insert it in field @@@PGM defined by statement 7 as occupying the first 10 bytes of the SDS.

@@@PGM is moved to PGMQ by statement 10, and PGMQ is used in statements 11 and 21 of Figure D-1b. In principle, there is no reason why the program name should not have been moved in by means of a literal:

```
    1000 C                     MOVEL  'MSFL_EG'     PGMQ
```

rather than going to the trouble of a program status data structure. However the method shown is general purpose and may simply be copied into any new program, whereas a literal would need to be changed.

At statement 12 an EXFMT is issued against format MAIN, in order to give the user an initial screen to look at. When he presses Enter, the program first executes the loop on statements 14 through 17.

Statement 14 also serves to declare the variable X, as 1 digit numeric. (Not 10 bytes alphameric! Note the alignment compared to the alignment of the 50 on statement 16.)

Statement 15 calls subprogram MSFL_EG1, and uses statement 16 to declare the variable MSG, and to load into it the X-th element of array LM1 – i.e. each line of the limerick in turn.

The lines of the limerick are thus sent one at a time to the program message queue. After 5 times round the loop all have been sent, and we drop through to statement 19, which writes the message subfile to the screen. Note that the WRITE uses the control format, not the subfile format.

To recap, the SFLPGMQ parameter gives OS/400 the name of the variable (PGMQ) containing the name of the program message queue to be displayed. We have loaded PGMQ with the name of our program.

At statement 20 we issue another EXFMT against format MAIN to allow the user to see the revised screen, which will now have on it the literal 'DUMMY SCREEN' on line 8, and on lines 22, 23 and 24 the first three lines of the firstlimerick.

He may look at the fourth and fifth lines by placing his cursor anywhere within the message area and pressing Roll Up. And he may then return to the first three lines by pressing Roll Down, and may repeat this as often as he wishes.

Note that all Roll requests are intercepted and actioned by OS/400, without our program even being aware of them.

Remember that EXFMT is in effect a WRITE followed by a READ, so our program will be waiting for the user to press Enter (or an enabled command key, if we had one).

As soon as he does so it will execute statement 22 which calls MSFL_EG2, the subprogram to clear the message queue. We now repeat, at statement 24 the write to the MSGCTL format. Because the message queue is now empty nothing will be written to the subfile, but it will be reinitialised by the unconditional SFLINZ parameter at statement 18 of Figure D-1b.

Another EXFMT, at statement 25, allows the user to see that his message subfile has been cleared.

Statements 27 through 33 repeat statements 14 through 20, this time using the second limerick, i.e. array NR2.

Finally, statement 35 sets on indicator LR. Because this is a fully procedural program (no

Primary file), RPG will not be able to terminate the program unless we issue an explicit command such as this – see section 10.6.

Example 2

This is a small CL program, intended to be used as a subprogram to an RPG (or COBOL or PL/I) program. It validates a supplied date by utilising indirectly the IBM-supplied date checking routines. As explained in section 10.3, it is often hugely profitable to take a "horses for courses" approach to programming languages.

Date validation is easy enough if you are content only to check that the month is not greater than 12. It becomes a considerable undertaking if you want to ensure that any date containing 29th February does in fact refer to a leap year. Not only have IBM done it for you, but they have done it within the operating system, and that has to be more efficient than anything you could hope to do in a high-level application language such as RPG.

The program in Figure D-2 receives two parameters, &RTN and &DATE, defined respectively as 3 and 6 character alphanumeric fields. A further 6 character field, &TODATE, is required only by the syntax of statement 12 – we have no other use for it.

```
SOURCE FILE . . . . . . .    QTEMP/QCLSRC
MEMBER  . . . . . . . . .    DATVALID

SEQNBR*...+... 1 ...+... 2 ...+... 3 ...+... 4 ...+... 5 ...+... 6 ...+... 7 ...+... 8 ...+... 9 ...+... 0
    100 PGM          +
    200      (&RTN   +
    300       &DATE)
    400
    500         DCL      VAR(&RTN)    TYPE(*CHAR) LEN(3)
    600
    700         DCL      VAR(&DATE)   TYPE(*CHAR) LEN(6)
    800         DCL      VAR(&TODATE) TYPE(*CHAR) LEN(6)
    900
   1000         CHGVAR   VAR(&RTN) VALUE(' ')
   1100
   1200         CVTDAT   DATE(&DATE) TOVAR(&TODATE) +
   1300                    FROMFMT(*YMD) +
   1400                    TOFMT(*JUL)  +
   1500                    TOSEP(*NONE)
   1600         MONMSG   MSGID(CPF0555) EXEC(DO)
   1700         CHGVAR   VAR(&RTN) VALUE(ERR)
   1800         ENDDO
   1900
   2000         RETURN
   2100
   2200 ENDPGM

                        * * * *  E N D  O F  S O U R C E  * * * *
```

Figure D-2

At statement 10 &RTN is initialised to blanks (just in case the calling program omitted to do so). The most important command in the program is the CVTDAT (Convert Date) on statement 12, continued on statements 13, 14 and 15.

The from format of the date is specified as *YMD, so the dates to be validated must conform to this. The to format is given as *.JUL (Julian), but any valid option could have been used – we are not interested in the output.

What we are interested in is whether CVTDAT detects any errors before it performs the conversion. If an error is detected, message CPF0555 is issued.

The next three statements monitor for CPF0555 and, if it has been issued, set &RTN to ERR. Control is then returned to the CALLing program.

Assuming that the date to be tested is in field XXDAT and in the stipulated format (YMD), the RPG calling and testing sequence would look like this:

```
C                   CALL 'CVTDAT'
C                   PARM *BLANK    RTN     3
C                   PARM XXDAT     DATE    6
C*
C         RTN       IFEQ 'ERR'
C                   EXSR SRERR
C                   ELSE
C                   EXSR SROK
C                   END
```

Example 3

The example in Figure D-3 demonstrates RPG's unique ability to work with entire arrays. Most languages require you to work with individual elements.

It is intended to supply a list of the claim numbers of claims changed by a previous program. The claim numbers are 6 digits numeric, and are to be printed scanning from left to right, 16 to a line.

File JCR is declared as Input Primary, which means that the cycle is switched on. It is Externally defined, and Keyed. The IBM-provided printer file QSYSPRT is defined to the program in statement 2. It is internally defined, and uses the overflow indicator OF.

The array CS is defined in statement 4. It has 16 elements, each 6 digits with 0 decimal positions. As the changed claims are read into the program their numbers will be stored in this array until it is full. It will then be printed, cleared, and the process repeated until end of file.

Statement A000018 is clearly an odd man out. It is one line (the 18th line) generated by the

```
    100  FJCR        IP  E           K           DISK
    200  FQSYSPRT O      F      132       OF     PRINTER
    300   *
    400  E                       CS          16   6 0
    500   *
A000018                                      126 1310CSNO          CASE NUMBER
    600  C                        ADD   1         X          30
    700  C                        MOVE CSNO       CS,X
    800  C*
    900  C              X         IFEQ 16                                          B001
   1000  C                        EXCPTDTL                                          001
   1100  C                        MOVE *ZERO      CS                                001
   1200  C                        MOVE *ZERO      X                                 001
   1300  C                        END                                              E001
   1400   *
   1500  OQSYSPRT H    2       1P
   1600  O          OR  2 1    OF
   1700  O                                         1  ' '
   1800  O                                         +  0 'JCR.QTEMP'
   1900  O                                           60 'CASE-SLIP FLAGS'
   2000  O                                         +  1 'CHANGED BY OTJ042'
   2100  O                                  UDATE Y  100
   2200  O                                  PAGE  Z  120
   2300   *
   2400  O          E  1                    DTL
   2500  O                                  CS    Z  132
```

Figure D-3

compiler by expanding the external definition of file JCR. The rest have been removed in order to condense the example, and because they are not relevant to it.

It defines the case number as being on columns 126 to 131, and having 0 decimal places. The external field name, which has not been over-ridden, is CSNO.

Variable X is declared at statement 6 as 3 digits numeric with 0 decimal places (not 30 characters alpha). Like most RPG variables (see section 7.11), X is automatically initialised to zero.

Each time a record is read from file JCR, statement 6 will increment X. The CSNO from that record will then be moved, by statement 7, to the X-th element of CS.

The program then checks, at statement 9, to see if the array is full. If not, processing drops through to the O-specs – the scope of the IF on statement 9 is terminated by the END on statement 13.

If it is full statements 10, 11 and 12 are executed. The EXCPT verb on statement 10 causes to be printed any E-type output lines named DTL. See section 7.13. In this example there is only one such line, statement 24. It contains only one field, the array CS, specified in statement 25 without a subscript.

Because there is no subscript, the entire array will be printed, following the rule that numeric arrays are printed with their elements separated by two blanks. The edit code Z will cause leading zeros to be suppressed.

Note that the end position is given as 132, i.e. the last possible position in the output record. When using this technique it is nearly always easiest to make the end position 132.

In any event, it must allow enough space to hold the entire array, plus the blanks between the elements, plus any edit characters which may have been specified.

We can now see why the array CS was defined with 16 elements. Each element is 6 digits long, and will be preceded by 2 blanks, requiring a total of 8 positions. The maximum number of elements we have space for is therefore 16 (16 x 8 = 128, whereas 17 x 8 = 136, which exceeds our page width of 132 characters).

Once the EXCPT is complete the array is initialised by statement 11. Note that because CS is not subscripted the value in Factor 2 will be moved to all elements of the array. The subscript X is reset by statement 12.

The first header O-spec, statement 15, specifies the output file as QSYSPRT. This remains in effect until another file is specified, which is why columns 7-14 of statement 24 may safely be left blank.

Output will take place when indicator 1P is on, i.e. before the first record is read from file JCR. (If you are in doubt as to why this should be, review Chapter 8 and particularly the detailed cycle diagram in section 8.3).

The OR line, statement 16, specifies that output will also take place if OF, the overflow indicator from statement 2, is on. Note the spacing commands: if 1P is on the printer will space 2 after printing, if OF is on the printer will again space 2 after printing, but will also skip to 1 before printing.

Statements 17 and 18 work as a pair. In effect, the literal JCR.QTEMP is being specified as beginning on position 1 – which saves working out that its end position would be 9. (In RPG II end positions must be used.)

Similarly, the literals contained in statements 19 and 20 are printed as a single heading. In RPG II it would have been necessary to calculate the end position for statement 20.

Field UDATE, the system supplied date, is output ending on position 100 and with a standard date edit specified by the edit code Y.

The automatically incremented page number field, PAGE, is output at statement 22, ending in position 120.

Note how the program is paragraphed by means of blank comment lines at statements 5, 8, 14 and 23.

Can you spot the bug in this program? If the number of records in file JCR is not an exact multiple of 16, the last few will never be printed.

The solution is to repeat statement 10 at the end of C-specs, with LR coded in positions 7-8.

Example 4

Figure D-4a contains a small contrived example of a sales reporting program. Figure D-4b shows the input file (printed by the VIEW utility – see Appendix B). Figure D-4c is the printed output. The program prints statistics for three cities for the six years 1986 to 1991 inclusive. Provision has been made for the number of cities to be increased to five.

File SALES is declared as Input Primary, which means that the cycle is switched on. It is Externally defined, and Keyed. Immediately beneath statement 1 the compiler tells us where it found the file and what format(s) it contained.

It also tell us that the external format name is RSALES, and the RPG name is RSALES. If we had wanted a different name within RPG we would have provided a RENAME statement on a continuation F-spec.

The IBM-provided printer file QSYSPRT is defined to the program in statement 2. It is internally defined, using overflow indicator OF.

The alternating arrays CCDX and CCD are defined in statement 4. They are loaded at compile-time, and a glance at the input data in Figure D-4a3 will show more clearly than words what is intended.

Array MTX, at statement 5, is more easily understood in the context of arrays YR and YRC, defined at statements 7 and 8.

YR provides for a 5 digit numeric field with 0 decimal positions for each of the 6 years in question. YRC replicates YR in character form, and is needed because the MOVEA command will not work on numeric arrays except on the AS/400, and then only under restricted conditions.

MTX provides, in effect, an iteration of YRC for each of the three cities. Array YRX is loaded at compile-time, and lists the six years in which we are interested. The input may be seen on statements 98 to 103 on Figure D-4a3.

Statements A000000 to A000003 are the I-specs generated from the external definition of file SALES. Note the comment on the right of statement A000001, which was drawn from the TEXT parameter within the DDS from which the file was created. A multiple occurrence data structure is defined by statements 10 and 11. The 3 in column 47 (immediately under the 5 in the preceding line) tells us that it occurs 3 times.

The variable YR in statement 11 is not 30 digits long. Because it has the same name as the array defined in statement 7, that array becomes part of the data structure. The program structure consists essentially of three subroutines, the initialising subroutine SRINIT, the main subroutine SRMAIN, and the wrap-up subroutine SRLR.

Appendix D - Examples

```
PROGRAM COMPILED AT 10:23:28 ON 15/05/91

PGM         REPORT.QTEMP
SRCFILE     QRPGSRC.QTEMP

    100   FSALES    IP  E             K        DISK
          RECORD FORMAT(S):  FILE SALES LIB QTEMP
                    EXTERNAL FORMAT RSALES RPG NAME RSALES
    200   FQSYSPRT  O   F      132      OF     PRINTER
    300   *
    400   E                  CCDX    1   3  2 0 CCD   8 CITIES
    500   E                  MTX         3 30           MATRIX (6 * 5)
    600   E                  YRX     1   6  2 0         REQ YRS
    700   E                  YR          6  5 0         YR ACCUMULTORS
    800   E                  YRC         6  5           YR IN CHARACTERS
    900   *
A000000   INPUT FIELDS FOR RECORD RSALES FILE SALES FORMAT RSALES
A000001                                      1    20CITY                01 = London, 02 = New Yor
A000002                                      3    40YEAR
A000003                                      5    90VALUE
   1000   IDS1       DS                      9
   1100   I                                  1   300YR
   1200   *
   1300   C          FLAG1P    IFNE 'N'                                      B001
   1400   C                    MOVE 'N'      FLAG1P  1                        001
   1500   C                    EXSR SRINIT                                    001
   1600   C                    END                                           E001
   1700   *
   1800   C                    EXSR SRMAIN
   1900   *
   2000   CLR                  EXSR SRLR
   2100   *
   2200   ****************************************************************
   2300   C          SRMAIN    BEGSR
   2400   C*
   2500   C                    Z-ADD1        X       30
   2600   C          CITY      LOKUPCCDX,X                   31        3
   2700   C          *IN31     IFEQ '1'                                      B001
   2800   C*
   2900   C                    Z-ADD1        Y       30                       001
   3000   C          YEAR      LOKUPYRX,Y                    32        3     001
   3100   C          *IN32     IFEQ '1'                                      B002
   3200   C                    EXSR SRTOT                                     002
   3300   C                    END                                           E002
   3400   C                    END                                           E001
   3500   C                    ENDSR
```

Figure D-4a

```
3600   *
3700   ************************************************************
3800   C           SRTOT     BEGSR
3900   C*
4000   C           X         OCUR DS1
4100   C*
4200   C                     MOVEAMTX,X    YRC
4300   C                     MOVE  YRC     YR
4400   C                     ADD   VALUE   YR,Y
4500   C                     MOVE  YR      YRC
4600   C                     MOVEAYRC      MTX,X
4700   C*
4800   C                     ENDSR
4900   *
5000   ************************************************************
5100   C           SRLR      BEGSR
5200   C*
5300   C           1         DO    3       X                         B001
5400   C*
5500   C           X         OCUR  DS1                                001
5600   C*
5700   C                     MOVEAMTX,X    YRC                        001
5800   C                     MOVE  YRC     YR                         001
5900   C                     EXCPTLRLIN                               001
6000   C*
6100   C                     END                                     E001
6200   C*
6300   C                     ENDSR
6400   *
6500   ************************************************************
6600   C           SRINIT    BEGSR
6700   C*
6800   C                     MOVE  *ZERO   MTX
6900   C*
7000   C                     ENDSR
7100   *
7200   OQSYSPRT H  2 1   OF
7300   O        OR        1P
7400   O                                 1 '$'
7500   O                               - 1 'REPORT'
7600   O                                50 '$'
7700   O                               - 1 'SALES REPORT BY CITY'
7800   O                               + 1 'FOR 1986-91'
7900   O                     UDATE Y + 10
8000   O                     PAGE  Z   132
8100   O        H  2   OF
8200   O        OR        1P
8300   O                                25 '1986'
8400   O                               + 5 '1987'
8500   O                               + 5 '1988'
8600   O                               + 5 '1989'
8700   O                               + 5 '1990'
8800   O                               + 5 '1991'
8900   *
9000   O        E  1        LRLIN
9100   O                    CCD,X  16
9200   O                    YR     K  71
       TABLE/ARRAY ------ CCDX
       TABLE/ARRAY ------ CCD
9400   01LONDON
9500   02NEW YORK
9600   03PARIS
       TABLE/ARRAY ------ YRX
9800   86
9900   87
10000  88
10100  89
10200  90
10300  91

TABLE OF END POSITION OFFSETS FOR FIELDS DESCRIBED USING POSITION NOTATION
STMT NO      POS      STMT NO     POS     STMT NO    POS    STMT NO    POS
   7500        6         7700      69        7800     81      7900      99
   8400       34         8500      43        8600     52      8700      61
   8800       70
```

Figure D-4a (cont.)

Note how statements 13 and 14 create a user defined first-record flag, which does not suffer from the limitations of indicator 1P, discussed in Chapter 8.

Note also that SRMAIN begins at statement 23, whereas SRINIT is left till last, at statement 66. This makes the main processing line easier to follow, but has no effect on the compiler.

SRINIT is used solely to set array MTX to zeros. The result field in statement 68 is not subscripted, and the move will therefore be applied to all elements of the array.

The first action in SRMAIN is to establish whether the city of the current record is one of those in which we are interested. The subscript X is defined by statement 25 as 3 digits numeric with 0 decimal places, and set to 1.

Be careful with this. If a MOVE was used instead of a Z-ADD the high order two digits would not be affected. The only safe way to use MOVE would be to code

```
C                   MOVE 001     X         30
```

and even with this if we ever decided to change the size of X we should have to remember to change Factor 2 also. Z-ADD is safer. X needs to be set to 1, because the LOKUP in the following statement will begin with the X-th element of CCDX, whatever that might be.

The LOKUP uses the contents of the field CITY, from statement A000001, to search array CCDX. If it gets a hit it sets the appropriate value in X, and sets on indicator 31; if not X is left unchanged and indicator 31 is set to off. At statement 27 this indicator is tested, and the remainder of SRMAIN by-passed if it is not on.

Note the compiler generated "B001" etc. at the extreme right of statements 25 through 34. These tell us clearly that the END at statement 34 terminates the IF at statement 27, whereas the END at statement 33 terminates the IF at statement 31.

Just as statements 25 to 27 establish whether the city is one we are interested in, so statements 29 to 31 establish whether the year is one we are interested in. If it is, statement 32 performs subroutine SRTOT. At statement 40 the value which has just been set into X is used to set the current occurrence of data structure DS1, defined by statement 10.

The appropriate chunk of matrix MTX is moved at statement 42 to the whole of array YRC. Because neither Factor 2 nor Result is subscripted in the MOVE at the next statement, each element of YRC is moved to the corresponding element of YR, and converted from character to numeric in the process.

The input field VALUE, from statement A000003, is added to the appropriate field in YR, and then statements 45 and 46 reverse the actions of statements 42 and 43.

At the end of the Primary file, indicator LR is automatically set to on, and SRLR invoked by statement 20. The "LR" in columns 7 and 8 of statement 20 stipulate that this statement is to be executed only at total-time, and only if indicator LR is set.

SRLR simply goes round a loop three times, once for each city, printing the accumulated figures as it goes. This is controlled by the DO at statement 53, the value of X being set to 1, 2 and 3 on succeeding passes.

As soon as X has been set it is used, at statement 55, to establish the current occurrence of DS1. Statements 57 and 58 perform exactly the same function as statements 42 and 43, and the EXCPT verb on statement 59 causes to be printed any E-type output lines named LRLIN. See section 7.13.

In this example there is only one such line, statement 90. At statement 91 it uses the second part of the alternating array pair CCDX/CCD to extract the name of the city. See statements 4 and 94 through 96.

The next field is the array YR, specified in statement 92 without a subscript. Because there is no subscript, the entire array will be printed, following the rule that numeric arrays are printed with their elements separated by two blanks. The edit code K will cause the elements to be printed with minus signs if negative, with commas separating the hundreds and thousands, and zero entries will be blank.

The first header O-spec, statement 72, specifies the output file as QSYSPRT. This remains in effect until another file is specified, which is why columns 7-14 of statements 81 and 90 may safely be left blank.

Output will take place when indicator 1P is on, i.e. before the first record is read from file SALES. (If you are in doubt as to why this should be, review Chapter 8 and particularly the detailed cycle diagram in section 8.3). Output will also take place if OF, the overflow indicator from statement 2, is on.

Statements 74 and 75 work as a pair. In effect, the literal "REPORT" is being specified as beginning on position 1 – which saves working out that its end position would be 6. (In RPG II end positions must be used.) Similarly, the literals contained in statements 78 and 79 are printed as a single heading, beginning on position 50. In RPG II it would have been necessary to calculate end positions for each.

Field UDATE, the system supplied date, is output 10 positions beyond the end of the heading, and with a standard date edit specified by the edit code Y.

The automatically incremented page number field, PAGE, is output at statement 80, ending in position 132. The edit code Z is supplied automatically for PAGE by RPG III, but in most dialects of RPG II must be specified if required.

Note, at the end of Figure D-4a3, the table of end positions provided by the compiler for all statements for which relative positioning has been specified.

Example 5

Figure D-5a is a structured RPG II program, using an external file definition, and over-ride I-specs. Figure D-5b is the printed test results.

The program prints statistics for Eire for insurance claims opened in the stipulated period. S.33s are pending claims, which sometimes are closed before they develop into full-blown claims. Separate totals are provided for open and closed claims.

File LOG133 is declared as Input Primary, which means that the cycle is switched on. It is Externally defined, and Keyed. It is a temporary Logical File, built over a Physical File called CASEREC.

It selects cases of types CLAIM and S.33, opened in 1986-1990, and presents them in the sequence Closed-flag within Type within Opening- year.

The IBM-provided printer file QSYSPRT is defined to the program in statement 5. It is internally defined, using overflow indicator OF.

The format name of the only format in LOG133 is RCASEREC, and this is specified in the header I-spec at statement 7 to link it and the body I-specs in the following three statements to that format. Statement 7 also specifies the resulting indicator 01.

Statement 8 amplifies the external definition of field CSOPYR – the year in which the claim was opened – by making it the control field for control breaks at level 3. Similarly statements 9 and 10 specify the control fields for levels 1 and 2.

The entries on statements 8 through 10 are made in descending order of "seniority" of control break. This is purely to make the program easier to follow – it makes no difference to the compiler.

Contrast statements 12-14 with statements 18-20. The conditioning indicators for statements 12-14 are in columns 9-17, meaning that they take effect at detail-time, whereas those for statements 18-20 are in columns 7-8, meaning that they take effect at total-time. See section 8.8.

The names of the subroutines are contrived to make clear what is happening. The first two characters are SR, for subroutine. The next two are Ln, where n is the level number, and finally there is a D or T, for Detail or Total.

Obviously the compiler does not mind what names you give to your subroutines. But the maintenance programmer does.

Note that the detail-time calculations work downwards from the highest level, whereas the total-time calculations work upwards from the lowest level. Again, there is no compulsion about this, but it is highly recommended.

```
                              VIEW                                           Page:   1
File: SALES                                                 10:39:33
Libr: QTEMP         Fmt: RSALES                                VIEW
Mbr:  SALES         Rec:      1 of 3

      CITY YEAR VALUE
        1   86   123
        2   88   456
        3   91   789
```

Figure D-4b

In the example, the detail-time subroutines are merely to clear accumulators, so the order in which they are executed makes no difference.

But imagine what would happen if SRL2T were to be executed before SRL1T. L2CNT would be added to L3CNT before L1CNT had been added to L2CNT.

Note how the program is broken up by comment lines containing rows of asterisks and equals signs. The asterisks suggest a stronger break than the equals signs.

The dates printed on the right of the example are the change dates from the source file headers – i.e. field SRCDAT – and tell us when that line was last changed.

Turning to Figure D-5a2, there is little to be added to the descriptions of the O-specs in the previous examples.

Note that the total-time output lines are ordered beginning with L1 and ending with LR, for exactly the same reasons as the total-time C- specs are so ordered.

```
REPORT                                       SALES REPORT BY CITY FOR 1986-91

                    1986    1987    1988    1989    1990    1991
        LONDON       123
        NEW YORK                     456
        PARIS                                                789
```

Figure D-4c

Appendix D - Examples

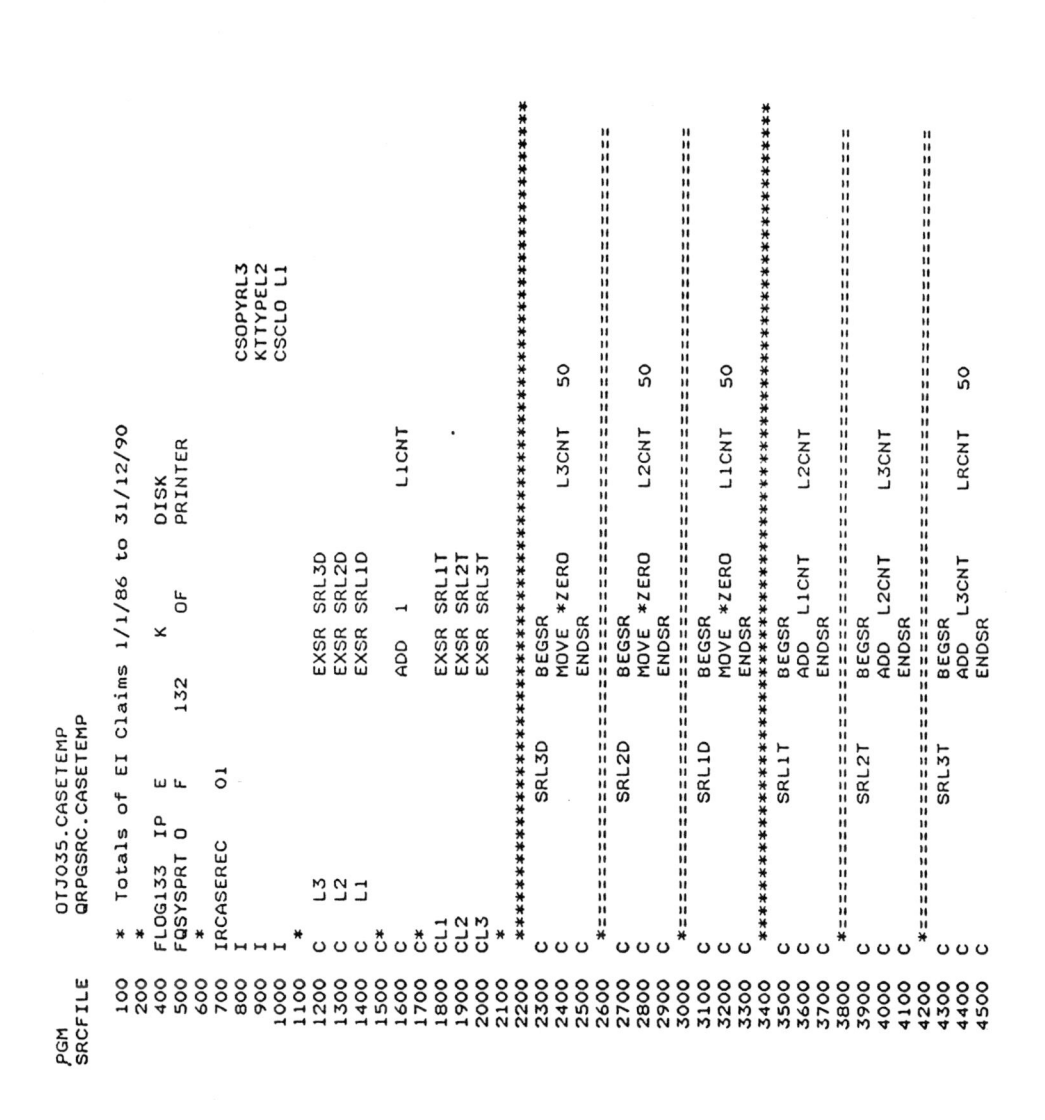

```
PGM         OTJ035.CASETEMP
SRCFILE     QRPGSRC.CASETEMP

 100     *
 200     * Totals of EI Claims 1/1/86 to 31/12/90
 300     *
 400     FLOG133  IP  E                           DISK
 500     FQSYSPRT O   F     132         OF        PRINTER
 600     *
 700     IRCASEREC    01
 800     I                                                   CSOPYRL3
 900     I                                                   KTTYPEL2
1000     I                                                   CSCLO L1
1100     *
1200     C           L3                EXSR SRL3D
1300     C           L2                EXSR SRL2D
1400     C           L1                EXSR SRL1D
1500     C*
1600     C                             ADD  1    L1CNT
1700     C*
1800     C           CL1               EXSR SRL1T
1900     C           CL2               EXSR SRL2T
2000     C           CL3               EXSR SRL3T
2100     *
2200     C*********************************************************
2300     C           SRL3D   BEGSR
2400     C                   MOVE *ZERO L3CNT    50
2500     C                   ENDSR
2600     C*========================================================
2700     C           SRL2D   BEGSR
2800     C                   MOVE *ZERO L2CNT    50
2900     C                   ENDSR
3000     C*========================================================
3100     C           SRL1D   BEGSR
3200     C                   MOVE *ZERO L1CNT    50
3300     C                   ENDSR
3400     C*********************************************************
3500     C           SRL1T   BEGSR
3600     C                   ADD  L1CNT L2CNT
3700     C                   ENDSR
3800     C*========================================================
3900     C           SRL2T   BEGSR
4000     C                   ADD  L2CNT L3CNT
4100     C                   ENDSR
4200     C*========================================================
4300     C           SRL3T   BEGSR
4400     C                   ADD  L3CNT LRCNT    50
4500     C                   ENDSR
```

Figure D-5a

```
4700 OQSYSPRT H   2  1           OF
4800        OR                   1P
4900                        -  1     '$'
5000                        -  1     'OTJO35'
5100                        - 50     ' '
5200                        -  1     'COUNT OF EIRE CLAIMS'
5300                        -  1     '1/1/86 TO 31/12/90'
5400                     UDATE Y + 10
5500                     PAGE  Z 132
5600        H   2                OF
5700        OR                   1P
5800                        -  9     '$'
5900                        -  1     'OPEN'
6000                        +  1     'TYPE'
6100                        +  1     'CLOSED'
6200      *
6300        T   1                L1
6400                   CSOPYR    - 11     '$'
6500                   KTTYPE    +  1
6600                   CSCLO     +  2
6700                   L1CNT  J  +  1
6800
6900        T   1                L2
7000                   CSOPYR    - 11     '$'
7100                   KTTYPE    +  1
7200                   CSCLO     +  2
7300               NL2 L2CNT  J  +  1     '*'
7400
7500        T   2                L3
7600                   CSOPYR    - 11     '$'
7700               NL3 KTTYPE    +  1
7800               NL3 CSCLO     +  2
7900                   L3CNT  J  +  1     '**'
8000
8100        T   1                LR
8200                   LRCNT  J  29
8300                            +  1     '***'
8400                            +  1     'GRAND TOTAL'
8500
8600
```

```
TABLE OF END POSITION OFFSETS FOR FIELDS DESCRIBED USING POSITION NOTATION
STMT NO   POS   STMT NO   POS   STMT NO   POS   STMT NO   POS
 5000       6    5200      69    5300      88    5400     106
 5900      12    6000      17    6100      24    6500      12
 6600      18    6700      21    6800      29    6900      31
 7200      12    7300      18    7400      21    7500      29
 7600      32    7900      18    8000      18    8100      21
 8200      29    8300      33    8600      41
```

Figure D-5a (cont.)

```
OTJ035
         OPEN  TYPE  CLOSED

           86  CLAIM   N      54  *
           86  CLAIM   Y      47  *
           86  CLAIM        101  **
           86  S.33    N       6  *
           86  S.33    Y       2  *
           86  S.33            8  **
           86                109  ***

           87  CLAIM   N      93  *
           87  CLAIM   Y      47  *
           87  CLAIM         140  **
           87  S.33    N      14  *
           87  S.33    Y       5  *
           87  S.33           19  **
           87                159  ***

           88  CLAIM   N     108  *
           88  CLAIM   Y      28  *
           88  CLAIM         136  **
           88  S.33    N      38  *
           88  S.33    Y       2  *
           88  S.33           40  **
           88                176  ***

           89  CLAIM   N     122  *
           89  CLAIM   Y       6  *
           89  CLAIM         128  **
           89  S.33    N      27  *
           89  S.33    Y       1  *
           89  S.33           28  **
           89                156  ***

           90  CLAIM   N     145  *
           90  CLAIM   Y       6  *
           90  CLAIM         151  **
           90  S.33    N      41  *
           90  S.33           41  **
           90                192  ***

                             792  GRAND TOTAL
```

Figure D-5b

Example 6

Figure D-6 contains an example of how to use one of the IBM-supplied service programs to convert an ASCII file to EBCDIC.

This program was intended to run on System/38 as well as AS/400, and therefore uses (on statement 12) the System/38 version of the IBM service program. The AS/400 version is QTBXLATE; when QDCXLATE is called on an AS/400 the call is automatically converted to a call to QTBXLATE.

File CAPSCAN is declared to the program on statement 3. It is declared as Update Primary,

```
    Z 5738PW1 V2R1M1                    SEU SOURCE LISTING

       SOURCE FILE . . . . . . .   WJTLIB/QRPGSRC
       MEMBER  . . . . . . . . .   ASCII_EBC

       SEQNBR*...+... 1 ...+... 2 ...+... 3 ...+... 4 ...+... 5 ...+... 6 ...+... 7 ...+... 8 ...+... 9 ...+... 0
         100        *   SEE PAGES 27-8/9 OF CPF PROG GUIDE
         200        *
         300        FCAPSCAN UP  F      41           DISK
         400        *
         500        ICAPSCAN NS  01
         600        I                                        1   41 XXX
         700        *                                                                .
         800        C                       Z-ADD41          FLDLEN  50
         900        C                       MOVEL'QEBCDIC'   TBL     10
        1000        C                       MOVEL'QSYS'      LIB     10
        1100        *
        1200        C                       CALL 'QDCXLATE'
        1300        C                       PARM             FLDLEN
        1400        C                       PARM             XXX
        1500        C                       PARM             TBL
        1600        C                       PARM             LIB
        1700        *
        1800        OCAPSCAN D   01
        1900        O                                XXX     41

                         * * * *  E N D   O F   S O U R C E  * * * *
```

Figure D-6

which means that the cycle is switched on. The F on column 19 means that it is internally defined, and the 41 on columns 26 and 27 is the record length.

AS/400 handles blocking and de-blocking outside of RPG, so block length is left blank. No keys are specified, so it will be read in RRN sequence, whether or not keys exist.

Because the file is internally defined the I-specs must be supplied, and statement 5 must refer to the file name rather than to a format name. The NS switches off an archaic checking feature which has not been used since the unit record machines were scrapped (see section 7.11.1).

Record identifying indicator 01 is assigned. Because no record identification tests have been applied in columns 21-41, every record in file CAPSCAN will cause 01 to be set to on.

There is no need to divide the record into its component fields, so at statement 6 the whole record is defined as a single field, called XXX for want of a better name.

Statements 8,9 and 10 set up the parameters for QDCXLATE in the format required. After statement 12 has been executed, control is returned from QDCXLATE with field XXX converted to EBCDIC, and all that remains is to replace it in the record.

This is achieved by statements 18 and 19. The file name is repeated on statement 18, and the D on column 15 stipulates that output is to occur at detail-time. The conditioning indicator is 01, which is also the record identifying indicator from statement 5.

Example 7

Figure D-7 contains only the relevant parts of a large program. The installation uses two standard types of printer forms, one of which is called A4PT.

The requesting user's terminal ID is used to discover the nearest printer with A4PT loaded, and the output is directed to it.

File CSC420P is defined at statement 3 as an Externally defined printer file, with indicator 88 as its overflow indicator. The UC on the extreme right means that the file is under User Control: it is not opened automatically by RPG.

Array QCA, defined at statement 22, contains 2 elements each 70 bytes long, and is loaded at compile-time, 1 element per record. The input records are shown at statements 173 and 174, and constitute part of an OVRPRTF (Over-ride Print File) CL command.

The OUTQ parameter is missing from statements 173-174, and is supplied by the program. In this instance the printer name is the same as the OUTQ which routinely feeds it.

The program status data structure is defined at statements 24-26, and the terminal and user IDs are extracted. (The user ID is required elsewhere in the program.)

Before looking at the data structure defined in statements 27-34, we must examine the CALL at statement 57. Program TRMPRT is a small RPG program which uses the terminal name to retrieve a record containing the names of the nearest printers with each of the two types of stationery. These are then passed to the CALLing program.

The first parameter, statement 58, contains the terminal ID retrieved via the program status data structure. When control is returned from TRMPRT, the next two parameters contain the names of the printers.

Only one is required, and the other is named UNUSED. (TRMPRT expects three parameters, and therefore three must be passed, even if not all of them are needed.)

The data structure defined in statements 27-34 is used in statement 68 as the main parameter to the QCAEXEC at statement 67.

The component field LINE1 (statement 30) is loaded with the first element of array QCA at statement 63, and LINE2 (statement 34) is similarly loaded with the second element of array QCA at statement 64.

The name of the printer (field PRTR, statements 32 and 59) is prefixed by the key word OUTQ and enclosed in parentheses by statements 65 and 66. For example, if PRTR contained P3, the net effect would be:

```
             OUTQ(P3    )
```

Trailing blanks within parentheses are permitted in CL.

```
CSC420/QI33SRC/QTEMP
 300 FCSC420P O    E                    PRINTER                              UC
2100  *
2200  E                    SDS
2300  *
2400  I              QCA           1   2 70
2500  I                                        88  PRINTER
2600  I     DS
2700  I                                        244 253 TRMNAL
2800  I                                        254 263 USERID
2900  I*
3000  I                                          1 156 OVR
3100  I                                          1  70 LINE1
3200  I                                         71  75 OUTQA
3300  I                                         76  85 PRTR
3400  I                                         86  86 OUTQZ
5500  *
5600  C*  Find nearest printer with A4PT
5700  C            CALL 'TRMPRT'
5800  C            PARM           TRMNAL
5900  C            PARM           PRTR     10
6000  C            PARM           UNUSED   10
6100  C*
6200  C*  OVRPRTF with nearest printer etc.
6300  C            MOVE QCA,1     LINE1
6400  C            MOVE QCA,2     LINE2
6500  C            MOVE 'OUTQ('   OUTQA
6600  C            MOVE ')'       OUTQZ
6700  C            CALL 'QCAEXEC'
6800  C            PARM           OVR
6900  C            PARM 156       LENGTH  155
7000  C*
7100  C            OPEN CSC420P

       TABLE/ARRAY ------- QCA
17300         OVRPRTF   FILE(CSC420P) FORMSIZE(72) LPI(6) OVRFLW(68)
17400                                 FORMTYPE(A4PT) HOLD(*YES)
```

Figure D-7

The call to QCAEXEC at statement 67 causes the CL command contained in the first parameter (i.e. statement 68) to be executed. That is, of course, the OVRPRTF we have just completed.

Note that the second parameter is the length of the command, and must be supplied in a numeric field 15 digits long, with 5 decimal places (the default size for numeric fields).

QCAEXEC works on System/38 and in the System/38 environment on the AS/400. The "pure" AS/400 version is QCMDEXC.

Once the OVRPRTF has been carried out we may safely open the print file, and this is done at statement 71.

Example 8

Figure D-8 contains a program designed to read source programs from a file created on a System/36, and load them into appropriate members within a source file on a System/38. The obvious application is for a conversion.

It would work in the AS/400's System/38 environment, alternatively a few minor changes would be needed, mainly to convert the "filename.libname" format to the AS/400's "libname/filename".

The source statements from the System/36 are contained in a single file. Each program is preceded by a header record beginning

//bCOPY

with the program name on columns 24-33, and followed by a trailer record beginning

//bCEND

The processing logic is that whenever the beginning of a new program is recognised a member with the same name as the program is added to source file QXYZSRC. QXYZSRC is then over-ridden to point to this member, OPENed, and all source records copied to it.

When the beginning of the next program is detected, QXYZSRC is CLOSEd, and the over-ride is deleted.

A minor complication is that each member is date-stamped as it is created, by inserting "RCVD dd/mm/yy" in its text entry.

File INPUTPF is declared to the program on statement 1. It is declared as Input Primary, which means that the cycle is switched on. The F on column 19 means that it is internally defined, and the 128 on columns 25-27 is the record length.

```
5738PW1 V2R1M1                    SEU SOURCE LISTING

SOURCE FILE . . . . . . .  WJTLIB/QRPGSRC
MEMBER      . . . . . . . . .  USPLIT

SEQNBR*...+... 1 ...+... 2 ...+... 3 ...+... 4 ...+... 5 ...+... 6 ...+... 7 ...+... 8 ...+... 9 ...+... 0
  100     FINPUTPF IP   F       128            DISK
  200     FQXYZSRC O    F        92            DISK                     UC
  300     E                          AR     1    3 71
  400     IINPUTPF NS   01   1 C/   2 C/   3 C
  500     I            AND        4 CC   5 CO   6 CP
  600     I            AND        7 CY   8 C
  700     I                                             24 33 MBRNAML1
  800     *
  900     I            NS   02   1 C/   2 C/   3 C
 1000     I            AND        4 CC   5 CE   6 CN
 1100     I            AND        7 CD   8 C
 1200     *
 1300     I            NS   03
 1400     I                                              1 80 STMT
 1500     *
 1600     I            DS
 1700     I                                              1 80 ADDPFM
 1800     I                                             31 40 MBR1
 1900     I                                             58 59 DD
 2000     I                                             61 62 MM
 2100     I                                             64 65 YY
 2200     *
 2300     I            DS
 2400     I                                              1 80 OVRDBF
 2500     I                                             31 40 MBR2
 2600     I            DS
 2700     I                                              1  6 DATEA
 2800     I                                              1  2 DDA
 2900     I                                              3  4 MMA
 3000     I                                              5  6 YYA
 3100     C       NL1            GOTO NOTL1
 3200     C                      TIME            TIMDAT 120
 3300     C                      MOVE TIMDAT     DATEA
 3400     C                      MOVE *ZERO      PAGE
 3500     C                      Z-ADD71         LENGTH 155
 3600     C                      MOVEAR,1        ADDPFM
 3700     C                      MOVEAR,2        OVRDBF
 3800     C                      MOVE MBRNAM     MBR1
 3900     C                      MOVE DDA        DD
 4000     C                      MOVE MMA        MM
 4100     C                      MOVE YYA        YY
 4200     C                      MOVE MBRNAM     MBR2
 4300     C                      CALL 'QCAEXEC'
 4400     C                      PARM            ADDPFM
 4500     C                      PARM            LENGTH
 4600     C                      CALL 'QCAEXEC'
 4700     C                      PARM            OVRDBF
 4800     C                      PARM            LENGTH
 4900     C                      OPEN QXYZSRC
 5000     C       NOTL1          TAG
 5100     C*
 5200     CL1                    CLOSEQXYZSRC
 5300     CL1                    MOVE AR,3       DLTOVR 71
 5400     CL1                    CALL 'QCAEXEC'
 5500     CL1                    PARM            OVRDBF
 5600     CL1                    PARM            LENGTH
 5700     OQXYZSRC D         03
 5800     O                                       12 '000000000000'
 5900     O                              PAGE      4
 6000     O                              STMT     92
 6100     **
 6200     ADDPFM   QXYZSRC.QTEMP              TEXT('RCVD  XX/XX/XX    ')
 6300     OVRDBF   QXYZSRC QXYZSRC
 6400     DLTOVR   QXYZSRC

                     * * * *  E N D  O F  S O U R C E  * * * *
```

Figure D-8

AS/400 handles blocking and de-blocking outside of RPG, so block length is left blank. No keys are specified, so it will be read in RRN sequence, whether or not keys exist.

Output file QXYZSRC is declared to the program on statement 2. The F on column 19 means that it is internally defined, and the 92 on columns 26-27 is the record length.

The 92 bytes represents the standard source statement length of 80 bytes, plus the 12 bytes of header information carried on each record of an AS/400 source file (see section 1.8).

Because INPUTPF is internally defined the I-specs must be supplied, and statement 4 must refer to the file name rather than to a format name. The NS switches off an archaic checking feature which has not been used since the unit record machines were scrapped (see subsection 7.11.1).

Statements 4 to 6 check for records beginning //bCOPYb and assign record identifying indicator 01 to them.

Any record which fails this test is checked by statements 9-11 to see if it begins //bCENDb. If it does, record identifying indicator 02 is assigned to it.

Any record which fails both of these tests is assumed to be a program source statement, and record identifying indicator 03 is assigned to it.

Note that the file name does not have to be repeated for statements 9 and 13. The name supplied in the first header I-spec holds good until another is supplied.

Only one field, MBRNAM, is defined for record type 01, at statement 7. It is designated to cause an L1 control break when its contents change, and L1 is used to control the process of adding a new member, over-riding QXYZSRC etc.

No fields are required from record type 02, and the first 80 bytes of record type 03 form a single field, defined at statement 14 as STMT. The only reason for identifying //bCEND records is to ensure that they are not mistaken for source statements.

The program contains three data structures. The first, at statements 16-21, is used to build an ADDPFM (Add Physical File Member) CL command.

The second, at statements 23-25 is used to build an OVRDBF (Over-ride Database File) CL command.

The third, at statements 26-30, is used to extract the day, month and year from the system date, as 2-byte alphanumeric fields.

Statement 31 contains a conditioned GOTO, against all the advice given elsewhere in this book. Do as I say, not as I do! The effect of statements 31 and 50 is to separate the L1 detail time statements into a paragraph. A much better way of doing so is shown in statement 14 of Figure D-5a1.

The system date and time are extracted by statement 32. Only the date is required, and this is isolated by statement 33, the Result field of which is also a component of the data structure at statements 26-30, so fields DDA, MMA and YYA are automatically filled.

The automatically incremented counter PAGE is reset at statement 34, and the length of the CL commands is loaded to the length field at statement 35. Note that the length field must be defined as 15 digits with 5 decimal places

The next two statements load the other two data structures from the array defined at statement 3 and loaded via statements 62-64.

The ADDPFM command is not yet complete, and the member name is added by statement 38. The Xs in the date entry in the first array (obtained from AR,1) are overwritten with the correct values by statements 39- 41.

The member name is added by statement 42 to the OVRDBF command.

The two CL commands are now ready for use, and are executed by statements 43-45 and 47-48. Once this has been done, the file is ready to be opened, and this is done by statement 49.

There being no more detail-time calculations, processing drops through to the O-specs until there is a level break.

Statement 57 specifies QXYZSRC as the output file, that output is to happen at detail-time, and that it is to take place for every record for which indicator 03 is set. (Indicator 03 is the resulting indicator set for source statements by statement 13.)

There will therefore be no output for the //bCOPY record, because its resulting indicator is 01, not 03.

The next input cycle will retrieve a program source record, and indicator 03 will be set to on, triggering output. The first 12 bytes of the output record – i.e. the source record header – are filled with zeros by statement 58. The first 4 bytes are then overwritten by the automatic counter, PAGE, at statement 59. (PAGE is intended primarily to provide automatic page numbering for printed reports; this is an example of how it can be used for other purposes.)

Finally, the remaining 80 bytes of the output record are filled with the System/36 source statement.

This process continues until the entire source program has been copied, and the //bCEND record is encountered. Because this sets on indicator 02, no output will take place.

The next record to be read is the //bCOPY for the next program, and this causes the program to enter total-time calculations, identified by entries on columns 7 and 8 of the C-specs. (If you are in doubt as to why this should be, look at the detailed flowchart in Chapter 8.)

The output file QXYZSRC is closed at statement 52, and statements 53-56 use the contents of the third element of the array to delete the over-ride established by statements 46-48.

No total-time output has been specified, so the new record will be made available, and the L1 detail-time processes contained in statements 31-50 will be repeated for the new program.

When the last program has been read, end of file will be sensed for INPUTPF, and indicator LR will be set to on, forcing on L1 for the last program. (If you are in doubt as to why this should be, look at the detailed flowchart in Chapter 8.)

With regard to statements 43, 46 and 54, note that QCAEXEC works on System/38 and in the System/38 environment on the AS/400. The "pure" AS/400 version is QCMDEXC.

APPENDIX E

Version 2 – Upgrade to RPG

Murphy's Law decrees that just as one finishes writing a book on a technical subject, the subject changes!

IBM has announced a number of enhancements to RPG which mean that there is at last a significant difference between RPG III and RPG/400. The latter now includes 11 new verbs, plus an additional use for the existing UNLCK verb (see section 7.12.76), and new forms of the END pseudo-verb (see section 7.12.24).

There are also two new figurative constants, *ON and *OFF. These may look less momentous than the new verbs, but in everyday use they are likely to be more significant. For programmers who appreciate the pitfalls of using GOTOs, the most common cause of bugs in RPG programs is problems with indicators. It is so easy to test for "on" when you mean "off", and vice versa. Now, instead of writing:

    C *IN11 IFEQ '1'

we can write:

    C *IN11 IFEQ *ON

While the existing form of END remains valid – as always, upward compatibility is imperative in IBM – there are new, more specific forms:

              ENDCS   End a CASxx group
              ENDDO   End a DOxx, DOWxx, or DOUxx group
              ENDIF   End an IFxx group
              ENDSL   End a SELECt group (see below)

Appendix E – Version 2 - Upgrade to RPG

The uses of these are self-evident; their purpose perhaps less so. The best way to explain is with an example. Consider the following:

```
C           PAWS        DOWEQ 4
                          .
C           ANIMAL      IFEQ  'DOG'
C                       MOVE  'BARK'  SOUND
C                       END
                                        .
C                       END
```

and

```
C           PAWS        DOWEQ 4 _ _ _ _
                                              |
                          .                   |
C           ANIMAL      IFEQ  'DOG' _ _ _ |_ _
C                       MOVE  'BARK'  SOUND   |   |
C                       ENDDO  _ _ _ _ |      |
                                              |
                          .                   |
C                       ENDIF _ _ _ _ _ _|
```

The first example has a DO, an IF, and two END statements, so it will compile even if it is logically incorrect. The error in the second example is obvious – the IF group straddles the end of the DO group. (This situation is sometimes called a "software knot".) The point is that in the second example the compiler will be able to detect a syntactical error; in the first it will not. In a simple case such as this, the benefit may appear trivial, but in real life DO and IF groups are often nested 8 or 10 deep, and any help that the compiler can give is more than welcome.

The UNLCK verb may now be used to release a locked database record, in addition to its long-standing function of releasing data areas. Until now, the only way to release a database record, which had been read for update, was to issue an UPDAT command, with all fields containing the same information as when the record was read. Not only was this untidy, it generated considerable unnecessary channel activity, with detrimental effects on performance.

Factor 2 may contain either a file or a format name.

Three of the new verbs – SELEC, WHxx and OTHER – are designed to be used in combination with one another, so we shall consider them as a group. Note that they have their own form of END, ENDSL, though the plain END will also work.

E.1 SELEC Start a Select group

Usage: Very frequent, Frequent, **Occasional**, Seldom, Very seldom

Indicators		Fact 1	Fact 2	Result	Resulting Indicators		
7 - 8	9 - 17				54 - 55	56 - 57	58 - 59
Blk	Blk	Blk	Blk	Blk	Blk	Blk	Blk

This verb is used to start a select group. To be meaningful the group should contain one or more WHxx or OTHER verbs, and be terminated by an END or ENDSL. Conditioning indicators are permitted, though they fly in the face of structured programming.

After the SELECT, control passes to the first WHxx group whose conditions are satisfied. If no WHxx condition is satisfied, control passes to the OTHER group, if present.

Note that only one WHxx or OTHER is executed – depending on which conditions are satisfied first – then control passes to the statement following the ENDSL (or END) statement.

E.2 WHxx When True, Select

Usage: Very frequent, Frequent, **Occasional**, Seldom, Very seldom

Indicators		Fact 1	Fact 2	Result	Resulting Indicators		
7 - 8	9 - 17				54 - 55	56 - 57	58 - 59
Blk	Blk	Req	Req	Blk	Blk	Blk	Blk

Factor 1 and Factor 2 are compared and, if the specified condition is satisfied the instructions which follow are executed. The WHxx group is terminated by another WHxx command, an OTHER, or an END[SL].

Note that ANDxx and ORxx lines may be used to create complex WHEN conditions.

Conditioning indicators are not permitted, but control level entries in positions 7 and 8 are permitted, meaning that SELECT groups may be used in programs which use the RPG cycle.

E.3 OTHER Other (catch-all) Selection

Usage: Very frequent, Frequent, **Occasional**, Seldom, Very seldom

Indicators		Fact 1	Fact 2	Result	Resulting Indicators		
7 - 8	9 - 17				54 - 55	56 - 57	58 - 59
Blk	Blk	Blk	Blk	Blk	Blk	Blk	Blk

The OTHER command is used as a catch-all within a SELECT group if all specified WHxx tests have failed. Only one OTHER command is permitted per SELECT group.

Conditioning indicators are not permitted, but control level entries in positions 7 and 8 are permitted, meaning that SELECT groups may be used in programs which use the RPG cycle.

The following is an example of a SELECT group:

```
C                       SELEC
C                         .
C           ANIMAL      WHEQ 'DOG'
C                       MOVE 'BARK'      SOUND
C           ANIMAL      WHEQ 'CAT'
C                       MOVE 'MEOW'      SOUND
C                       OTHER
C                       MOVE '????'      SOUND
C                         .
C                       ENDSL
```

Of course, this could have been written:

```
        C           ANIMAL      IFEQ 'DOG'
        C                       MOVE 'BARK'      SOUND
        C                       ELSE
        C           ANIMAL      IFEQ 'CAT'
        C                       MOVE 'MEOW'      SOUND
        C                       ELSE
        C                       MOVE '????'      SOUND
        C                       ENDIF
        C                       ENDIF
```

but the SELECT group method is clearer. That means that it is less prone to errors, and easier for a maintenance programmer to follow.

E.4 CAT Concatenate

Usage: Very frequent, Frequent, Occasional, **Seldom**, Very seldom

Indicators		Fact 1	Fact 2	Result	Resulting Indicators		
7 - 8	9 - 17				54 - 55	56 - 57	58 - 59
Blk	Blk	Req	Req:n	Req	Blk	Blk	Blk

The character strings specified in Factors 1 and 2 are concatenated. If the entry in Factor 2 is followed by a colon and a number, then that number of blanks is inserted after the last non-blank character in Factor 1 before concatenating. The combination is placed in the field specified in Result. A new use has been found for the half-adjust entry (column 53). If a P is entered in column 53 the field in Result is padded with blanks if necessary. Otherwise, if the field in Result is longer than the concatenated string, the low-order bytes of Result are left undisturbed – in effect a MOVEL to Result is carried out.

The main value of the CAT command is that it avoids having to CALL a CL program whenever concatenation is required. However, sophisticated concatenation will require a somewhat inelegant multiple use of CAT verbs, and the CL approach may therefore still be preferred in these circumstances.

Suppose we wish to construct a single 20-character name entry, NAME, from the following fields, all 10 characters long:

```
FORNM1 contains "Johnbbbbbb"
FORNM2 contains "Hirambbbbb"
SURNAM contains "Jonesbbbbb"
```

The elegant way to do it is in CL:

```
        CHGVAR    VAR(&NAME)                  +
                  VALUE(&FORNM1      *BCAT    +
                        &FORNM2      *BCAT    +
                        &SURNAM)
```

The difficulty is that CALLing subprograms for such small tasks can lead to over-modularisation.

We now have the alternative to do it in RPG:

```
    C         FORNM1    CAT     FORNM2:1    NAME   P
    C         NAME      CAT     SURNAM:1    NAME
```

Note that a P on column 53 in the second statement would be redundant, because the P in the first statement would already have set the remainder of NAME to blanks.

E.5 CHECK Check for existence of characters

Usage: Very frequent, Frequent, Occasional, Seldom, **Very seldom**

Indicators		Fact 1	Fact 2	Result	Resulting Indicators		
7 - 8	9 - 17				54 - 55	56 - 57	58 - 59
Opt	Opt	Req	Req:n	Opt	Blk	Err	Fnd

Each character in Factor 2, beginning with the optional start position after the colon, is checked to see whether it appears in the list in Factor 1. If no invalid characters are found, the numeric field in Result is set to zero, and the indicator in positions 58 and 59 is set off. Either Result or the indicator must be specified. However, if an invalid character is found, the position of that character is entered in the numeric field in Result, the indicator in positions 58 and 59 is set on, and processing ends.

In the case where Result is a numeric array, processing will continue until the supply of elements in the array is exhausted. If the end of Factor 2 is reached before the array is filled, any remaining elements will be set to zero.

This verb is the converse of SCAN (section E.10). It would be used to scan for a not condition, e.g. for the first non-blank character in a line.

E.6 CLEAR Clear a Field or Data Structure

Usage: Very frequent, **Frequent**, Occasional, Seldom, Very seldom

Indicators		Fact 1	Fact 2	Result	Resulting Indicators		
7 - 8	9 - 17				54 - 55	56 - 57	58 - 59
Blk	Blk	Opt	Req	Blk	Blk	Blk	Blk

This is likely to be a useful and popular addition to the RPG programmer's tool-box.

The variable or data structure in Factor 2 is cleared, i.e. set to blanks or zeros depending on the data type of each element. This is likely to be of limited value for single fields, but will be very useful indeed for initialising data structures. At present that task involves coding a MOVE for each field in the data structure.

If Factor 2 contains a database format name, the figurative constant *NOKEY may be entered in Factor 1, meaning that any key fields are not to be cleared.

E.7 ITER Iterate

Usage: Very frequent, Frequent, **Occasional**, Seldom, Very seldom

Indicators		Fact 1	Fact 2	Result	Resulting Indicators		
7 - 8	9 - 17				54 - 55	56 - 57	58 - 59
Blk	Blk	Blk	Blk	Blk	Blk	Blk	Blk

This new verb provides a way of abandoning the current iteration of a DO loop. Control passes to the ENDDO statement, and then back to the DOxx, where the next iteration will proceed provided the conditions are met. Contrast this with the next new verb, LEAVE, which causes control to be passed to the statement after the ENDDO, so that the loop is unconditionally abandoned.

E.8 LEAVE Leave [a DOxx group]

Usage: Very frequent, Frequent, **Occasional**, Seldom, Very seldom

Indicators		Fact 1	Fact 2	Result	Resulting Indicators		
7 - 8	9 - 17				54 - 55	56 - 57	58 - 59
Blk	Blk	Blk	Blk	Blk	Blk	Blk	Blk

When this statement is encountered, control is passed to the statement following the ENDDO for the DOxx group, thus effectively abandoning the loop.

Contrast this with ITER (Iterate), which abandons only the current iteration of the loop.

Suppose we are asked to search an array for a dog with a black tail and white paws. There are of course many ways of doing this, but use of the new verbs offers an elegant solution.

```
C              DO           99        X
     C*
     C        TAIL,X        IFNE      'BLACK'
     C                      ITER
     C                      ENDIF
     C*
     C        PAWS,X        IFEQ      'WHITE'
     C                      MOVE      'Y'      FOUND
     C                      LEAVE
     C                      ENDIF
     C*
     C                      ENDDO
```

The DO loop retrieves details of the dogs from two arrays. First we check to see whether the dog has a black tail. If not, it is clearly not the one we are looking for, so we pass on to the next one.

If it does have a black tail we check to see whether the paws are white.

If not, the second test fails, and again we pass on to the next one. If it does have white paws then both conditions have been satisfied, we have found our dog, and there is no point in continuing with the loop.

E.9 RESET Reset a Field or Data Structure [to its initial value]

Usage: Very frequent, Frequent, Occasional, Seldom, **Very seldom**

Indicators		Fact 1	Fact 2	Result	Resulting Indicators		
7 - 8	9 - 17				54 - 55	56 - 57	58 - 59
Blk	Blk	Opt	Req	Blk	Blk	Blk	Blk

The field or data structure specified in Factor 2 is reset to its initial value i.e. its value at the beginning of the program. Contrast with the CLEAR verb, which resets each element to blank, if alphanumeric, or zero if numeric.

If Factor 2 contains a database format name, the figurative constant *NOKEY may be entered in Factor 1, meaning that any key fields are not to be reset.

E.10 SCAN Scan [for a character string]

Usage: Very frequent, Frequent, Occasional, **Seldom**, Very seldom

Indicators		Fact 1	Fact 2	Result	Resulting Indicators		
7 - 8	9 - 17				54 - 55	56 - 57	58 - 59
Blk	Blk	Req:m	Req:n	Req	Blk	Blk	Blk

It is probably not quite fair to describe the expected usage of this new verb as "seldom": "spasmodic" would be better. Not many programs require this sort of processing, but it will be a real blessing for the few that do.

The string in Factor 2 is scanned to see if it contains the string in Factor 1. A start position may be specified for each string by means of a colon and a number following the string name. If it is not found, the numeric field in Result is set to zero, and the indicator in positions 58 and 59 is set off. Either Result or the indicator must be specified.

If the string is found the position of its first character is entered in the numeric field in Result, and the indicator in positions 58 and 59 is set on.

Suppose that field XYZ contains "THEbCATbSATbONbTHEbMAT". The following statement will leave a value of 9 in field X.

```
C       'SAT' SCAN XYZ:4      X
```

Scanning begins with the 4th character in Factor 2, the C in CAT. The 9th, 10th and 11th positions of XYZ contain the word SAT, so the first of these will be entered in X. Scanning will end when the search argument is found, unless Result contains the name of a numeric array. Scanning will then continue, placing the start position of each occurrence of the search argument in successive elements of the array, until no more elements are left. If the scan completes before all the elements in the array are used up, any remaining elements will be set to zero.

E.11 SUBST Substring

Usage: Very frequent, Frequent, Occasional, **Seldom**, Very seldom

Indicators		Fact 1	Fact 2	Result	Resulting Indicators		
7 - 8	9 - 17				54 - 55	56 - 57	58 - 59
Blk	Blk	Req	Req:n	Req	Blk	Blk	Blk

The purpose of this verb is identical to that of the %SST operator in CL, and its chief value is that it avoids having to CALL a CL program whenever a substring is required.

The number of characters specified in Factor 1 is extracted from the string specified in Factor 2, and placed in Result. Optionally, a start position may be specified for Factor 2, by means of a colon and a number, which may itself be contained in a field.

If the Result entry is longer than the length specified in Factor 1, the low order (rightmost) positions will be left undisturbed unless a P is entered in column 53, in which case they will be padded with blanks.

Suppose that field XYZ contains "THEbCATbSATbONbTHEbMAT", and that field PQR is 5 characters long.

```
C             Z-ADD 4        X
C       3     SUBST XYZ:X    PQR      P
```

After executing these instructions, PQR will contain CATbb. (The start position could have been specified with a literal; field X was used merely to demonstrate how to do it with a field.)

APPENDIX F: The Coding Forms

266 RPG on the IBM AS/400

Appendix F

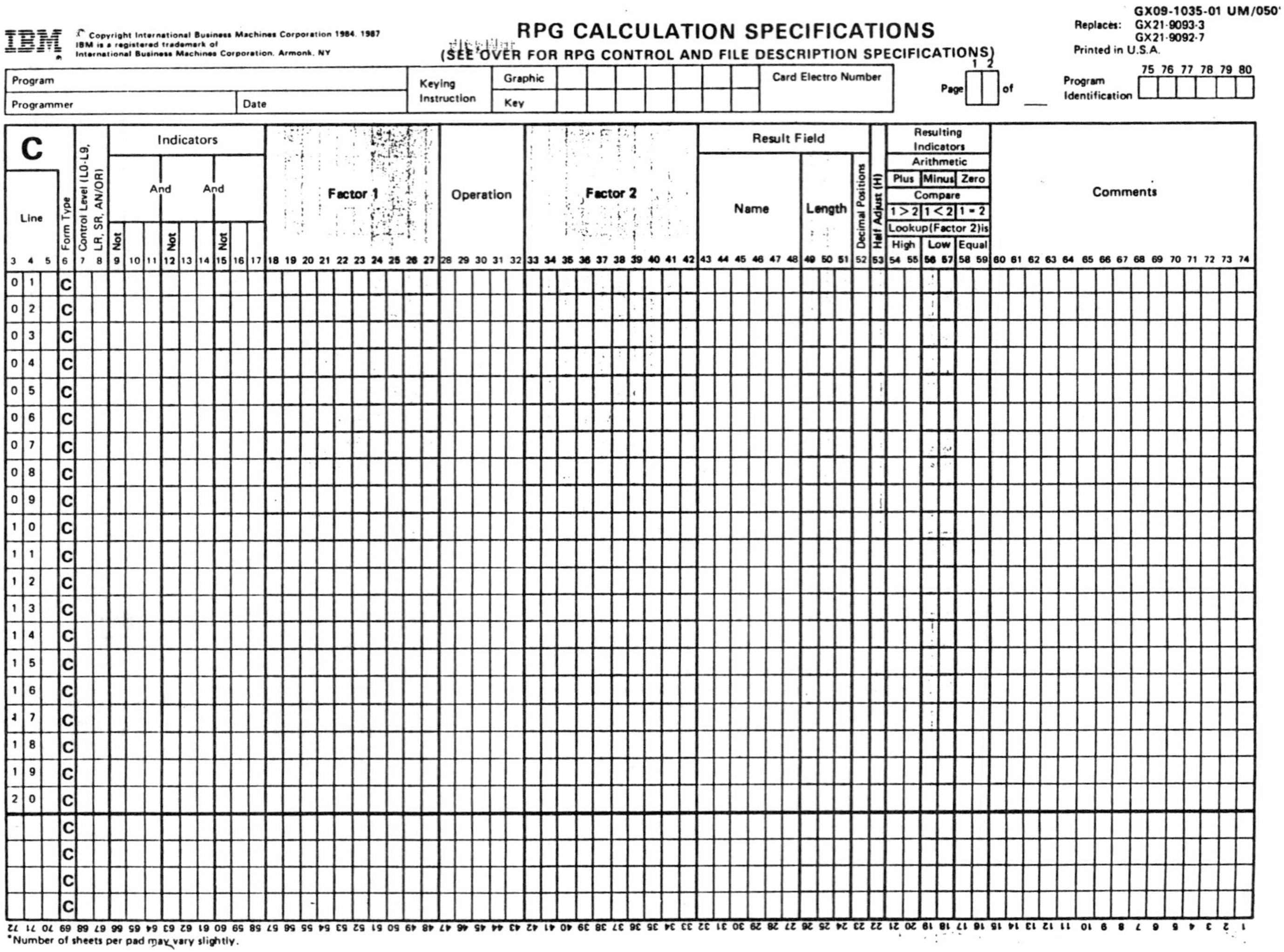

IBM © Copyright International Business Machines Corporation 1984, 1987
IBM is a registered trademark of International Business Machines Corporation, Armonk, NY

RPG CALCULATION SPECIFICATIONS

(SEE OVER FOR RPG CONTROL AND FILE DESCRIPTION SPECIFICATIONS)

GX09-1035-01 UM/050*
Replaces: GX21-9093-3
GX21-9092-7
Printed in U.S.A.

Program | Programmer | Date | Keying Instruction | Graphic | Key | Card Electro Number | Page 1 2 of __ | Program Identification 75 76 77 78 79 80

C Line (3 4 5)	Form Type (6)	Control Level (L0-L9, LR, SR, AN/OR) (7 8)	Indicators: Not (9 10 11), And Not (12 13 14), And Not (15 16 17)	Factor 1 (18–27)	Operation (28–32)	Factor 2 (33–42)	Result Field: Name (43–48)	Result Field: Length (49 50 51)	Decimal Positions (52)	Half Adjust (H) (53)	Resulting Indicators — Arithmetic: Plus / Minus / Zero; Compare: 1>2 / 1<2 / 1=2; Lookup (Factor 2) is: High / Low / Equal (54 55 / 56 57 / 58 59)	Comments (60–74)
0 1	C											
0 2	C											
0 3	C											
0 4	C											
0 5	C											
0 6	C											
0 7	C											
0 8	C											
0 9	C											
1 0	C											
1 1	C											
1 2	C											
1 3	C											
1 4	C											
1 5	C											
1 6	C											
1 7	C											
1 8	C											
1 9	C											
2 0	C											
	C											
	C											
	C											
	C											

*Number of sheets per pad may vary slightly.

Appendix F

RPG OUTPUT SPECIFICATIONS (IBM form UK25-7803-0-UM/50)

IBM® International Business Machines Corporation

AS/400™ DATA DESCRIPTION SPECIFICATIONS

GX21-9891-0 UM/050•
Printed in U.S.A.

File		Keying Instruction	Graphic							
Programmer	Date		Key							

Description	Page of

A

Sequence Number (1 2 3 4 5)	Form Type (6)	And/Or/Comment (A/O/*) (7)	Not (N) (8)	Conditioning – Condition Name: Indicator (9 10)	Not (N) (11)	Indicator (12 13)	Not (N) (14)	Indicator (15 16)	Type of Name of Spec (b/R/H/J/K/S/O) (17)	Reserved (18)	Name (19 20 21 22 23 24 25 26 27 28)	Reference (R) (29)	Length (30 31 32 33 34)	Data Type (b A/P/S/B/F A/S/X/Y/N/I/W/D/M) (35)	Decimal Positions (36 37)	Usage (b/O/I/B/H/M/N/P) (38)	Location – Line (39 40 41)	Location – Pos (42 43 44)	Functions (45 46 47 48 49 50 51 52 53 54 55 56 57 58 59 60 61 62 63 64 65 66 67 68 69 70 71 72 73 74 75 76 77 78 79 80)
	A																		
	A																		
	A																		
	A																		
	A																		
	A																		
	A																		
	A																		
	A																		
	A																		
	A																		
	A																		
	A																		
	A																		
	A																		
	A																		
	A																		
	A																		
	A																		
	A																		

•Number of sheets per pad may vary slightly.

RSLY013-0

Index

A
acceptable response, 163
access paths, 5
    shared, 24
ACQ, 78
action stub, 102
Adabas, 2, 3, 5, 15, 17
ADD, 78
ADDBKP, 189
ADDPFM, 253
ADDTRC, 193
ALIAS, 31
all, 54
alternating
    arrays, 238
    table, 49
AND relationship, 71
ANDxx, 79
areas, data, 215
arrays, 39, 47, 127, 135
    alternating, 238
    compile-time, 135
    of structures, 51
    output, 50
ASCII, 247
assembler, 12, 34, 35
asterisk protection, 134
attribute, 25
audit trails, 185

B
back-ups, 183
BEGSR, 80
BGNCMTCTL, 179, 181
binary
    fields, 44
    search, 68
binder, 155
BITOF, 80, 122
BITON, 81, 122
BKPCOND, 191
blank, 54
    after, 133
breakpoint, 189
bugs, 97
Burroughs, 36, 155, 187, 196

C
CA (Command Attention), 161
CABxx, 82, 121
California Software, 35
CALL, 82, 111, 151, 156
card
    images, 56
    sorters, 145
CASE, 35
CASEQ, 218
CASxx, 83
CAT, 260
CF, 161
CHAIN, 56, 62, 84, 125
CHANGE indicator, 66
change notes, 214
chart, printer spacing, 32
CHECK, 261
checking, level, 225

checkpoints, synchronised, 184
checks, existence, 85, 118
cheques, 134
CHGDBG, 189, 193
CHGINPDFT, 160
CHGPGMVAR, 192
CHGVAR, 154, 260
CICS, 2, 3, 159, 208
CICS BMS, 208
CL commands, 9
CLEAR, 261, 263
CLOSE, 56, 85, 179
CLRPFM, 63, 223
CMS, 59
COBOL, 5, 12, 26, 31, 34, 40, 44, 45, 48, 52, 54,
    57, 59, 60, 68, 69, 73, 75, 89, 90, 96-98, 101,
    106, 115, 121, 143, 147, 151, 153, 162, 166,
    168, 171, 173, 176, 217, 234
CODASYL, 15, 17, 211
Codd, 4, 25
code,
    commented-out, 218
    edit, 132
COLHDG keywords, 26
collators, 145
COMIT, 64, 86, 117, 178, 179, 181, 182
Command Function (CF), 161
command-key indicators, 46
commands, CL, 9
commented-out code, 218
commitment control, 146, 177, 178, 215
COMP, 86
compatibility, upward, 48
compile-time arrays, 135
COMPUTATIONAL-2, 26, 44
COMPUTATIONAL-3, 26
constants, figurative, 38
control
    breaks, 139, 243
        commitment, 177
controlling format, 167
conventions, 210
    format naming, 215
    indicator, 216
    library, 213
    naming, 30, 167
Convert Date, 235
converting
    data, 104
    source, 225
CPF9898, 232
CPYF, 203, 220

CPYFRMDKT, 220
CPYFRMTAP, 220
CPYSPLF, 225
CPYTODKT, 63, 220
CPYTOTAP, 63, 220
CRTDUPOBJ, 8, 222
CRTPF, 126
CRTPRTF, 67
CRTRPGPGM, 60
currency symbol, 134
CVTDAT, 55, 235
cycle, 58, 137, 142, 147, 148, 182, 217, 235, 238,
    243
cycling languages, 12

D

daily saves, 211
DAM, 25
data,
    areas, 12, 99, 110, 125, 215
    atoms, 14, 29
    dictionary, 6
    queues, 12
    structures, 68, 172, 238
    structures, multiple occurrence, 51
    structures, program status, 249
    structures, status, 232
    converting, 104
    intersection, 211
Data Description Specifications (DDS), 21
Data Dictionary, 18, 26
databases,
    network, 211
    mirror, 185
    networked, 17
date edit, 132
Date, 14
    Convert, 235
dates, julian, 55
DDM, 222
DDS, 21, 47, 55, 134, 135, 160, 167, 203, 208, 229
    rules, 133
    syntax, 26
deadly embrace, 6, 16, 19, 183
DEBUG, 86, 187
decision table, 101
decompiling, 9
DEFN, 40, 49, 75, 87, 218
DELET, 88
dense key, 17
detail time, 144
DFTPGM, 188

Direct Access Method (DAM), 25
DISK, 63
display files, 216
DITTO, 221
DIV, 76, 88, 107
DL/I, 15
DLYJOB, 184
DO, 89, 90, 242
documentation, 32
DOUxx, 90
DOWxx, 91
DOxx, 262
DSPDBR, 27
DSPFD, 27
DSPFFD, 33
DSPJOB, 182
DSPJRN, 202
DSPLY, 91
DSPOBJD, 27, 214
DSPPGMREF, 27
DSPPGMVAR, 192, 202
DSPTRCDTA, 193
dual receivers, 180
DUMP, 92
dumps, 196
dynamic storage allocation, 157

E
EBCDIC, 247
edit
   code, 132
     date, 132, 132
     time, 132
     words, 134
editor, link, 155
ELSE, 92
END, 89-91, 93
end-users, 137
ENDCMTCTL, 179, 181
ENDCS, 256
ENDDBG, 189, 193
ENDDO, 256
ENDIF, 256
ENDSL, 256
ENDSR, 93
ENTDBG, 188
entity, 25
entry, NS, 72
ERRMSG, 165
error bucket, 83
exception names, 94
EXCPT, 94, 131, 148, 236

EXFMT, 95, 113, 162, 171, 233
existence checks, 85, 118
EXSR, 95, 151
external
   files, 134
   indicators, 46
   print files, 148, 249
eye strain, 57

F
feasibility study, 33
FEOD, 96
Fetch overflow, 130
Field Record Relation, 73
Field Reference File (FRF), 26, 216
fields,
   hidden, 170
   root, 216
figurative constants, 38, 54
file,
   definition, multiple, 217
   display, 216
   external, 4
   external print, 148
   internal display, 160
   intersection, 28
   joined logical, 22, 206
   logical, 5
   matching, 145
   pointer, 56, 85, 109, 113, 117, 125, 126
   physical, 5
   prefix, 30
   primary, 61, 138, 145
   record address, 60
   secondary, 61, 145
   source, 222
   source, physical, 6
   spooled, 225
   table, 61
   work, 212
first-page indicators, 46
Flip-flop logging, 180
FMTOPT, 203, 225
FORCE, 96
Ford, 34
formal specification, 33
formalised interfaces, 153
format,
   names, 42
     naming conventions, 215
     controlling, 167
FRCDTA, 162

FREE, 97
FRF, 26, 216
FROMKEY, 223
FS (Future Systems), 2
full procedural, 147
function, Full, 61

G
Goldberg, 51
GOTO, 97, 121, 205, 217, 256

H
H1-H9, 116
halt indicators, 46
hash number, level check, 161
HELP, 197
    ([CF4]), 7
    key, 161
hidden fields, 170
hierarchies, 15
hierarchy chart, McCracken, 148, 151
hival, 54
Hollerith,
    cards, 56
    machines, 36

I
IBM 1401, 33, 196
IBM 360, 196
IBM 4331, 101
ICCF, 2, 59
ID, 64
IDMS, 15
IFxx, 98
IGNORE, 64, 162
images, card, 56
IN, 98
INCCHAR, 223
INCREL, 223
IND, 64
indicators, 45, 46
    CHANGE, 66
    command-key, 46
    external, 46
    first-page, 46
    halt, 46
    level, 46, 144
    match, 46
    overflow, 130
    summary form, 65
    resulting, 71
    return, 46

INFDS, 64, 69, 70, 112
Input Primary, 235, 238, 243
interfaces, formalised, 153
internal display file, 160
intersection,
    data, 18, 211
    files, 27
IP, 124
ISAM, 22
ITER, 262

J
Jackson, 151
JCL, 60
joined logical files, 206
journals, 179, 183, 202, 211
    receiver, 179
journalling, 177
Julian dates, 55

K
key,
    compound, 84
    dense, 17
    HELP, 161
    partial, 84
    roll, 174, 174
    search, 174
    sparse, 17
keywords, COLHDG, 26
KFLD, 99
KLIST, 84, 99

L
L0-LR, 142
L1-L9, 182
languages, cycling, 12
LEAVE, 262
level,
    breaking, 148
    check hash number, 161
    checking, 225
    indicators, 46, 144
    nesting, 93
    locking, 182
level check, 160
library conventions, 213
line,
    time, 164
    traffic, 164
    editor, 155
LOCK, 162

locking levels, 182
logging, flip-flop, 180
logical files, 5
    joined, 22, 206
LOKUP, 49, 67, 100, 241
LOVAL, 54, 81
LR, 46, 116, 140, 142, 149, 157, 233

M

M1 through M9, 145
mainframes, 60, 157, 207
market penetration, 34
match indicators, 46
matching, 138, 145, 148
    file, 145
MAXTRC, 188, 193, 196
McCracken, 153, 226, 228
    hierarchy, 148, 151
message subfile, 8, 176
messages, second-level, 197
MFCM, (Multi Function Card Machine), 130
MHHZO, 103
MHLZO, 103
mirror databases, 185
MLHZO, 103
MLLZO, 104
Modified Data Tags, 208
modular programming, 150
monitoring, 197, 219
MOVE, 104, 127, 241
MOVEA, 105
MOVEL, 106, 107
MR, 145, 182
MS-DOS, 227
MSGCTL, 229
MSGLOC, 176
MSGSFL, 229
mule team, 29
MULT, 107
multi-lingual programming, 154
multi-threading, 157
multiple occurrence, 238
    data structures, 108
MVR, 76, 89, 107
MVS, 207

N

names,
    format, 42
    program, 213
naming conventions, 30, 167
Nassi-Schneidermann, 15, 151

Native Software, 35
Natural, 2, 12
NBRRCDS, 223
nesting level, 93
networked databases, 17, 211
NEXT, 108
Normalisation, 14
notes,
    change, 214
    program amendment, 214
NS entry, 72

O

objects, standard, 9
OCL, 60, 204
OCUR, 108
OF, 134, 143
OPEN, 64, 85, 109, 179
OPNQRYF, 23, 217, 224
OR relationship, 71
ORxx, 109
OTHER, 257, 259
OUT, 99, 110
overflow indicator, 130
OVERLAY, 162
OVRATR, 164
OVRDBF, 10, 42, 212, 217, 253
OVRDTA, 164
OVRPRTF, 67, 249, 251

P

page,
    fault, 156
    overflow, 46
PAGE, 55, 242, 254
PAGE1, 55
PAGE7, 55
PAGEn, 142
paging algorithm, 156
PAGNBR, 55
parameters, 12, 146, 152
PARM, 82, 111
partial key, 84
Partitioned Data Set, 6
passwords, 69
physical files, 5
    source, 6
PL/I, 31, 91, 157, 176, 187, 234
PLIST, 82, 111
PLIST/PARM, 146
pointers, file, 56
position, start, 133

POST, 112
Primary file, 61, 138, 145
PRINT, 160
printed reports, 32
printer,
    file, Externally, 249
    spacing chart, 32
program,
    amendment notes, 214
    names, 213
programming,
    modular, 150
    multi-lingual, 154
PRTFMT, 221
PS/2, 227
PSDS, 69
pseudo-verb, 92, 99
PUTOVR, 164, 216

Q

QADSPJRN, 202
QCAEXEC, 10, 158, 179, 232, 249, 251, 255
QCMDEXC, 10, 158, 179, 232, 251, 255
QDATFMT, 55, 124
QDCXLATE, 247
QSECOFR, 27
QSYSOPR, 92
QSYSPRT, 8
QTBXLATE, 247
QTEMP, 3, 23

R

RCLRSC, 97, 158
READ, 56, 95, 113, 115, 125, 162, 171, 191, 208
READC, 113, 125, 171
READE, 56, 114, 115
READP, 56, 115, 115
receivers, dual, 180
record address files, 60
REDPE, 56, 115
REFFLD, 162
REL, 116
relative record number, 62
remote screens, 164
reports, printed, 32
reserved words, 54
RESET, 263
resetting, 133
response times, 163
Result, 75
resulting indicator, 71
RETRN, 46, 116, 143, 149, 157, 219

return indicators, 46
reverse,
    engineer, 152
    image, 66
RG1, 36
RMVBKP, 189
ROLBK, 116, 179, 181, 182, 215, 217
Roll Down, 173, 176
roll keys, 174
Roll Up, 166, 173, 176
root,
    definition, 30
    fields, 216
rows, 16
RPG rules, 30
RRN, 62, 84, 167, 223
RT, 46, 140, 143, 157, 219
rules,
    DDS, 30, 133
    RPG, 30
run-program, 155

S

SAVLIB, 213
SAVOBJ, 213
SBMDBJOB, 60, 217
SBMJOB, 60
SCAN, 261, 263
SDA, 32, 148, 160
SDS, 232
SEARCH, 101
SEARCH ALL, 68, 101
search,
    argument, 84, 99, 100
    keys, 174, 174
    binary, 68
second-level messages, 197
Secondary file, 61, 138, 145
SELEC, 257, 258
SEQ, 63
SETGT, 56, 117
SETLL, 56, 85, 117
SETOF, 118
SETON, 119
SFLCLR, 168
SFLCTL, 167, 229
SFLDLT, 168, 176
SFLDROP, 170, 176
SFLDSP, 168
SFLDSPCTL, 168
SFLEND, 168
SFLINZ, 169, 233

SFLLIN, 169, 176
SFLMSGRCD, 229
SFLNXTCHG, 171
SFLPAG, 169
SFLPGMQ, 231
SFLRCDNBR, 171
SFLROLVAL, 171
SFLSIZ, 169
SHTDN, 119
single-level storage, 155, 163
skipping, 130
SNDJRNE, 179, 184
SNDPGMMSG, 232
SORTA, 120
sorters, card, 145
source,
    file, 222
    physical files, 6
    converting, 225
spacing, 130
sparse key, 17
SPECIAL, 63
specification, formal, 33
spooled file, 225
SQRT, 120
SRCDAT, 222
SRCSEQ, 222
standard objects, 8
standards, 210
start position, 133
statistical survey, 97
status data structure, 232
storage, single-level, 24, 155, 163
STRDBG, 188
structures,
    arrays of, 51
    data, 68, 172, 238
    program status data, 249
    system data, 232
SUB, 120
sub-schemas, 17
subfile, 95, 126, 166
subfiles, 161
subscript, 48
SUBST, 264
survey, statistical, 97
symbol, currency, 134
synchronised checkpoints, 184
Synon/2, 35, 36, 37
System/36, 47, 60, 138, 162, 165, 204, 251

T

tables, 47
    files, 61
    alternating, 49
    decision, 101
    truth, 101
tabulators, 145
TAG, 82, 93, 121
TAPE, 63
tape, carriage, 67
terminal, 159
TESTB, 121
TESTN, 122
TESTZ, 123
TEXT, 26
Third Normal Form (3NF), 14
thrashing, 156, 173
time edit, 132
TIME, 124
time,
    detail, 144
    line, 164
    total, 144
time-out, 19
times, response, 163
TOKEY, 223
total time, 144
Total, 15
trace, 192
    augmentor utility, 193, 226
transaction, 178
TRCFULL, 188, 196
truth table, 101
tuples, 16, 25

U

UDATE, 55, 124, 242
UDAY, 55, 124
UMONTH, 55, 124
UNIQUE, 22, 256, 25, 212
UNIX, 35, 227
UNLCK, 125, 275, 257
Until, 90
UPDAT, 125, 181
UPDPROD, 189
UPSI, 47
upward compatability, 48
User Control, 63, 249
user-id, 69
userviews, 5, 17
utility, trace augmentor, 193
UYEAR, 55, 124

V
VIEW, 192, 203, 226, 238
VM, 3, 59, 207
VSAM, 16
VSE, 47, 59, 207, 221

W
WAITCRD, 182
WAITRCD, 183
whip-round programs, 184
WHxx, 257, 258
words,
    edit, 134
    reserved, 54
work files, 212
workfields, 39
WORKSTN, 63, 159
WRITE, 94, 95, 126, 162, 208, 233

X
XFOOT, 50, 126

Z
Z-ADD, 105, 127, 241
Z-SUB, 128
zero, 54

Symbols
%SST, 264

*BCAT, 154, 260
*CVTSRC, 225
*DROP, 225
*DSPF, 32, 160
*ENTRY, 147
*FROMMBR, 222
*INZSR, 124
*LIKE, 87
*LOCK, 99
*LOVAL, 85
*MAP, 225
*MSGF, 165
*NAMVAR, 87
*NOCHK, 225
*OFF, 256
*ON, 256
*PRTF, 32
*PSSR (Program Status Subroutine), 80
*PSSR, 94
*TCAT, 154
*ZERO, 105, 127

/COPY, 155
/EJECT, 216

//JOB, 60

1NF, 14
1P, 124, 130, 142
2NF, 14
3NF, 14, 14, 31
4GL, 35
    capability, 7